WY ③
24
KUH

Caring

FHSW

Caring:
Nurses, Women and Ethics

Helga Kuhse

 BLACKWELL
Publishers

First published 1997

2 4 6 8 10 9 7 5 3 1

Blackwell Publishers Ltd
108 Cowley Road
Oxford OX4 1JF
UK

Blackwell Publishers Inc.
350 Main Street
Maldon, MA 02148.
USA

British Library Cataloging in Publication Data

A CIP catalogue record for this book is available from the
British Library.

Library of Congress Cataloging-in-Publication Data
Kuhse, Helga.
    Caring : nurses, women, and ethics / Helga Kuhse.
        p.   cm.
    Includes bibliographical references and index.
    ISBN 0–631–20210–2 (hbk. : alk. paper). — ISBN 0–631–20211–0 (pbk. : alk. paper)
    1. Nursing ethics.   2. Nursing—Decision making.   3. Nurse and physician.   4. Nurses—Social conditions.   5. Women—Social conditions.   6. Nurses—Public opinion.   7. Caring.   8. Sex differences (Psychology)   I. Title.
    [DNLM: 1. Nursing Care. 2. Ethics, Nursing. 3. Philosophy, Nursing. 4. Nurse-Patient Relations. WY 85 K96c 1997]
RT85.K84   1997
610.73—DC20
DNLM/DLC
for Library of Congress   96–30173
                                                                              CIP

Typeset in 11 on 13 pt Bembo
by Graphicraft Typesetters Ltd., Hong Kong

Printed and bound in Great Britain by
Marston Lindsay Ross International Ltd,
Oxfordshire

Contents

Preface

This book had its beginning in 1985 when Margaret Brumby (of the Monash University Faculty of Education) and I were awarded a two-year grant by the Victorian Nursing Council to examine the 'ethical and legal issues raised by the role of the nurse'.

Since that time I have continued to take a special interest in the ethical issues faced by nurses, but it was not until the early 1990s that this book was conceptualized in its present form. By that time I was no longer satisfied with analysing particular ethical issues from 'the nursing perspective'; rather, it had become abundantly clear to me that the special ethical issues faced by contemporary nurses have their source in the historical and moral conceptions of the role of nurses and doctors, and of women and men.

Doctors make decisions and nurses carry them out. That is the traditional assumption. But is this how it should be? Nurses care for patients on a continuing basis, and are often acutely aware of the patient's needs and wants. Doctors, on the other hand, see their patients only briefly and consequently often lack the particularized caring understanding that is a precondition for good patient care. Why, then, should it be the doctor rather than the nurse who will write – or refuse to write – not-for-resuscitation orders, or who decides how much pain and symptom control is sufficient for a suffering and dying patient? Should it not rather be the nurse?

Taking the accounts of two nurses of two very different medical end-of-life decisions as my starting-point, I question the traditional relationship between doctors and nurses, and between medicine and nursing, and show that the exclusion of nurses from decision-making is not serving patients well. This means that the traditional role responsibilities of doctors and nurses need challenging, on moral grounds. There is, however, an increasing trend in nursing to reject traditional 'male' ethical thinking in favour of a feminine ethics of care. Such an ethics, I argue, will reinforce the traditional subordinate role of nurses and will facilitate the continued exclusion of nurses from ethical discourse. As a consequence, it will not allow nurses to press their own legitimate moral claims or to argue on behalf of those for whom they care.

Care is a necessary but not a sufficient basis for ethics. An adequate ethics needs justice as well as care. In the context of an ethical framework of 'just caring', I argue that authority for the making of end-of-life decisions for terminally ill and competent patients should be vested in nurses. Moreover, based on the impartial consideration of the interests of all patients, health care policies and laws should be such that nurses will not only be permitted to withhold or withdraw life-sustaining treatment, administering adequate pain and symptom control, but also to provide direct help in dying to terminally ill patients who request it.

I owe thanks to many people, especially to Margaret Brumby for helping to conceptualize the first nursing project, and to the Victorian Nursing Council for funding it. Thanks are also due to our then research assistants, Marilyn Evans, Megan-Jane Johnstone and Amalda Langslow. Their experiences in nursing and nursing law respectively provided me with many valuable practical insights. So did my occasional work, undertaken as part of the research project, at Dandenong Hospital. Provided with the uniform of a Nursing Aid, I was able to spend many hours working in different wards, and had an opportunity to talk to many patients, including those who were nearing the end of their lives. My thanks to the patients, the nurses and the hospital.

Special thanks are due to my colleague and friend, Peter Singer, whose support throughout the writing of this book and comments on various sections have been invaluable. I should also like to thank another good friend and collegue, Robert Young, and an anonymous referee for their critical reading of an earlier draft of this book. Their comments have been most helpful. Many thanks also to Ann Woodruff, who read the manuscript from a nursing point of view.

Working on this book and on the the so-called justice/care debate in ethics stimulated my interest in the central question of partiality and impartiality in ethics, and in the question of whether nurses and doctors and women and men approach ethics differently. Funded by the Australian Research Council (ARC), Peter Singer and I were able to examine this question in some detail. We were assisted by research assistants Jessica van Dyke, Leslie Cannold and Maurice Rickard. Some of their work is reflected in chapters 5, 6 and 7. My thanks to the ARC, and to Jessica, Leslie, Maurice and Peter.

I must not forget to thank Scott Wagstaff. Scott is a physiotherapist in an outer suburb of Melbourne, where I live. On a number of occasions, Scott relieved me, miraculously I thought, of a most crippling headache caused by spending long hours at my computer in preparing the final manuscript of this book.

And last, and most of all, I owe special thanks to my partner of many years, Bill. Throughout our life together, Bill has been a pillar of support and encouragement. Without his support, this book would not have been completed.

Helga Kuhse
May 1996

Acknowledgements

The extracts from Barbara Huttman, 'One nurse's story', are reproduced with the kind permission of the Springhouse Corporation, the publishers of *Nursing Life* (now called *Nursing*) in which the article first appeared in the issue dated January–February 1984 (p. 21). The extracts from 'Dr Cox: The Nurse's Story', by Janet Snell, are reproduced with the kind permission of the editor of *Nursing Times*, in which the article first appeared on 7 October 1992 (p. 19).

1

Two Nurses

In this chapter, two clinical nurses tell their stories. The first is Roisin Hart, a British nurse, who reported Dr Nigel Cox for having ended the life of one of his patients, Lillian Boyes. The second is Barbara Huttmann, an American nurse who helped her patient Mac to die.

The stories are similar in some crucial respects and different in others. Both patients were terminally ill and wanted to die. In the case of Mac, the treating doctor ignored the patient's wishes and refused to write a 'not-for-resuscitation' order. In the case of Lillian Boyes, on the other hand, the doctor injected a fatal dose of a non-therapeutic drug. What makes the cases significantly similar is not only that both nurses disagreed with the respective doctor's decision, but also that they were prepared to act on their convictions – one, Barbara Huttmann, by acting contrary to medical orders, existing policies and the law; and one, Roisin Hart, by upholding her professional code of conduct and the law.

These cases raise a variety of important ethical issues. This book is about ethics, and about the connection between nursing and ethics. It is also about the relationship between doctors and nurses, medicine and nursing, and between women and men. The central question occupying us throughout this book will be whether nurses should think and act for themselves in ethical questions in health care.[1]

There are various ways in which this question can be understood. We shall focus on two important and different ways. First, we shall interpret it as raising questions about the role of nurses:

whether nurses should see themselves as autonomous moral agents
and health-care professionals, or whether they should, as has traditionally been the case, accept a subservient role. Second, we shall
interpret the question as raising issues about ethics: whether nurses
should adopt their own ethical approach – an approach that distinguishes nursing ethics from traditional medical ethics. We shall
examine these questions both in general terms and, towards the
end of the book, more specifically in the context of medical end-
of-life decisions.

The stories of Roisin Hart and Barbara Huttmann will serve as
an introduction to these questions.

Roisin Hart

In August 1991 a respected English rheumatologist, Nigel Cox,
injected 10 ml of potassium chloride to end the life of his long-
time patient Lillian Boyes. Mrs Boyes had been experiencing excru-
ciating pain, which Dr Cox had been unable to relieve, and she
had repeatedly begged him to end her life. Following a report by
the ward sister, Roisin Hart, Dr Cox was convicted of attempted
murder.[2]

Public opinion was on the side of Dr Cox. He was hailed as a
hero. Roisin Hart, on the other hand, was made a public scapegoat. Based on an exclusive interview with Roisin Hart, Janet
Snell wrote the following article for *Nursing Times*:

> Roisin Hart has lived through hell recently. Threats of violence
> have been made against her, she has had crank phone calls, she has
> been vilified by some sections of the media. All because she acted
> on her code of conduct. But she is hoping that her experience, far
> from discouraging other nurses from following her example, will
> lead to lessons being learnt so that no other nurse will be made a
> scapegoat in the way she feels she has been.
> Roisin and her husband, Ted, who is also a nurse in the combined
> rheumatology and surgical unit at the Royal Hampshire County
> Hospital in Winchester, went on holiday in August 1991 wonder-
> ing if they would ever see 70-year-old patient Lillian Boyes again.
> Her condition had been deteriorating and she was not expected to
> live.

'She was a lovely lady,' said Roisin. 'A few weeks earlier, when her sister died, we had a long chat about death and she told me she would like to go quickly, like her husband had done, when her time came. But she never asked me to hurry things along.'

'She didn't want to suffer, but then nobody does, and in this day and age, I don't think anyone should with all the pain control techniques available.'

'She was having subcutaneous diamorphine. I had asked for venous access but they said they couldn't get it.'

When the Harts came back from holiday, Mrs Boyes was still holding on, though she was going downhill rapidly. On August 16, as Roisin arrived for the late shift, she met the Boyes family in the corridor. 'They said to me: "Mum has died." I noticed there was an atmosphere when I got to the ward, but I assumed it was because people were upset.'

'As sister, I took report, and when we came to Lillian someone said: "He gave her potassium chloride." Another nurse said: "Look at the notes afterwards." They read "10 mmol [*sic*] potassium chloride".'

'I was totally stunned. The notes had been left in the nurses' station for all to see. I didn't know what to do. Every nurse on the shift knew what had happened, and they all seemed to be looking at me as if to say: "What happens now?"'

Sister Hart tried to contact Dr Cox but could not reach him and she was reluctant to talk to other doctors and nurses for fear of involving them too.

'By documenting what he had done, Dr Cox involved the nurses and touched so many people's lives. It was so blatant I knew we couldn't cover it up. I'd have been an accessory. The notes would go out to audit and it would come out then or leak out some other way.'

'I was off for three days and I discussed it with Ted and, by the end of the weekend, I had decided I had no choice but to report the incident.'

'It was a difficult decision, as I knew some people would disagree with me. I told my manager and I was sent to see the director of nursing services and the unit general manager.'

The Harts expected the matter to be sorted out within the hospital, so it was a shock to hear the police had been called.

'I carried on working, but when the guilty verdict came it was a horrible shock – of course it must have been awful for Dr Cox, too. There was a press conference at the hospital and I was sent home. Then we got a phone call from a manager saying someone had given out my address, the *News of the World* were on their way round and to get out of the house. I just broke down. I'm seven months pregnant with a two-and-a-half-year-old son. I didn't want people shouting through the letterbox.'

'I left, but they didn't turn up anyway. Then shortly after that I switched on the local television news. There was a picture of the hospital and a voiceover said: "Should Roisin Hart feel guilty?" It was awful. Then the press calls started and people coming to the door. Ted dealt with it all – he's been marvellous.'

'There have been a lot of letters at the hospital and here at home. They got a call at the hospital from someone saying that now the nights are getting darker, he'd get me in the staff car park.'

'We've also had crank phone calls going on about me being a Catholic. I am, but it has nothing to do with what for me was a purely professional decision.'

'Because that's what it was. I'm disappointed the UKCC [United Kingdom Central Council for Nursing, Midwifery and Health Visiting] didn't come out early on with some sort of statement supporting me. They could have used it as a chance to reinforce the code of conduct.'

'I think hospitals could learn from all this too. We were told to go away for a while, but we couldn't afford it and, anyway, why should we have to leave our home? We were also advised not to say anything to the media, but because of that I ended up being made a scapegoat in the eyes of the public.'

'I've support from my colleagues, nursing, and medical, and, of course, from Ted and his family. Without that I would have cracked up, I'm sure.'

'I also have to say that, despite everything, I would do it over again if I had to. I just want the system changed so that other nurses faced with a similar dilemma can make the right decision without having to put up with the sort of persecution my family and I have been through.'[3]

Barbara Huttmann

Barbara Huttmann is an American nurse educator. In the following article, reprinted from *Nursing Life*, she recounts how she contravened medical orders and US state law to allow her patient Mac to die:

'Murderer,' a man shouted. 'God help patients who get *you* for a nurse.'

'What gives you the right to play God?' another one asked.

It was the Phil Donahue show, where the guest is a fatted calf and the audience a 200-strong flock of vultures hungering to pick at the bones. I had told them about Mac, one of my favorite cancer patients. 'We resuscitated him 52 times in just one month. I refused to resuscitate him again. I simply sat there and held his hand while he died.'

There wasn't time to explain that Mac was a young, witty, macho cop who walked into the hospital with 32 pounds of attack equipment, looking as if he could single-handedly protect the whole city, if not the entire state. 'Can't get rid of this cough,' he said. Otherwise, he felt great.

Before the day was over, tests confirmed that he had lung cancer. And before the year was over, I loved him, his wife Maura, and their three kids as if they were my own family. All the nurses loved him. And we all battled his disease for six months without ever giving death a second thought. Six months isn't such a long time in the whole scheme of things, but it was long enough to see him lose his youth, his wit, his macho, his hair, his bowel and bladder control, his sense of taste and smell, and his ability to do the slightest thing for himself. It was also long enough to watch Maura's transformation from a young woman into an old lady.

When Mac had wasted away to a 60-pound skeleton kept alive by liquid food we poured down a tube, I.V. solutions we dripped into his veins, and oxygen we piped to a mask on his face, he begged us: 'Mercy . . . For God's sake, please just let me go.'

Miracles

The first time he stopped breathing, the nurse pushed the button that calls a 'code blue' throughout the hospital and sends a team rushing to resuscitate the patient. Each time he stopped breathing, sometimes two or three times in one day, the code team came again. The doctors and technicians worked their miracles and walked away. The nurses stayed to wipe the saliva that drooled from his mouth, irrigate the big craters of bedsores that covered his hips, suction the lung fluids that threaten to drown him, clean the feces that burned his skin like lye, pour the liquid food down the tube attached to his stomach, put pillows between his knees to ease the bone-on-bone pain, turn him every hour to keep the bedsores from getting worse, and change his gown and linen every two hours to keep him from being soaked in perspiration.

At night I went home and tried to scrub away the smell of decaying flesh that seemed woven into the fabric of my uniform. It was in my hair, the upholstery of my car – there was no washing it away. And every night I prayed that Mac would die, that his agonized eyes would never again plead with me to let him die.

Every morning I asked his doctor for a 'no code' order. Without that order, we had to resuscitate every patient who stopped breathing. His doctor was one of several who believed we must extend life as long as we have the means and knowledge to do it. To not do it is to be liable for negligence, at least in the eyes of many people, including some nurses. I thought about what it would be like to stand before a judge, accused of murder, if Mac stopped breathing and I didn't call a code.

And after the 52nd code, when Mac was still lucid enough to beg for death again, and Maura was crumpled in my arms again, and when no amount of pain medication stilled his moaning and agony, I wondered about a spiritual judge. Was all this misery and suffering supposed to be building character or infusing us all with a sense of humility that comes from impotence?

Had we, the whole medical community, become so arrogant that we believed in the illusion of salvation through science? Had we become so self-righteous that we thought meddling in God's work was our duty, our moral imperative, and our legal obligation? Did we really believe that we had the right to force 'life' on a suffering man who begged for the right to die?

Such questions haunted me more than ever early one morning when Maura went home to change her clothes and I was bathing Mac. He had been still for so long, I thought he at last had the blessed relief of coma. Then he opened his eyes and moaned, 'Pain . . . no more . . . Barbara . . . do something . . . God . . . let me go.'

Death

The desperation in his eyes and voice riddled me with guilt. 'I'll stop,' I told him as I injected the pain medication.

I sat on the bed and held Mac's hands in mine. He pressed his bony fingers against my hand and muttered, 'thanks'. Then there was a soft sigh and I felt his hands go cold in mine. 'Mac' I whispered, as I waited for his chest to rise and fall again.

A clutch of panic banded my chest, drew my fingers to the code button, urged me to do something, anything . . . but sit there alone with death. I kept one finger on the button, without pressing it, as a waxen pallor slowly transformed his face from person to empty shell. Nothing I have ever done in my 47 years has taken so much effort as it took not to press that code button.

Eventually, when I was as sure as I could be that the code team would fail to bring him back, I entered the legal twilight zone and pushed the button. The team tried. And while they were trying, Maura walked into the room and shrieked, 'No . . . don't let them do this to him . . . for God's sake . . . please, no more.'

Cradling her in my arms was like cradling myself, Mac and all those patients and nurses who had been in this place before who do the best they can in a death-denying society.

So a TV audience accused me of murder. Perhaps I am guilty. If a doctor had written a no-code order, which is the only *legal* alternative, would he have felt any less guilty? Until there is legislation making it a criminal act to code a patient who has requested the right to die, we will all of us risk the same fate as Mac. For whatever reason, we developed the means to prolong life, and now we are forced to use it. We do not have the right to die.[4]

The cases of Roisin Hart and Barbara Huttmann are just two of many similar cases that have led to a serious debate about the role nurses can and should play, when morally significant decisions are at issue. Most if not all nurses will have experienced ethical dilemmas in their professional lives. These dilemmas can arise in varying contexts. A patient may, for example, repeatedly ask her nurse whether she has terminal cancer. The oncologist in charge has allowed the patient to maintain the belief that she can be treated. The nurse knows the facts are wrong, but has been told by the doctor that the patient would not be able to cope with the truth and that any disclosure on her part would be inconsistent with her role as a nurse. Is the oncologist right? Should she lie to the patient?

A nurse knows it is common practice in her hospital to allow groups of medical students to perform vaginal examinations on anaesthetized women without consent. The argument is that the women will never know about this, and are consequently not harmed by it, and that students must be given an opportunity to practise. She has unsuccessfully argued that consent should be obtained, or the practice stopped. Should she now blow the whistle?

Ethical issues in health care, foremost among them issues concerning the end of life, have been the subject of much discussion – not only in the professional literature but also in the popular press. This is not surprising. After all, these kinds of issue are of concern not only to nurses and doctors, but are of universal concern. For example, the question of whether human life has 'sanctity' and must always be prolonged, or whether there are times when a patient should be allowed or helped to die, touches not only nurses, doctors and patients, but also prospective patients – that is, all of us. There is, however, another set of question – much less discussed – that is of particular interest to nurses and to nursing: it is the type of conflict that can arise between doctors and nurses. Most nurses care for patients in a medical framework in institutional settings. They are accountable not only to the institution and to patients, but also to doctors: they are expected to follow the doctors' orders and to implement medical treatment plans. At times, there will be strong conflict between what nurses think ought to be done and what they are expected to do. The case of Barbara Huttmann is, of course, a case in point.

This type of situation, involving conflict between a course of action proposed by a doctor and the nurse's own ethical judgement about what ought to be done, is at the heart of what is sometimes called 'the nurse's dilemma'. It is also at the heart of the central theme of this book.

The traditional assumption is that nurses will implement the lawful orders of doctors. But does and should this traditional assumption also apply when *ethical*, rather than purely *medical* decisions are at issue? Are doctors better ethical decision-makers than nurses or patients? And what should individual nurses do when there is ethical conflict between the demands imposed on them by their responsibilities to patients on the one hand, and to colleagues, their professional association, their employing institution, and to society and the law on the other?

While such situations of conflict, and the question of an appropriate response in the face of divided loyalties, are of great importance to many practising nurses, we will not specifically address these kinds of issue. They have been competently and sensitively considered in many other volumes.[5] Rather, we will take a broader view and ask questions about the proper *role* of hospital-based nurses in ethical decision-making, and about the moral basis of this role. First, we will critically examine the claim that there are good reasons why nurses should continue to accept a subservient role to doctors and to medicine; and second, examine the soundness of recently articulated nursing ethics of care – nursing ethics that see themselves as distinct from traditional medical ethics. We shall ask whether these ethics can and should guide the practice of nursing. From time to time, we will look at practical examples from various areas of health care, but it will not be until chapter 8 that we will focus more closely on medical end-of-life decisions – the kinds of decision raised by the cases of Roisin Hart and Barbara Huttmann. At that point, the cases will serve to consolidate our earlier discussions, and to illustrate concretely how reasoning in and about ethical issues in health care would proceed, on the basis of the view of ethics defended in this book.

Until not so long ago, the question of whether nurses should think and act for themselves was relatively rare. Nurses have traditionally seen themselves as loyal and dependent functionaries who rarely questioned a doctor's order. When American nurses, at the end of the nineteenth century, took the so-called Nightingale Pledge, they swore to loyally 'aid the physician in his work,'[6] and the motto of the first Canadian school of nursing was 'I see and I am silent.'[7]

In 1977 Margaret Steinfels made the following observation:

> The subordination of nursing to doctoring mirrors society's expectation that women will defer to men, nurses to doctors. This is true even though nurses have independent as well as overlapping functions in patient care. Doctors and patients expect nurses to act as subordinates of the doctor; most nurses have been socialized to do so.[8]

The traditional relationship between nurses and doctors, and women and men, more than any other aspect of nursing, has determined the way in which nursing has developed. Many of today's better-educated and highly skilled nurses are, however, questioning their traditional role. They no longer see themselves as the mere handmaidens of doctors and of medicine, but rather as health-care professionals, who have a role to play in the making of morally significant health-care decisions. After all, doctors are experts in medicine and not experts in ethics. Why, then, should nurses accept the value judgements of doctors as morally superior to their own?

Nurses have begun to think and act for themselves. As we shall see, nurses have not only devised new professional codes of ethics and engaged in discussions about their role as 'patient advocates'; there are also attempts to ground nursing in a 'female ethics of care'. Such an ethics, it is frequently claimed, is clearly distinguishable from traditional male ethics and is the appropriate one for nurses to adopt. It focuses not on abstract moral principles, rules and rights, but rather on particular patients and on their needs and wants. As Jean Watson, a nurse and prominent proponent of a nursing ethics of care, sums it up: an ethics of care 'ties us to the people we serve and not to the rules through which we serve them'.[9]

In this book, we shall examine the idea of a 'female ethics of care' and ask whether it is an appropriate basis for the practice of nursing, and for the resolution of practical ethical problems in health care. A central question is whether an ethics of care can do without universal and impartial ethical principles, rules and rights or, as it is often put, without 'justice'.

We might, for example, agree that rigid rules will not always serve individual patients well, but can we do without principled ethical thinking altogether? Do we not, at the very least, need principles that give direction to our caring? We might agree that it is desirable for nurses to be caring rather than uncaring. But what should they be caring about? To say that nurses should care for, or about, their patients will not do – for it does not answer questions of the kind raised by the cases of Lillian Boyes and Mac. Does 'caring' entail keeping patients like Lillian Boyes and Mac alive, or does it entail that they should they be allowed or helped to die? Are there any limits to care? Must nurses always do what serves an individual patient best, even if means acting contrary to their own legitimate interests, to hospital policy and the law? Moreover, what does the rejection of 'justice' amount to, in terms of feminist concerns with the oppression of women, and the traditional exclusion of women and nurses from ethical discourse? After all, will not the adoption by women and nurses of an ethics of care become a 'compassion trap' that keeps women in their traditional place?[10]

As we shall see, there is much we can learn from recent discussions of 'care'. Some traditional 'justice'-based approaches to ethics have paid insufficient attention to a range of morally significant issues now being raised by nurses and women. As we will also find, no adequate ethics can do without universal principles and justice. To the extent that contemporary 'care' approaches reject universal ethical principles and the idea of impartiality, they constitute, at best, an inadequate ethics and, at worst, a dangerous one. In not allowing the articulation of principled claims, these care approaches facilitate the continued exclusion of nurses from ethical discourse and are unlikely to serve either nurses or patients well.

Questions about the possibility of a 'female ethics of care' are of considerable philosophical and practical interest. It would hence be tempting to plunge straight into that debate, and to examine the central philosophical and ethical issues involved. This would have been the traditional philosophical approach. I have decided to depart from this practice, to take a closer look at the recent history of nursing.

I recount this brief history of nursing not merely because it will provide texture and background to the subsequent theoretical discussions, but also because I believe that an ahistorical purely philosophical approach cannot provide us with an adequate understanding of the complex issues before us. While there is a definite place, as I hope my subsequent discussions will show, for careful discussion of the various philosophical and ethical issues involved, this should not blind us to the fact that ethical discourse always takes place in particular social and historical settings, and that nursing is a function almost exclusively performed by women. When we are looking at the way in which women and men have shaped their intellectual and practical lives, we are not only concerned with abstract philosophical and ethical questions, but also with important social or political issues, such as the relations between the sexes, power and powerlessness, and subjection and domination.

Rather than adopt gender-neutral personal pronouns, I have decided to use female pronouns to refer to nurses and male pronouns to refer to doctors. While it is true that changes are beginning to occur (particularly in the ratio of male to female doctors), historically the vast majority of nurses have been women, and the vast majority of doctors have been men. In 1986 around 90 per cent of all nurses, worldwide, were reported to be women,[11] and in the United States the figure was 97 per cent.[12] Gender-neutral language would obscure this significant historical fact, and some of the contemporary role-related nursing problems connected to it.

In her feminist tract, *Cassandra*, Florence Nightingale asked: 'Why have women passion, intellect, moral activity . . . and a place in society where none of these three can be exercised?'[13] A very similar question might still be asked today with regard to contemporary nurses. In the next chapter, and throughout the book, we will attempt to find some answers.

2
A History of Subservience

And here is an opportunity for showing how a woman's work may complement man's in the true order of nature. Where does the character of the 'helpmeet' come out so strikingly as in the sick-room, where the quick eye, the soft hand, the light step, and the ready ear, second the wisdom of the physician, and execute his behests better than he himself could have imagined.

Charlotte Haddon, 'Nursing as a Profession for Ladies',
St Paul's Monthly Magazine (1871)

Nursing is a metaphor for subordinated femininity.
Margaret Thornton, 'Foreword' in Megan-Jane Johnstone,
Nursing and the Injustices of the Law (1994)

Many of the contemporary assumptions regarding the role of the nurse have their roots in the cultural tradition of the nineteenth century, a tradition that gave an unequal status to women and men, and placed much emphasis on hierarchical social organization and authoritarian lines of command. The second half of the nineteenth century was also the time when medicine learned more than ever before about the transmission of disease, its treatment, cure and prevention. It became a discipline that could increasingly benefit patients and, for its implementation, needed assistants to administer the treatment prescribed by doctors. Since modern nursing was born at the time, since nursing was done by women and medicine by men, it would almost have been surprising had nurses and nursing *not* succumbed to a position of subservience and deference in relation to doctors and medicine.

In this chapter, we shall not ask critical questions, for example, whether it is appropriate for nursing to be subservient to medicine, and we shall not probe the question of what role, if any, nurses should play in ethical decision-making. These are central issues to which we shall return later. For the moment, let us just take a brief look at the historical period in which modern nursing had its beginning.

The word 'nursing' itself comes from the word 'nourish' and is derived ultimately from the Latin *nutrire*, 'to nourish or suckle'. Even today, the first meaning of the verb 'to nurse' is still 'to nourish at the breast: suckle'.[1] Writing at the beginning of this century, Lavinia Dock and Isabel Stewart were among the first nursing writers to suggest that '[n]ursing is a development of the mother-care of the young.'[2] This theme has since been taken up by other writers as well. Lisa H. Newton, for example, suggests that the function of the nurse is in many ways identical with that of a mother because sick people are childlike in their dependence on others. The nurse's assumption of the mother-role, she argues, is therefore justified not only etymologically and historically, but also in terms of the psychological demands of the patient.[3]

Whether or not contemporary nurses *should* take on the role of a surrogate mother is again a question we must postpone for later. There is little doubt, however, that even though there have been times when nursing was performed by men,[4] and even though men are entering nursing in larger numbers today, nursing is and probably always has been typically a woman's task. Looking at the history of nursing, Barbara Melosh thus reflects that 'women's dominance in nursing nearly equals women's monopoly of motherhood.'[5]

The understanding of nursing as a natural extension of a woman's role means that there are close historical links between the status of women in a given society and the status of nurses and of nursing. There have been times when women were highly regarded as 'healers', when their skills and expertise were greatly valued by the members of the groups or societies in which they lived.[6] In our more recent tradition, however, the understanding of nursing as 'a woman's task', and the social constraints that have traditionally severely curtailed women's opportunities and status outside the home, combined to make nursing in many ways a subservient profession.

The nineteenth and twentieth centuries saw the women's emancipation movement, and medical care became more complex and tied to hospitals. As more and more patients were treated in hospitals, nursing was gradually separated from the sphere of women's domestic duties and became a paid occupation requiring training. Despite these moves, nursing remained for a long time a largely subservient profession and nurses today are still trying to determine how they should answer the most basic contemporary question for nurses identified in chapter 1: whether nurses 'should act and think for themselves in matters involving ethical questions in health care'.[7]

Why should this be so?

Metaphors and Nursing

Karl Marx remarked that the 'tradition of all the dead generations weighs like a nightmare on the brains of the living',[8] and that our consciousness is, from the very beginning, 'burdened' by language.[9] But one need not be a Marxist to agree that history and tradition can have a profound influence on the way in which we perceive, and act in, the world. One way in which our consciousness is shaped is through figurative language (metaphor, analogy, simile and so on).[10] Take the metaphor 'A good nurse is a good mother/woman,' encapsulated in Florence Nightingale's famous statement: 'You might as well register mothers as nurses. A good nurse must be a good woman.'[11] Thinking of the nurse as a woman/mother will not only draw attention to the overlapping 'natural' functions of women/mothers and those of the nurse – such as promoting the well-being of particular others, nurturing and caring for the patient/child – but will also shape our interpretation of the role, and create expectations as to how the role ought to be understood. If a historical tradition understands a woman's role essentially in terms of 'wife and mother', sees a wife and mother as subservient, self-effacing and submissive, and expects her to leave all non-domestic decisions to the male head of the household, then it is not surprising that very similar historical and social expectations should also shape the relations between doctors and nurses, and medicine and nursing. After all, as the metaphor asserts, nurses *are* women, and women *are* wives and mothers, and wives and mothers *are* subservient, self-effacing and so on, and their role is quite properly limited to the care of particular others. Thus, if it is socially expected that the role of the woman/mother is defined in this way, then it will seem almost natural that the role of the nurse/mother should take a rather similar form.

Moreover, to assert that 'A good nurse is a good mother/woman' may also suggest that nurses are not professionals, that is, that they lack a special area of expertise characteristic of professionals. While nurses have certain skills and capacities, these capacities are not acquired through education or training; rather, the special skills possessed by nurses – their maternal caring qualities – are biologically given; they are inborn and largely unteachable female characteristics.

By asserting that 'A good nurse is a good mother/woman,' the metaphor is thus not only drawing attention to similarities that already exist, but is also *creating* similarities.[12] Gerald Winslow puts it well when he says that metaphors are not mere 'niceties of language'. Rather, because of their capacity 'to focus attention on some aspects of reality while concealing others', they are powerful shapers of our understanding of the world.[13] Depending on whether they are forward- or backward-looking, they can be a tool or a toil – being supportive and productive of change, or giving implicit support to practices and institutions that we would be better off without.

History has burdened nurses with a number of metaphors that may well have inhibited their self-perception as autonomous and self-determining professionals, and hampered their ability to make their moral voice heard. Some of these – the nurse as mother-substitute in a patriarchal family, as nun or saint, domestic servant, as obedient soldier fighting death and disease, or as handmaiden of the physician – have received frequent discussion in the literature.[14] These discussions can help us understand how certain aspects of nursing practice came to be accepted and appeared quite natural to nurses, doctors, administrators and the general public. But each of these metaphors focuses on only one aspect, or at most a few aspects, of the historical role of the nurse; they cannot give us the complex picture that will allow us to see why nurses have for a long time worked from a position of subservience and deference, and have been largely mute on matters of ethics. There is, however, a common strand which binds these metaphors together. This common strand is the notion that the nurse is not autonomous or self-determining, but in one way or another subservient – to God, if her role is seen as that of a nun or religious ascetic; to a military authority, if her role is regarded as that of a soldier fighting disease; to a husband or father if her role is seen as that of a wife and mother in a patriarchal family; to a master if her role is seen as that of a domestic servant; and to the physician if her role is equated with that of doctor's handmaiden. These views of subservience are reinforced and supported by the overarching metaphor which asserts that a good nurse equals a good woman, and the historical context in which women were seen as in some sense subservient to men.

These metaphors of subservience, and the social conditions in which they were born, can go a long way towards helping us to understand why nurses so readily, and apparently without much challenge, accepted a subservient role; why nurses sometimes saw themselves merely as 'intelligent machine[s] for the purpose of carrying out [doctors'] orders',[15] and why doctors could refer to them as 'useful parasites' to the medical profession.[16]

Our initial focus will be on Britain, where modern nursing had its beginning.

The Pre-Nightingale Period

There were virtually no trained nurses in Britain before 1840, and nursing was seen as little more than a 'specialised form of charring'.[17] It was, in the words of Davis and Aroskar, 'a poorly paid, confining discipline of unpleasant routines'.[18] If nurses were not religiously motivated nuns or deaconesses, they were largely illiterate women of the so-called 'lower classes' – widows, unmarried women, or impoverished married women.[19] As Florence Nightingale saw it, nursing was generally done by those 'who were too old, too weak, too drunken, too dirty, too stolid, or too bad to do anything else'.[20]

While such descriptions would undoubtedly have done an injustice to some nurses of the time,[21] there is little doubt that they were frequently correct. Charles Dickens – intent on revealing the evils of the time – satirized and immortalized the stereotypical early nineteenth-century nurse in his vivid creation of the unsavoury characters of Sarah Gamp and Betsy Prig in his book *Martin Chuzzlewit*.[22]

This is how Dickens described Mrs Gamp:

> The face of Mrs Gamp – the nose in particular – was somewhat red and swollen, and it was difficult to enjoy her society without becoming conscious of the smell of spirits. Like most people who have attained to great eminence in their profession, she took to hers very kindly; insomuch as setting aside her natural predilections as a woman, she went to a lying-in or a laying out with equal zest and relish.[23]

For Sarah Gamp and Betsy Prig the welfare of the patient was very much a secondary concern. When Mrs Gamp arrives to take over the care of a patient from Mrs Prig, Charles Dickens has the two nurses engage in the following dialogue:

> 'Anythin' to tell afore you goes, my dear?' asked Mrs Gamp . . .
> 'The pickled Salmon,' Mrs Prig replied, 'is quite delicious. I can partick'ler recommend it. Don't have nothink to say to the cold meat, for it tastes of the stables. The drinks is all good! He [the patient] took his last slime draught at seven. The easy-chair ain't soft enough. You'll want his piller.'[24]

Part of the reason why nursing in general was so unattractive lay in hospitals and infirmaries themselves. There was little if any infection control and the death rate in hospitals was very high.[25] As a consequence, hospitals were feared by the general public and were generally used only by those who could not be cared for at home: they were often seen as the last step to the grave. It was not until the twentieth century that hospitals were used by the rich.[26]

This, then, was the situation the young Florence Nightingale faced in the 1840s: insanitary hospitals staffed by untrained and undisciplined nurses – a combination that was doing patients more harm than good. If nursing was thus, as Florence Nightingale later put it, to be 'raised from the sink',[27] then it would not only be necessary to sanitize hospitals, but also to turn untrained, undisciplined and slovenly nurses of 'low morals' into trained and disciplined professionals who displayed 'high moral character'. Charles Dickens' Sarah Gamp and Betsy Prig may have been caricatures, but, as *Fraser's Magazine* put it at the time, Mrs Gamp's 'likeness is very traceable'.[28]

The Nightingale Period

Things were, however, beginning to change. Not only had a number of prominent women become involved in hospital reforms,[29] the second half of the nineteenth century also saw revolutionary changes in science and medicine. Medicine began to understand how diseases were transmitted and how they could be prevented and cured. Treatments were becoming more sophisticated, and it was frequently difficult to administer them at home. In this way, the care of the sick gradually moved from the family to the hospital. As a result, nurses were confronted by new conditions, had to carry out novel and increasingly complex tasks, and were faced with new responsibilities. It soon became obvious that it was important for patients to be cared for by skilled nurses.

All these factors are important in explaining why there should have been reforms in nursing, but they cannot explain why these reforms took the somewhat paradoxical form they did. For the first time in history, a substantial number of women were beginning to see themselves as professionals who would be able to perform valuable functions in public life. This change in perception gave women a new sense of freedom and autonomy. That autonomy was not reflected in the nursing role that so many of them subsequently adopted. Why?

In many ways, the nineteenth century was a time of great intellectual ferment and excitement. This included the raising of questions regarding the role of women. In 1792 Mary Wollstonecraft had published her famous *Vindication of the Rights of Woman*, arguing that the same educational, professional and political opportunities should be open to women and men, and that the double standards of male and female morality should be abandoned.[30]

Half a century or so later, John Stuart Mill was to publish his landmark essays 'On Liberty' and the 'Subjection of Women',[31] and the first claims for female suffrage were heard in countries such as England, the USA and Australia. Some pioneering women began to move into new areas – medicine, philosophy, law, politics and even the church. A quarter of a century later still, surprisingly radical undertones could even be detected in editorials and articles in journals such as *The Australian Women's Magazine and Domestic Journal* and *Women's World*. There, scattered among advice on how to make jam and mend socks, readers could find serious discussions on the role of women.[32] In addition to these new trends, demographic factors such as the late age of marriage, low marriage rates and migration created a pool of 'idle spinster labour'.[33] Some of these 'idle spinsters' were to become the new nurses. But before this could occur, some formidable obstacles had to be overcome.

England was, as one writer puts it, 'in the grip of an ideology that worshipped the woman in the home'. Women had no identity of their own: they were regarded 'as wives and mothers, as potential wives and mothers, or as failed wives and mothers'. If a woman was neither wife nor mother, she was not only 'the odd woman' or 'the redundant woman',[34] she was also frequently unable to support herself.

In a pamphlet, *Women and Work*, the political activist Barbara Leigh-Smith (a first cousin to Florence Nightingale) outlined the economic plight of women and argued that there were no good reasons why women could not become clerks, shopkeepers, nurses, doctors – indeed, anything they were competent to do.[35] Her ideas, like the similar ones of others, were not well-received and, in response, the *Saturday Review* swiftly reminded its readership of the traditional role of women:

> Married life is a woman's profession; and to this life her training – that of dependence – is modelled. Of course, by getting no husband, or losing him, she may find that she is without resources. All that can be said to her is, she has failed in business and no social reform can prevent such failures.[36]

An increasing number of well-to-do intelligent young women, Florence Nightingale among them, experienced a mounting sense of frustration with the kind of life society and convention sought to enforce on them. Florence Nightingale poured out her frustration and her loathing of such a life – described by her friend Mary Clarke as consisting of 'faddling, twaddling and the endless tweedling of nosegays in jugs'[37] – in her early feminist essay *Cassandra*[38] and in many letters and private notes.

At the time, the performance of good works – what Nightingale called 'poor peopling'[39] – was already sanctioned as a suitable pastime for 'good' (higher-class) women, and was promoted by the High Church movement. Professional nursing could be seen as an extension of such good works. Indeed, when Florence Nightingale finally gained her parents' permission to leave her home as an unmarried woman, it was on the understanding that she would dedicate her life to the care of the sick.

Metaphors of Subservience

To learn about nursing, Florence Nightingale went to Germany, to the Protestant Institute of Deaconesses at Kaiserwerth, where she admired the 'high tone' of the Institute and the 'pure devotion' of the religiously motivated carers.[40] There is little doubt that this experience had a profound influence on her subsequent understanding of the role of the nurse. An even greater influence was perhaps her experience as an army nurse in the Crimea during the 1850s.

Florence Nightingale's successes in the Crimea – she reportedly reduced the death rate from over 40 per cent to 2.2 per cent[41] – had turned her into a hero and living legend. After her return to England, there was no opposition to her proposal to use the large Nightingale Fund, collected in her honour while she was in the Crimea, to set up a training school for nurses at St Thomas's Hospital in London.

The changes Florence Nightingale made to nursing were truly revolutionary – but only in the sense that they distinguished the devoted and disciplined 'new nurse' from the slovenly and undisciplined 'old nurse'. They did not seriously challenge the Victorian conception of the role of women[42] or encourage critical thought and self-reflection. In line with Nightingale's own experiences and vision, nurses were expected to portray the single-minded devotion of the Protestant sisters at Kaiserwerth, the military discipline and hierarchical structure of the Crimea, and the value system of her prosperous Victorian background.[43] 'Good women' were trained to be obedient and loyal soldiers, who – like soldiers – were expected reliably to follow the commands of those in charge.[44]

Obedient soldier and deferential handmaiden to medical men

Modern nursing not only had its beginning in the military setting of the Crimean War, it also emerged at a time when medicine was appropriating the military metaphor.[45] As Gerald Winslow notes, it is now difficult to imagine a more pervasive metaphor in contemporary medicine.

> Disease is the *enemy*, which threatens to *invade* the body and overwhelm its *defenses*. Medicine *combats* disease with *batteries* of tests and *arsenals* of drugs. And young staff physicians are still called house *officers*.[46]

Nursing, perhaps even more so than medicine, adopted the military metaphor. It was used to turn undisciplined pre-Nightingale nurses into disciplined and uniformed soldiers, battling disease under the leadership of doctors. In the second half of the nineteenth century, nurses at St John's Hospital in London were thus issued with a pamphlet, entitled 'Hints for Nurses', which described their role as that of a sentinel on duty: 'The sentinel on duty has to keep watch and protect human life against any sudden assault, and warn the garrison . . . of the approach of danger.'[47]

The metaphor demanded of nurses not only that they stand by their posts and endure the hardships engendered by their soldierly role, it also stressed the virtues of loyalty and obedience to those of superior rank. Nurses in Victoria, now one of the Australian states but then a British colony, had apparently adapted well to the role implied by the metaphor of soldiers at war. They accepted long hours of work, squalid accommodation, bad food and extremely low pay. Grace Jennings Carmichael, a nurse at the Children's

Hospital in Melbourne in the 1890s, left a detailed account of her experiences as a special nurse in her book *Hospital Children: Sketches of Life and Character at the Children's Hospital Melbourne.*[48]

'Special nursing' in those days usually involved nursing infectious patients; it could mean weeks or months of quarantine. When told of her posting, the author wrote:

> I remember some secret rebellion lay under my outward obedience. However, there is no question of personal inclination in hospital regime; a nurse must obey as promptly and unquestioningly as a soldier, and stand to her post.[49]

Unquestioning soldierly obedience, self-sacrifice and ready subordination meant not only that nurses could easily be exploited, it also meant that they were, for years to come, discouraged from forming their own ethical or professional judgements. Seeing themselves as dutiful soldiers fighting death and disease, they became something Florence Nightingale had most likely never intended them to become – the subservient and obedient handmaidens of medicine and doctors.[50]

The military metaphor was soon to shape nursing and nurses in countries other than Britain and her colonies. This is evidenced in the writings of Charlotte Perry, one of America's leading nurses at the turn of the century. Writing in 1906, in the recently established *American Journal of Nursing*, on nursing ethics and etiquette, Charlotte Perry reflected on the education required to produce what she called the 'nursing character'. Upon entering training, Perry wrote, the student 'soon learns the military aspect of life – that is a life of toil and discipline'. Such discipline, she held, is part of the 'ethics of nursing' and should be evident in the 'look, voice, speech, walk and touch' of the trained nurse. The nurse's whole being, the author continued, 'bristles with the effect of the military training she has undergone and the sacrifices she has been called upon to make. A professional manner is the result.'[51]

A few years earlier, another leading American nurse, Isabel Hampton Robb, had also made use of the military metaphor when she outlined her thoughts on nursing ethics: 'The head-nurse and her staff should stand to receive the visiting physician, and from the moment of his entrance until his departure, the attending nurses should show themselves alert, attentive and courteous, like soldiers on duty.'[52]

There appears to have been little difference between the 'nursing ethics' that shaped generations of American and Australian nursing students. Between 1895 and 1913, Martha Farquarson served as matron at two Australian hospitals. Like her American counterpart, she insisted that when on duty in wards 'nurses should always rise and remain standing whilst doctor, matron, sisters or other officials visit the ward . . . it is necessary for peace that we should all learn obedience.'[53]

Here it is interesting to note that the nurses' obedience, subservience and deference seemed to focus quite naturally on doctors. Doctors were not only seen as authorities in medicine, but also as being *in* authority. Even if nurses had to rise and remain standing for matrons, sisters and other officials as well, it was none the less always the doctor who was at the apex of the hierarchical hospital pyramid. It was he to whom deference was due, and it was he who gave orders that had to be obeyed without question. As one writer in the *Australasian Nurses' Journal* of 1910 put it: '[O]ne of the first requirements a physician exacts of a nurse is obedience.'[54]

Many a nurse, at the beginning of her career, may have found such unquestioning subordination and obedience difficult. Writing in 1917 in the *American Journal of Nursing*, Sarah Dock impressed on young nurses the need to overcome this 'stumbling block', which was incompatible with becoming a good and reliable nurse:

> In my estimation, obedience is the first law and the very cornerstone of good nursing. And here is the first stumbling block for the beginner. No matter how gifted she may be, she will never become a reliable nurse until she can obey without question. The first and most helpful criticism I ever received from a doctor was when he told me that I was supposed to be simply an intelligent machine for the purpose of carrying out his orders.[55]

Similar sentiments were voiced by other nursing leaders. The first trained matron at the Melbourne Hospital, Isabelle Rathie, thus warned nurses of the danger 'of making too much of our knowledge . . . [for] we are in a great measure the handmaid of the medical man, and our function in this particular is to be obedient in every detail.'[56]

Obedience, readers of the English *Nursing Times* were told in 1913, did not just mean carrying out orders which, in the opinion of the nurse, were soundly based, but also those with which she disagreed:

> Obedience implies the immediate compliance not only with those directions which commend themselves to the good judgement or convenience of the staff, but with all orders, even though in the private opinion of the nurse others better might be issued.[57]

Doctors did not, apparently, mind this state of affairs; on the contrary. In 1903 the *American Medical Journal* complained that the nurse is 'often conceited and too unconscious of the due subordination she owes to the medical profession of which she is a sort of useful parasite'.[58] Three years later the same journal published a resolution which held that

> Every attempt at initiative on the part of nurses . . . should be reproved by the physician and the hospital administration . . . physicians charged with [the instruction of nurses] should never forget, in the course of their lectures, to insist on the possible dangers of the initiative on the part of . . . [the] nurse.[59]

Nurses, then, were to be completely subordinate to doctors, so much so that they were but 'the physician's hands lengthened out to minister to the sick'.[60] The military metaphor had thus not only turned nurses into obedient soldiers, but had also put them under the command of medical men.

Obedience and loyalty to physicians, and subservience to medicine, remained a central focus of nursing ethics teaching until the rebirth of feminism in the 1960s and 1970s. Although the tone had been softened somewhat, some of the central virtues associated with the military metaphor – subordination, loyalty and obedience to those in command – were still affirmed in a 1950 Australian textbook for nurses:

> Loyalty is the first essential . . . your training and the lectures you receive are given so that you can intelligently cooperate with the doctor in the treatment of the patient. The little knowledge you will have gained during your years in hospital in no way fits you

to diagnose disease or to prescribe treatment, nor does it place you in a position to criticise the doctor or his methods. Accord to him always that deference and respect which is his due.[61]

But these exhortations, although commonplace, have probably never been meant to be understood as absolutes. As Andrew Jameton rightly points out, nurses have, for example, never been expected by the writers of these texts to obey doctors making obvious mistakes. Florence Nightingale herself, while stressing the importance of obedience, emphasized that what was demanded was *intelligent* obedience. While blind obedience 'might . . . do for a horse', it was, Florence Nightingale insisted, but 'a very poor thing' for a nurse.[62] Similar qualifications were made by Isabel M. Stewart. Writing in 1916, she restated the traditional virtues of the nurse, but then also emphasized initiative and self-reliance:

> The traditional virtues of the good nurse are: obedience, the spirit of self-sacrifice, courage, patience, conscientiousness, and discretion. These are good, but under the newer conditions they are not alone sufficient. I think we have not placed enough emphasis on the more positive and vigorous qualities, such as self-reliance, the power of leadership, and initiative.[63]

But whatever potential qualities of self-reliance, initiative and leadership nurses may have had, they were not encouraged to give expression to them. Another metaphor, that of the nurse as a good or virtuous woman, weighed heavily on the consciousness of generations of nurses.

Nursing – a profession for virtuous women

To distinguish the new Nightingale nurses from the nurses of the past, it was necessary for them to be 'good women' of 'high moral character'. As Florence Nightingale put it at the time: 'It should naturally seem impossible to the most unchaste to utter even an immodest jest in her presence.'[64]

Strict insistence on high moral character was necessary if nursing was to become an acceptable profession for 'better class' women and their daughters. While many women had begun to question their traditional role as solely that of wife and mother and were beginning to seek some independence outside the home, they were still under great social pressure to refrain from doing anything that was perceived as unbecoming to women. As Florence Nightingale saw it, '[o]ne piece of indiscretion, one false step, and hopes of reforming the nursing profession and elevating its status might be set back for years.'[65]

By pointing to the congruence between the 'good woman' and 'the good nurse' the metaphor did more than affirm such traits as temperance, chastity and cleanliness. It also gave prominence to some other characteristics or virtues associated with the good or virtuous Victorian woman – submissiveness, selfless devotion to the care of particular others, and intellectual passivity. As a consequence, many of the qualities fostered in the 'new nurse' looked remarkably like the qualities thought desirable in Victorian women.

This congruence between the virtues possessed by 'the good woman' and 'the good nurse' had one almost immediate result: nursing became respectable and was now seen as a suitable profession for 'ladies'. In 1871, only 11 years after the Nightingale training school had opened, sentiments such as the following were expressed in the popular press:

> The want of remunerative occupations suitable for gentlewomen is, in these days, painfully felt and universally acknowledged; and fresh schemes are continually being started to remedy the evil. It has been proposed to throw open the learned professions to the competition of women, and to remove the various disabilities which keep the sex in a position of inferiority. But it appears that there is one department of activity peculiarly their own, which they have hitherto failed to make the vantage-ground it might become. We refer to nursing . . .
>
> Waiving the question whether women might or might not be made capable, with man's advantages of doing man's work, it surely will not be denied that a sphere of action would be preferable in which she would not have to compete with him, but in which her own peculiar endowments would give her a special advantage. And here is an opportunity for showing how a woman's work may complement man's in the true order of nature. Where does the character of the 'helpmeet' come out so strikingly as in the sick-room, where the quick eye, the soft hand, the light step, and the

ready ear, second the wisdom of the physician, and execute his behests better than he himself could have imagined.[66]

While many other factors would have contributed to nursing becoming an acceptable occupation for women – demographic changes, the need for more and better-trained attendants in hospitals, the increased momentum of the women's liberation movement and so on – there is little doubt that an important (perhaps *the* most important) factor was that nursing did not infringe the then prevalent conception of the role of women. Rather, because there was, as the metaphor asserted, congruence between the good nurse and the good woman, nursing was not only an *acceptable* occupation for women, it was a natural and highly commendable one.[67]

While Florence Nightingale had stressed that '[a] good nurse must be a good woman,'[68] she did not believe that being a woman was either a sufficient condition for being a good nurse or that women could do little else but nursing. Rather, she emphasized that in her view there was more to nursing than 'a loving heart, the want of an object, and a general disgust or capacity for other things to turn a woman into a good nurse';[69] she also made it quite clear that she thought women had numerous talents or gifts, and that they should neither allow themselves to be pushed into traditionally male professions nor allow themselves to be held back by those seeking to recall them to 'a sense of duty as women'.[70] Many of those who came after her did, however, understand the equation 'good woman = good nurse' as ultimately resting on a view about the natural role of women and men. Witnesses before a Royal Commission conducted in Australia in 1890 thus believed that Florence Nightingale had shown that women were 'natural nurses'. As one witness, Dr Balls-Headly, elaborated, 'I think women are fitted for nursing better than men; they sit up better and endure better, and . . . are apt to be kinder . . . I think it is natural for every woman to be, to some extent, a nurse.'[71]

Another doctor, Dr James Blair, an eminent physician in Melbourne, took a similar view. Lecturing to nurses in 1893, he claimed that woman 'is pre-eminently suited for a position at the side of the sick bed, a position for which nature evidently intended her'.[72]

Perceptions about women's natural fitness for nursing connected neatly with traditional ideas about their roles as wives and mothers in the Victorian and post-Victorian family. The role they had until then played inside the family was merely transferred from the home to the hospital. Indeed, hospitals came to be seen as a 'home away from home'. One commentator paints the following picture of the traditional 'hospital family':

> Early hospitals followed closely the Victorian concept of the home. The early nurse functioned as 'mother'. She worked inside the home, in other words, the hospital, and took charge of the house-keeping and hospital finances . . . The nurse as mother also bore direct responsibility for patient care. Like children, patients were the central figures and intended beneficiaries of the hospital family. At the same time, patients were expected to have little say-so in the conduct of hospital affairs. The nurses cared for, cleaned up after, managed, and educated their 'children'. The physician, to complete this all-too-real image, functioned as 'father'. Like the typical urban male worker, he spent much of his time absent from home. He only visited briefly to leave instructions with 'mother' for the care of the 'children'. In addition, he took major responsibility for the conduct of hospital affairs, was the head of the 'household', and often owned the hospital, just as the patriarchal male owned the home. As owner, the physician was the primary financial beneficiary of this arrangement, while nurses made financial sacrifices to support the industrialisation of health care.[73]

In health care, as in the Victorian home, Nature had apparently neatly fitted each sex for its particular sphere of activity. If some nurses found their role too restrictive and wanted to venture into what was regarded as the male sphere of medicine, it was easy to dismiss these ambitions as aberrations, as contrary to nature. As one commentator put it at the time: 'Woman as a nurse is the natural help of man as a doctor. Woman as a doctor is a conceit contrary to nature.'[74]

Raised from the Sink

Women were only too willing to accept the role that Nature had apparently mapped out for them. It offered them some independence, the opportunity – in the words of Florence Nightingale

– to do something more than tend the 'domestic hearth'.[75] There were plenty of nursing recruits, and some hospital books recorded hundreds of applications. Some of these applicants had to wait for months before their names were even registered for consideration.[76] These applicants were not only willing to function in the overlapping roles of obedient soldier, doctor's handmaiden and hospital wife and mother, but were also prepared to accept long hours of work, low pay, 'perpetual risk' and 'self-surrender'. As one nurse put it at the time:

> The intense desire, latent in the breast of every true woman, for occupation and to be of use in the world, is a powerful incentive to many in their desire for a life which everyone knows, entails much hard work, self-surrender and perpetual risk.[77]

Nurses who lacked the spirit of self-surrender and were interested in monetary rewards were not only bad nurses but also, as the *Una Journal of Nursing* thundered, 'poor specimens of womanhood'.[78]

There is no doubt that patients and doctors preferred the 'new nurse' to the 'old nurse'. In 1848, an English magazine lamented that 'it is notorious that the present race of hospital nurses do not come up to the standards';[79] and four years later the *Medical Times and Gazette* pointed out that '[w]e in the Profession well know what [a paid nurse of the old school] means – a hardminded, ignorant and lazy woman, who sleeps when she should be awake and is cross when she should be patient.'[80]

The nurse of the Nightingale school was strikingly different. She was often of the 'better classes', thoroughly trained in all aspects of nursing and of 'high moral character'. The reputation of Nightingale nurses soon spread beyond England to other parts of the Empire. In 1880 an article in the *Australian Medical Journal* had already called for the training of nurses.[81] During the next few years these calls increased in strength. As one Australian doctor put it, after his return from England in 1885:

> The difference between working in wards with the co-operation of educated gentlewomen on the one hand and of domestic servants on the other is so great that it would be with repugnance that I would go back to the old system.[82]

When, in the same year, the Australian daily paper *Argus* provided a public forum for the debate of the nursing question, the general public joined in the debate. This is what one recent recipient of nursing care had to say:

> Having only just risen from an illness, I have vivid recollections of the 'fever and the fret' of being in the power of vulgar, half-educated and wholly unfeeling women: and I cordially agree . . . that it is desirable that a superior class of women should turn their attention to this most important sphere of women's work.[83]

With all three groups – nurses, doctors, patients – working towards the object of making nursing an acceptable occupation for a 'superior class of women', it is hardly surprising that they were successful. This success ultimately rested on nursing being perceived as a natural extension of woman's function as wife and mother, and as the natural helpmate of man – a role which has, so we are told, been assigned to woman right from the start, when God decided to create a 'helpmate' for the first man, Adam.[84] As the previously cited article in *St Paul's Monthly Magazine* neatly summed it up: nursing is an ideal occupation for women because it gives them the opportunity to show 'how a woman's work may complement man's in the true order of nature', where woman can best display her character as 'helpmate' and execute the doctor's 'behests better than he himself could have imagined'.[85]

It would have been extremely difficult at the time to challenge social structures and roles which seemed to derive their legitimacy from such weighty authorities as God or Nature; and it would have been similarly difficult to challenge the notion that women and men who performed these social roles should portray certain given character traits or virtues. For women and nurses, as the fitting helpers of men, these traits were obedience and loyalty, submissiveness and self-sacrifice for particular others.

Conclusion

With this observation, we have come full circle. We have briefly looked at the two metaphors of subservience which were frequently interpreted as simple equations of the kind: 'woman = wife/mother/

helpmate to man = nurse = helpmate to doctor' and 'nurse = dutiful soldier = unthinking machine'. Few, if any, early nursing leaders would have accepted these simple equations. As we noted above, nursing leaders did not generally ask for the blind obedience one might expect from an unthinking machine; nor did these leaders have many of the self-effacing and subservient qualities thought so desirable in Victorian women. Rather, these early nursing leaders – including, of course, Florence Nightingale herself – were energetic and outspoken women, who would ably and vigorously assert themselves and, at times, go to great length to defend the rights of women.[86] It is tempting, therefore, to think that the legacy of deference, obedience and subordination should be seen as the price these early nursing leaders were willing to pay in their efforts to advance nursing.[87] Another and complementary explanation is, of course, that metaphors, once created, acquire a life of their own, thereby leading us along paths that are not of our own choosing.

Indeed, as we shall see in later chapters, the contemporary flirtation by some women and nurses with a 'feminine ethics of care' raises this very concern – that the identification of 'care' with 'women' will lead to consequences that few, if any, women would want.

Whatever Florence Nightingale and the early nursing leaders themselves may have thought, there is little doubt that the metaphors of subservience have structured the self-perception of nurses and of nursing for a very long time. Until the 1960s, nurses saw themselves largely as helpmates to doctors and medicine, and echoes of the metaphors of subservience could still be heard in the 1965 version of the *International Code of Nursing Ethics*. Item (7) of the *Code* states: 'The nurse is under an obligation to carry out the physician's orders intelligently and loyally.'

It was only the 1973 *International Council of Nurses' Code for Nurses* that pointed to a change in the perceived role of nurses. According to this code, the nurse's 'primary responsibility' is no longer seen to be to doctors, but to patients – 'to those people who require nursing care'; and instead of reminding nurses that they are under an obligation to carry out doctors' orders, the new *Code* admonishes the nurse to sustain 'a cooperative relationship with co-workers in nursing and other fields'.

This change in focus from obedience to doctors to responsibility to patients has usually been interpreted as a change from subservience to a degree of moral autonomy: nurses are no longer seen as the mere instruments of doctors, but rather as moral agents, whose primary responsibility is to patients. This raises a number of questions, including the following one: *should* nurses strive for a more autonomous role? While nurses may prefer to 'think and act for themselves', a number of arguments have been put to show that they ought to retain their traditional subservient role. Are these arguments sound? We will examine this question in the next chapter.

3

Advocacy or Subservience for the Sake of Patients?

Men of good conscience inherently know what is to be done or to be avoided.

Introduction to the 1972 Code of the
American Medical Association

Nurses are no longer willing to accept the hand-maiden role that has been their lot as an oppressed group, reflecting how society has viewed the role of women generally.

Nurse Educators, *Report of the Study of
Professional Issues in Nursing*, Health
Department, Melbourne/Australia
(1988)

The patient does not need another autonomous professional at his bedside, any more than the physician can use one or the hospital bureaucracy contain one.

Lisa Newton, 'In Defense of the
Traditional Nurse', *Nursing Outlook*
(1981)

As the previous chapter showed, the role of the nurse has traditionally been a subservient one. Guided by various metaphors, such as those of the loyal and obedient soldier and the good or virtuous woman, many nurses saw themselves as dependent and non-autonomous functionaries whose primary responsibility was to the doctor. One well-known Australian nurse, born at the beginning of this century, thus recounts how, as a young midwife in a Melbourne private hospital in the late 1920s, she was present when a deformed baby was born. The baby was alive, but no attempts were made to keep it alive. On the contrary, the attending doctor asked her to take the baby to the pan room and to leave it there until it died. Thinking back to this incident now, she said the baby could be heard crying in the pan room for a long time before it finally died. She clearly remembers feeling extremely uncomfortable about the doctor's order, 'But,' she said, 'it would never have occurred to me then to question that order. Doctors were regarded as gods in those days. They could do no wrong, and you just did as you were told.'[1]

A similar view was expressed by another nurse, the American Eunice Rivers. Nurse Rivers was a public health nurse and played a key role in the infamous Tuskegee syphilis study, conducted in Macon County, Alabama, from 1932 to 1972.[2] In this study, 400 black men were subjected to non-therapeutic research and denied effective antibiotic treatment, in an attempt to determine the natural history of untreated syphilis in blacks. Herself a black, Eunice Rivers was employed by the Public Health Service to serve as a liaison between the researchers and the subjects. She lived in Tuskegee, and knew the men and their families well. In fact, for most of her life, 'the men in the experiment were the closest thing Nurse Rivers had to a family in Tuskegee.'[3] She loved the men and their families, and they trusted her. And yet she never advocated treatment, and did not raise the matter for discussion. 'As a nurse,' she said. 'I didn't feel that was my responsibility. That was the doctors'.'[4] Any other response, Nurse Rivers explained, would have been unthinkable for a nurse of her generation. It is true, she had been taught that nurses must provide the best possible care for all patients, but her instructors, especially a Dr Dibble, had left no doubt in her mind what she was to do if there was a clash between a patient's interests and the instructions of the doctor: 'Obey the doctor's orders!'[5]

The view that doctors were gods whose commands must always be obeyed was beginning to be seriously questioned in the 1960s and 1970s. There had always been courageous nurses who had occasionally challenged orders,[6] but it is almost as if nurses needed a new metaphor to capture their new understanding of their role before they could finally attempt to free themselves from the shackles of the past. This new focus was provided by the metaphor of the nurse as patient advocate. Whereas the old metaphors had focused attention on such virtues as submissiveness and unquestioning obedience and loyalty to those in command, the new metaphor of patient advocate highlighted the virtues of assertiveness and courage, and marked a revolutionary shift in the self-perception of nurses and their role. The nurse's first loyalty, the metaphor suggested, is owed not to the doctor but to the patient. In thus focusing on the nurse's responsibilities to patients, that is, on the *recipients* rather than the *providers* of medical care, the metaphor of the nurse as patient advocate made it possible for nurses to see themselves as *professionals*. No longer were they, as the old metaphors had suggested, the loyal handmaidens of medical men: they were professionals whose primary responsibility – like that of all professionals – was to their clients or patients.[7]

A Change in Metaphor

Why is it that, after a century of largely unquestioning subservience to doctors and to medicine, nurses were beginning to reject their traditional role? There is no simple answer to this question. Various complex intellectual, social and technological developments have contributed to this change. There is little doubt, however, that the following factors have played a significant role.

New technology and consumer discontent

Medicine has traditionally occupied an exalted place in society, and doctors were treated with awe and respect, not only by nurses but also by patients. During the 1970s and 1980s, this began to change. Patients began to look more critically at doctors and their practices. Many countries were faced with escalating health-care costs, there was a fragmentation of services, dissatisfaction with the treatment and information provided by arrogant and business-like doctors, and the recognition that, far from being gods, doctors were fallible human beings who sometimes make mistakes, and who are occasionally tempted to put their own interests before those of their patients.

There were not only some widely publicized 'unfortunate experiments',[8] such as the Tuskegee syphilis study mentioned above, where doctors showed blatant disregard for the well-being of their patients, but it also became increasingly clear that new medical technology was not an unmixed blessing; inappropriately used, it could sometimes harm rather than benefit patients.[9] In his 1988 book *Some Doctors Make you Sick*, Stephen Rice estimated that in Australia alone some 70,000 patients are injured each year by their doctors,[10] and a health-care complaint line set up in Melbourne in 1986 recorded 2617 complaints during its first year of operation.[11] A more recent 1994 report, the authoritative *Australian Hospital Care Study*, based on surveys in New South Wales and South Australian hospitals in 1992, estimates that a total of 14,000 patients die unnecessarily each year, and a further 30,000 are disabled in Australian hospitals because of errors in decision-making.[12] Some years earlier, the social historian of medicine, Paul Starr, had already spoken of the 'stunning loss of confidence' experienced by medicine in the United States in the 1970s, and of a patients' rights movement which challenged 'the distribution of power and expertise'.[13]

If patients were potential victims of medicine because they lacked power and medical expertise, were unfamiliar with new medical technology, and were often too ill and too weak to assert themselves, it seemed clear that they needed help. Nurses – many of whom regarded themselves as the past victims of medicine and of doctors – were only too willing to render this help to patients, whom they saw as another oppressed group.[14]

New technology – new ethical questions

The distribution of power and of expertise, and with this the position of doctors as sovereign decision-makers, was also challenged by another related development. By the 1970s, advances in biomedical technology had created many new treatment options; it was, for example, now possible to sustain the lives of patients who, only a decade or two ago, would have died because the means were not available to sustain their lives. What became increasingly obvious, however, was that it was not always in the patients' best interests to be kept alive in this way.

At the time, the US case of a permanently comatose patient,

Karen Ann Quinlan, did much to stimulate the worldwide debate over the prolongation of life. Karen's parents wanted life-sustaining treatment discontinued because it was not, in their view, doing Karen any good. After extensive ethical and legal debates, the Supreme Court of New Jersey agreed to the withdrawal of artificial respiration.[15]

Fundamental questions were being raised about the value of life and the morally appropriate use of life-sustaining treatment and other technologies. These included the question of whether health-care professionals had a moral duty to prolong 'life', or whether they had, instead, a duty to act in the patient's best interests or in accordance with the informed patient's wishes. Was a patient whose brain had died alive or dead? Must such patients be kept alive? Is there a moral distinction between certain obligatory means of life-sustaining treatment and other 'extraordinary' treatments which may legitimately be forgone, and between active and passive euthanasia? These were the types of question that were now vigorously being discussed by doctors and nurses, by lawyers, philosophers, theologians and the general public.

In this climate of moral and legal uncertainty, it was not unusual for different doctors to make conflicting treatment decisions. As one nurse observed, 'the doctor on one shift will decide that a grievously ill person has no possibility of useful life and will suspend all active measures. The doctor on the next shift will start it all up again.'[16] The result of this moral uncertainty was that treatment decisions by doctors came to be seen for what they were: disputable and disputed ethical judgements.

Advances in medical technology thus raised questions not only about the fundamental ethical principles or values on which decision-making in the practice of medicine should be based, but also about the role of doctors as hitherto largely unchallenged decision-makers in such matters.

Better skilled and educated nurses

This insight was not lost on nurses, whose education and training had begun to change. The skills and responsibilities of nurses had expanded considerably, and an increasing number of nurses were now university-educated. As a consequence, they had developed a new appreciation of their own knowledge and expertise. Nurses with masters' and doctoral degrees were involved in research and teaching, and in the coordination and delivery of health care. These nurses not only commanded considerable knowledge, but also status – a status not enjoyed by nurses in the past. As it was summed up by A. M. and B. L. Sadler:

> It has been *the universities* which have endowed nursing with a respectability, freedom, and responsibility which embody the self-esteem that nursing had not been able to enjoy in the hospital sickroom despite a century of service.[17]

It is not surprising that these educated and highly skilled nurses were increasingly becoming dissatisfied with their traditional subservient role. They were also, as we noted above, working in an environment where revolutionary developments in medical technology had raised new and complex ethical questions. Moreover, as might be expected, nurses, like doctors, experienced moral uncertainty and their ethical judgements did not always correspond with those of doctors. That nurses were none the less expected to implement medical orders was not only morally troubling; nurses were also learning that they could be held legally responsible for the mistakes or wrongdoing of doctors. In short, it seemed abundantly clear that the interests of both patients and nurses were ill-served by meek nurses who saw themselves as mere physician-extenders.[18] When nurses in the Australian state of Victoria were engaged in a 50-day strike in 1986, one nurse summed up the feelings of many of her colleagues when she said:

> Yes, we want more money, but money is only part of it. More than anything we want recognition, we want to be treated as professionals, we want to be accepted as part of a team, which means we want to be consulted when decisions are made, and we want our ideas to count.[19]

The growth of feminism

That nurses so enthusiastically responded to the new challenges was undoubtedly also due to the growth of feminism. Feminism challenged the sex-role stereotyping inherent in the traditional metaphors of nursing, and many nurses were no longer willing to play the submissive and passive role traditionally assigned to them. A number of Australian nurse educators expressed these feelings in the following way:

> Nurses are no longer willing to accept the hand-maiden role that has been their lot as an oppressed group, reflecting how society has viewed the role of women generally. They have been at the beck and call of all others involved in health care, especially male doctors, and the role that they have played has been considered in parallel with the status of women generally. This is now widely challenged and the socialisation process is changing.[20]

Nurses wanted to be recognized as professionals in their own right, and they wanted their voice to count when morally significant decisions were at issue.

Factors such as these – the growth of feminism, nurse education, revolutionary developments in medical technology, consumer discontent and ethical uncertainty – can go a long way towards explaining why many nurses so eagerly appropriated the new metaphor of patient advocate. In focusing attention on responsibility to the patient and on new qualities or virtues, such as assertiveness, professional independence and courage to challenge traditional authority, the metaphor was able to capture the imagination of modern and well-educated nurses.

Rallying under the banner of patient advocacy, nurses began to take a stand, and to tell it to the world. A whole new genre of nursing literature sprang up:[21] the short story of 'The Courageous Nurse-Advocate'.[22] In these stories, nurses became intrepid female warriors who, much like the female private detective, V. I. Warshawsky, in Sara Paretsky's well-known feminist tales of crime and corruption,[23] were willing to defend the vulnerable against the harm and injustice inflicted by powerful others. The abstract of one such nursing story reads:

> Huddled in a cubicle during a shoot-out in a Detroit hospital or doggedly persisting until a callous welfare department gives in, this young public health nurse embodies the courage she calls on all nurses to display.[24]

A more recent article 'Helping Joanne Die with Dignity' has the subtitle 'A Nursing Profile in Courage', and the abstract tells prospective readers:

Paralysed by ALS, Joanne Benson was ready to die. But her primary doctors refused to help her remove the ventilator, and more than 20 other doctors declined to accept her as a patient when they learned what she wanted to do. Even so, her family – and several courageous nurses – didn't give up. This is the true story of how those nurses helped Joanne live her last days with dignity.[25]

Few dissenting voices could be heard,[26] and the general idea that they should take on the patient advocacy role was enthusiastically and widely embraced by nurses. Some nurses had already raised the question of patient advocacy in the 1960s,[27] and by the 1970s there was widespread agreement that advocacy was the 'mission of nursing'[28] and the nurses' 'hope for the future'.[29] By the late 1970s nurses like Patricia Fay wanted to scream the message to the world:

My plea to all practicing nurses is this: Please do not allow another group to take over the essential function of patient advocacy. We have all known deep in our hearts, even before the days of nursing process, nurse practitioners, and clinical nurse specialist, that our first priority was to the patient; but somehow, the patient and the world never received the message . . . We can no longer afford to leave the concept of patient advocacy implicit in the definition of nursing practice . . . We must scream it to the world![30]

Nursing – a Naturally Subservient Profession?

Until now, we have largely described what *is*, rather than what *ought* to be. This will now change. From now on, and for the remainder of this book, we will ask critical questions about the role of nurses, about ethics, about the relationship between ethics and nursing, between nursing and medicine, and between women and men.

Our first question must be this: *should* nurses reject their traditional largely subservient role and act as patient advocates?

As relatively recently as 1970, the American Medical Association approved a statement of its Committee on Nursing according to which nurses have a 'logical place at the physician's side', to function under the physician's supervision for the purpose of 'extending the hands of the physician'.[31] Objectionable as this statement will sound to many nurses, can we simply assume that it is based on nothing but sexist presuppositions about the role of women and men, or might it be the case that the nursing profession 'by its very nature' requires its members – women *or* men – to play a subservient role, for the sake of good patient care?

Before we examine this question, it is important to make one central presupposition clear. I shall, without argument, assume that a profession such as medicine or nursing does not exist for the sole or even primary purpose of benefiting its members. This view is widely shared and is implicit in most if not all professional codes;[32] it is also regarded as one of the necessary conditions for an organization to claim professional status.[33] For the purposes of our discussion, then, I shall assume that both nursing and medicine are professions which are, or ought to be, aiming at the welfare of others, where those others are patients or clients.

This raises the question of the relationship between medicine and nursing, and between doctors and nurses. Might it not be the case that the subordinate role of nurses has its basis not in objectionable sexism but rather in a natural hierarchy between the professions, a hierarchy that serves patients best?

Robert Baker is among those who have pointed out that we cannot simply assume that the nurse's subservient role has a sexist basis. He does not deny that sexism exists or that the subservient nursing role has traditionally been seen as a feminine one; but, he writes,

> it is not at all clear whether the role of the nurse is seen as dependent because it is filled by females, who are held to be incapable of independent action by a male-dominated, sexist society . . . *or* whether females have been channelled into nursing because the profession, *by its very nature*, requires its members to play a dependent and subservient role (i.e., the traditional female role in a sexist society).[34]

In other words, the facts that almost all nurses are women, that the traditional nurse's role has been a subservient one and that most societies were and are male-dominated and sexist, cannot lead us to the conclusion that the nurse's role necessarily rests on objectionable sexism. The nurse's role may, 'by its very nature', be a subservient one. But is nursing 'by its very nature' subservient to medicine – is it a naturally subservient profession?

There is clearly something odd about speaking of the 'natural subservience' of nursing to medicine, or for that matter of 'the natural subservience' of any profession in relation to another. To speak of 'natural subservience' suggests that the subservient or dominant character of the relevant profession is somehow naturally given and in that sense fixed and largely unchangeable. But is this view correct? As we have seen above, nursing has developed in a very particular social and historical context, in response to the then prevailing goals and purposes of medicine on the one hand and the social roles of women and men on the other. Would this not make it more appropriate to view the character of the two health-care professions, and the tasks and privileges that attach to them, as a historically contingent accident or social construct, rather than as a compelling natural necessity?[35]

It seems to me the answer must be 'yes'. There are no natural professional hierarchies that exist independently of human societies, and we should reject the idea that professions have fixed natures and instead view them as changing and changeable social institutions. When looking at professions in this way we may, of course, still want to think of them as having particular characteristics by which they can be defined ('social natures', if you like), but we would now view these characteristics as socially constructed, in much the same way as the institution itself is a social and historical construct.

How, then, might one go about capturing the 'social nature' or characteristics of a profession? One might do this in one of two ways: either by focusing on the functions or roles performed by members of the profession or by focusing on the profession's philosophical presuppositions or goals.

Function or role

What is the function or role of a nurse? What is a nurse? The clear and neat boundaries and distinctions presupposed by our everyday language and by the terms we use rarely accord with the real world.[36] We often speak of 'the role' or 'the function' of the nurse, or of the 'the role' or 'the function' of the doctor. These terms are problematical because nurses and doctors working in different areas of health care perform very different functions and act in many different roles, and there is a considerable degree of overlap between the changeable and changing functions performed by members of the two professions.

The expansion of knowledge, of nursing education, and of medical science and technology, has resulted in the redefinition and scope of nursing practice. Nurses now carry out a range of procedures that were formerly exclusively performed by doctors. Some nurses give injections, take blood samples, administer medication, perform diagnostic procedures, do physical examinations, respond to medical emergencies and so on.

Take diagnosis and medical treatment. The diagnosis and treatment of medical problems had always been regarded as the realm solely of doctors. But, as Tristram H. Engelhardt notes, if one looks closely at the diagnostic activities performed by nurses, it is difficult to see them as essentially different from medical diagnoses. Nursing diagnoses such as ' "Airway clearance, ineffective"; "Bowel elimination, alteration in: Diarrhoea"; "Cardiac output, alteration in, decrease"; "Fluid volume deficit",' Engelhardt points out, all have their medical equivalents; and the diagnosis of psychological or psychiatric disturbances, such as ' "Coping, ineffective individual", or "Thought processes, alteration in" can be given analogues in the *Diagnostic and Statistical Manual of Mental Disorders* of the American Psychiatric Association.'[37]

Nurses are not permitted by law to perform any 'medical acts', but in practice the line between medical and nursing acts has become rather blurred[38] and is, in any case, the result of social and historical choice. Moreover, as nurses have become more assertive and conscious of their own knowledge and expertise, there has been a broadening of the definitions of nursing practice. In 1981 the American Nursing Association thus produced a model definition of nursing practice, which included 'diagnosis . . . in the promotion and maintenance of health'. By 1984, 23 US states had included [nursing] diagnoses, or similar terms, in their nursing practice acts.[39]

To conclude, then, the fact that nurses work in very different areas of health care, where they perform very different functions, and the fact that there are considerable overlaps between contemporary nursing functions and the functions traditionally performed by doctors makes it difficult to see how it would be possible to define nursing in terms of a particular function or role performed by nurses. If we thus think of 'the nature' of nursing in terms of some specific function or role performed by all nurses, this suggests not only that nursing lacks a particular nature, but also makes it difficult to claim that nursing is 'naturally subservient' to medicine.

It is true, of course, that nurses frequently work under the direction of doctors, and that control over many of the functions performed by them is retained by the medical profession. It is also true that only doctors may, by law, perform operations, prescribe medical treatments and authorize access to certain drugs. This might lead one to the conclusion that nursing and medicine can be distinguished by the range of socially and legally sanctioned tasks and privileges that members of one but not of the other profession may lawfully engage in. Such a distinction would, of course, be possible. But it is not a distinction that allows one to infer anything about the subservient or dominant 'nature' of either one of the two professions. The distribution of socially and legally sanctioned privileges and powers between medicine and nursing is itself a historically contingent fact, and there is nothing to suggest that the current distribution of powers and privileges is either natural or that it is the one that we should, upon reflection, adopt.[40]

For example, why should it be the doctor who decides whether a patient like Mac, in Barbara Huttmann's case description, should be resuscitated or not? Should it not be the patient? And if not the patient, why not the nurse?

Philosophical commitment

Is it possible to distinguish the two professions by their philosophical commitment, that is, by the philosophical presuppositions that guide their respective health-care endeavours? It is, again, not easy to see how this might be done. Someone intent on rejecting the view that nursing is naturally subservient to medicine might point out that there is no essential difference between the philosophical commitment of the two professions that would allow one to speak of one of them as being subservient to the other. Both nursing and medicine are other-directed and committed to the welfare of clients or patients; members of both professions have a similar understanding of pain and of suffering, of well-being and of health, and both accept the same scientific presuppositions. If there are differences between individual doctors and nurses, these are no more pronounced than those found between individuals from the same professions. Hence, one might conclude, nursing does not have a nature which is different from that of medicine and can therefore not be said to be naturally subservient to medicine.

Another, diametrically opposed avenue is sometimes chosen by those writing in the field to prove wrong the claim that the nurse's role is a naturally subservient one. Rather than trying to show that the nurse's role is – either functionally or in terms of its philosophical commitment – *indistinguishable* from that of doctors, this second group of nurses claims that the nursing commitment is fundamentally *different* from that of medicine. In other words, those who take this approach start with the premise that medicine and nursing have different philosophical commitments or 'natures', and then go on to deny that this will necessarily lead to the conclusion that nursing ought to be playing a subservient role to medicine.[41]

This is generally done in one of two ways. The first involves drawing a distinction in terms of a commitment to 'care' and to 'cure'. Whereas medicine is said to be directed at 'cure', the therapeutic commitment or moral end of nursing is identified as 'care'. Medicine and doctors, it is said, often focus on treating or curing the patient's medical condition; nursing, on the other hand, is based on holistic care, where patients are treated as complex wholes. As a number of Australian nurses put it in their submission to a 1987 inquiry into professional issues in nursing:

> Medical science and technology is concerned with disease diagnosis and cure. This reductionist model of care inevitably dissects, fragments and depersonalises human beings in the process of caring. The nurse's caring role demands the preservation and integrity of the wholeness of human beings.[42]

The second way of attempting to draw a distinction between nursing and medicine involves an appeal to two different ethics. Whereas medicine is said to be based on principles and rules (a so-called [male] ethics of justice), nursing is said to be based on relational caring (a so-called [female] ethics of care). This means, very roughly, that doctors will put ethical principles or rules before the needs or wants of individual patients, whereas nurses regard the needs or wants of individual patients as more important than adherence to abstract principles or rules.

These two views do not deny that nursing is context-dependent or that nurses perform very different functions in different health-care settings; they also acknowledge that nurses and doctors sometimes perform very similar or identical functions and act in very similar roles. None the less, those who take this view assume that nursing is different from medicine because it has a different philosophical commitment or end – that of care. 'Care' – the nurture, the physical care, and the emotional support provided by nurses to preserve the 'human face' of medicine and the dignity of the patient – cannot, the suggestion is, 'be absent if nursing is present'.[43]

There are a number of reasons why I am pessimistic about the endeavour of distinguishing nursing from medicine and nurses from doctors in this way. We will discuss some of these at length in later chapters of this book. Here the following will suffice: it seems very difficult, in a straightforward and practical sense, to make philosophical commitments, such as the commitment to care, the defining characteristic of a profession. Such a definition would presumably include all nurses who have this commitment, but would exclude all those who do not. A registered nurse, who has all the relevant professional knowledge and expertise, who performs her nursing functions well, but – let us assume – subscribes to 'the scientific medical model' or to an 'ethics of justice' would now, presumably, no longer *be* a nurse. Would her philosophical commitment make her a doctor? And would a doctor, who subscribes to 'care' now more appropriately be described as a nurse?

The problem is raised particularly poignantly in settings, such as intensive care units (ICUs), where the emphasis is on survival and 'cure'. After Robert Zussman, a sociologist, had observed doctors and nurses in two American ICUs for some time, he reached the

conclusion that ICU nurses were not 'gentle carers' but technicians. Zussman does not deny that other nurses may well be differently motivated, but in the ICU, he says, they are 'mini-interns'.
'They are not patient advocates. They are not "angels of mercy".
Like physicians, they have become technicians.'[44]

For all practical purposes, attempts to define a profession in
terms of its philosophical commitment simply would not work.
How would one test a potential nursing candidate for it? How
could one ensure continued commitment – especially in a high-
technology environment such as intensive care? And why should
we assume that 'care' should always have priority over either principle or cure? Are there not times when proper care demands that
we attempt to 'cure' or when ethical principle ought to trump
care? If the answer is 'yes', as I think it should be, then we should
abandon the attempt to draw a distinction between nursing and
medicine in these ways.

There is, of course, another reason as well: Even if a sound
distinction in the philosophical or ethical commitments of nursing
and medicine could be drawn, this would not settle the question
of whether nursing is or is not a naturally subservient profession.
The fact (if it is a fact) that medicine has one philosophical commitment or nature and nursing another is quite independent of the
further question of whether one of the professions is, or ought to
be, subservient to the other. Further argument would be needed
to show that, for nothing of substance follows from establishing
that one thing, or one profession, is different from another.

Subservience for the Sake of Life or Limb?

What arguments could be provided to show that nurses and nursing ought to adopt a subservient role to doctors and medicine? In
accordance with our assumption that nursing is an other-directed
profession, a profession that primarily aims at the good of patients,
such arguments would have to show that nurses' subservience
would benefit patients more than nurses' autonomy.

One argument for nurses' subservience hinges on the saving of
life and on the achievement of various other therapeutic endeavours; a second argument focuses on meeting the patient's emo-

tional needs. We shall examine the first argument in this and the following section, and the second in the section after that.

Throughout this book, our main focus will be hospital-based nurses. Most nurses work in hospitals, and it is part of their role to carry out the treatment plans of doctors. Here a powerful argument is sometimes put that, regardless of what is true for other nurses, it is essential that nurses who work in acute-care settings adopt a subservient role. Those who take this view do not necessarily deny that it may be quite appropriate for some nurses, in some contexts, to play an autonomous role; but, they insist, when we are talking about hospitals matters are different.[45]

Hospitals are bureaucratic institutions and bureaucratic institutions, so a typical argument goes, rely for efficient functioning on vertical structures of command, on strict adherence to procedure and on avoidance of initiative by those who have been charged with certain tasks. While this is true of all bureaucratic institutions, strict adherence to rules and to chains of command becomes critically important when we are focusing on hospitals. In such a setting much is at stake. A patient's health, and even her life, will often depend on quick and reliable responses by members of the health-care team to the directions of the person in charge.[46]

Let us accept that efficiency will often depend on some of the central criteria identified above. This does not, however, answer questions regarding the proper relationship between nurses and doctors. Take the notion of a bureaucratic hierarchy. A simple appeal to that notion does not tell us how the bureaucratic hierarchy should be arranged.[47] Here it is generally assumed that it is appropriate for doctors to be in charge and appropriate for nurses to follow the doctors' orders. But why should this be so? Why is it so widely assumed that doctors should perform the role of 'captain of the ship'[48] and nurses those of members of the crew?

The argument from expertise

The reason most commonly given for this type of arrangement is that doctors, but not nurses, have the relevant medical knowledge and expertise to deal with the varied and often unique medical conditions that afflict patients, and the different emergencies that might arise. Just as it would not do to put crew-members with

only a limited knowledge of navigation in charge of a ship tra-
versing unpredictable and potentially dangerous waters, so it would
not do to put nurses with only a limited knowledge of medicine
in charge of the treatment plans of patients. Many a ship and many
a patient would be lost as a result of such an arrangement. Hence,
if we want ships and patients to be in good hands, it follows that
those with expertise – doctors and captains – must be in charge.

Such an argument is put by Lisa H. Newton, a vocal critic of
nursing's quest for autonomy. If the purpose of saving life and
health is to be accomplished in an atmosphere which is often tense
and urgent, then, Newton argues,

> all participating activities and agents must be completely subordin-
> ated to the medical judgements of the physician . . . [T]hose other
> than physicians, involved in medical procedures in a hospital con-
> text, have no right to insert their own needs, judgements, or per-
> sonalities into the situation. The last thing we need at that point is
> another autonomous professional on the job, whether a nurse or
> anyone else.[49]

There is something right and something wrong about the above
kind of argument. To see this, the argument needs untangling.

Shared goals, urgency and medical authority

In her argument Newton implicitly assumes that the therapeutic
goals of doctors are morally worthy ones, and that the ethical question of whether a doctor should, for example, prolong a patient's
life or allow her to die is not in dispute. This assumption is inherent in her observation that the tasks at hand are, or ought to be
'protective of life itself'.[50] While we know that this very question
is frequently in dispute, let us, for the purpose of our initial discussion, accept and work with that assumption. We shall question
it later.

There is no doubt that doctors have special medical expertise
that is relevant to the achievement of various therapeutic goals,
including the goal of saving or prolonging life. Extensive medical
studies and registration or licensing procedures ensure that doctors
are experts in medical diagnosis and medical therapy. Their educa-

tion equips them well to act quickly and decisively in complicated and unforeseen medical circumstances. As a general rule (but only as a general rule – there could be exceptions to this rule) doctors would thus be better equipped than nurses to respond to a range of medical emergencies. In emergency situations, then, where urgent action is required, it is likely that the best outcome for patients as a whole will be achieved if doctors are in charge. Moreover, since the outcome of medical measures in such contexts often depends crucially on the practical assistance of nurses, it is important that nurses will, as a general rule, quickly and unquestioningly respond to the doctor's orders.

It seems that we should accept this type of argument. During emergency procedures it is more likely that the desired outcome will be achieved if there is not only a single decision-maker, but if this single decision-maker is also the most expert medical professional in the field. This will typically be the doctor.

In addition to those cases where urgent action by a medical expert is required to achieve the desired therapeutic goal, there are also some other specialized contexts, such as the operating room, where it is appropriate for doctors to exercise and for nurses to recognize medical authority. As John Ladd has put it:

> In an operating room, the authority of the surgeon might be likened to the authority of the conductor of an orchestra; the surgeon is the chief performer and the one who 'orchestrates' the proceedings. Let us grant that the aim of the procedure is to save the patient's life, i.e., a morally worthy goal. But here, as with the orchestra, we are dealing with a precisely defined, limited enterprise involving goals that we may assume are shared by all the parties involved, or, to be more nearly accurate, we should say that they ought to be shared by all of them.[51]

There is a connection, then, between the possession of particular expertise and authority. Expertise can be crucial to the achievement of goals and, provided the goals are shared, it will frequently be appropriate for people who are authorities in a particular field to also be *in* authority.

If we accept this argument, it follows that doctors ought, other things being equal, to be in charge in medical emergencies and in other specialized contexts that are characterized by an element of urgency. They ought to be in charge because this arrangement best ensures that the therapeutic goal will be reached.

Acceptance of this view has, however, less far-reaching consequences than might be assumed. First, even if particular therapeutic treatment goals are most likely to be achieved if a single medically trained person is in charge *during*, for example, operations or resuscitation procedures, this does not entail that the doctor should have overall authority as far as the patient's treatment is concerned. The authority to decide on an operation or on the desirability of implementing resuscitation procedures might, for example, rest with the patient or her relatives, and the nurse could conceivably be in charge of the overall treatment plan of the patient.[52]

Second, it does not follow that nurses must, even during emergency procedures, *blindly* follow a doctor's order. Doctors, like the rest of us, are fallible human beings and sometimes make mistakes. This means that the nurse's obligation to follow a doctor's order, even in these specialized contexts, cannot be absolute and may at times be overridden by other considerations, such as the avoidance of harm to patients.

A study conducted in 1966, when nurses were probably more likely unquestioningly to follow a doctor's order than they are now, demonstrates that unquestioning obedience to doctors is likely to have some rather undesirable consequences for patients. In the 1966 study, nurses were asked by a doctor, by telephone, to prepare medication which was obviously excessive and to give it to a patient. Twenty-one out of 22 nurses followed the doctors' orders and were ready to give the medication to the patient when the researchers intervened. Commenting on their findings, the authors of the study wrote:

> In a real-life situation corresponding to the experimental one, there would in theory be two professional intelligences, the doctor's and the nurse's, working to ensure that a given procedure be undertaken in a manner beneficial to the patient or, at the very least, not detrimental to him. The experiment strongly suggests, however, that in the real-life situation one of these intelligences is, for all practical purposes, non-functioning.[53]

Given, then, that doctors will occasionally make mistakes and that nurses frequently have the professional knowledge to detect them, it will be best if nurses do not understand their duty to follow a doctor's order as an absolute and exceptionless one. If the doctor's order is, in the nurse's professional judgement, clearly wrong, then the nurse must bring her 'professional intelligence' into play and question it.

Benjamin and Curtis have introduced the useful concept of a 'spectrum of urgency'.[54] While the nurse's duty to follow a doctor's order is relatively high in emergency situations (where quick and efficient cooperation between doctors and nurses is often necessary if the desired goal of the medical intervention is to be achieved), it is much lower in cases where disagreements can be resolved at a more leisurely pace. In the latter type of case, there is time for questioning, reflection and discussion, and a nurse's refusal to act immediately on a doctor's order will not jeopardize the outcome for the patient.

Does a nurse who subscribes to the general proposition or rule that there are times when it will best serve the interests of patients that she accept the authority of doctors thereby necessarily adopt a subservient or non-autonomous role? Does she abrogate her autonomy? I think not. As long as a nurse does not *surrender* her autonomy or judgement, that is, does not blihdly follow every order she is given, but rather *decides*, after reflection, to adopt a general rule that it will be best to accept and act on the doctor's authority under certain circumstances, then she is not a subservient tool in the doctor's hands. She is not, as was once proposed, simply 'an intelligent machine'.[55] She is a moral agent who, in distinction from a mere machine, *chooses* to act in one way rather than another.

To sum up, then: the argument that nurses should – for the sake of achieving certain worthy therapeutic goals such as the saving of life – adopt a subservient role to doctors typically rests on at least two rather dubious assumptions. The first assumption is that all or most decision-making is characterized by great urgency. The second assumption is that the therapeutic goal is best achieved by nurses adopting an absolute rather than a prima facie rule to carry out the doctor's orders. But, as we have seen, both assumptions must be rejected, on the grounds outlined above.

In this connection, we should also note that nurses do not generally lament the fact that they are, while in an operating theatre, under the surgeon's direct command, nor do they generally question the fact that the urgency of some emergency situations requires them to submit themselves to the authority of doctors. As long as there is agreement on the worth of the therapeutic goals in question, relatively few problems arise. The situation changes, however, when the urgency may be low, but the ethical worth of the goal itself is in dispute. One example would be the case of Mac, described by Barbara Huttmann above. We will discuss these types of situation below. Before we do so, we should also briefly note that, if medical expertise is one reason why doctors should sometimes be in authority, the argument from expertise can also be used to show that there are some areas of health care where nurses should be in authority.

The goal of 'care' – and nursing experts

The argument from expertise has led some writers to the conclusion that nursing's quest for professional autonomy crucially depends on nurses having or acquiring a particular kind of expertise – an expertise different from that possessed by doctors – which would make them the equals or the superiors of doctors.[56] This argument is sometimes couched in terms of the distinction previously touched on between 'care' and 'cure'. Those who take this approach might agree that doctors are experts as far as curative efforts are concerned, but that nurses are experts in the area of 'care'. 'Care', they might say, comes into its own when 'cure' is no longer possible – in care of the aged, for example, and in the type of care provided to the incurably or terminally ill. As Robert Baker puts it:

> By their declaration of incurability physicians have admitted that nothing can be done to ameliorate sickness. But if death is inevitable, pain and incapacity need not be . . . The role of the nurse is to care for the sick in their sickness, even when cure is impossible.[57]

Baker gives the example of St Christopher's.

St Christopher's is a nursing facility for the incurably ill directed by Cicely Saunders – a nurse who, in order to have her theories of nursing the incurably ill listened to, had to qualify as a physician. At St Christopher's, care of the sick is primary; disease *per se* is untreated, and physicians are indeed ancillary to nurses.[58]

Based on the argument from expertise, Baker thus believes that in those areas where 'care' rather than 'cure' has primacy, nurses are the experts and ought to be *in* authority as far as the treatment or care of individual patients is concerned. While the medical expertise of doctors would still be relevant and could be drawn on by nurses (for example, a doctor might be called in to perform a palliative medical procedure), it would be nurses who are in charge of the overall care and treatment plans of patients.

This division of labour between 'cure for the curable' and 'care for the incurable' would give nurses an autonomous professional sphere: doctors would be in authority in the general area of 'cure' and nurses would be in authority in the general area of 'care'.

The appropriation of a particular and distinct sphere of professional responsibility is a possible approach to nursing's quest for greater professional autonomy and we will return to it in chapter 9. Nurses would still be working under the direction of doctors where cure is attempted, but they would be autonomous in all those areas where 'care' rather than 'cure' is the primary consideration.

This suggestion, while clearly worthy of consideration, would not resolve the underlying question of whether we should aim at 'cure' or provide 'care' only. Nor does it have anything to say on what role, if any, nurses should play in reaching that decision.

Professional Experts are not Ethical Experts

In a range of health-care settings, we find a set of shared assumptions about therapeutic endeavours and about the goals to be achieved. There is agreement, for example, that accident units and emergency departments should ordinarily attempt to save the lives of those admitted to their care. Generally, little is known about the victim of the accident, and a full assessment of the injuries may not have been possible. Preventing death in such circumstances will keep future options open and may restore the patient to good health. A similar agreement on goals – although not on the same goals – exists in terminal care facilities, such as hospices. When patients are admitted to hospices, the goal is no longer to prevent death, but rather to keep the patient pain- and symptom-free, and to allow her to die with dignity.

For the purposes of our discussion in the preceding section, we explicitly assumed that there was agreement on the medical goals, that is, that there was agreement on whether a particular patient, for example, should be kept alive or allowed to die. This agreement cannot always be assumed, and acute-care hospitals are frequently characterized not so much by its presence as by its absence. What if there is no such agreement? What if the nurse disagrees with a doctor's order not because the doctor has, for example, made a straightforward mistake in the medication ordered, but rather because she believes that the decision is ethically unsound?

There are many patients who are chronically ill and beyond cure, but whose lives can be prolonged for long periods of time through a range of medical interventions. Take Mac, the patient for whom Barbara Huttmann cared. The patient was terminally ill and wanted to die, but the doctor refused to write a not-for-resuscitation order. The disagreement between Barbara Huttmann and the treating doctor was thus not about whether resuscitation was an appropriate and effective treatment in a narrow *medical* sense, but rather about the moral appropriateness of that decision. Barbara Huttmann regarded the doctor's decision as morally wrong.

The question before us is this: should nurses adopt a subservient role when *ethical* rather than *medical* questions are at issue? As we have seen, doctors might quite properly be described as experts or authorities in medicine, and we have granted that there is a link between the possession of professional expertise and authority if there is agreement on the moral worth of the goals in question. But does expert professional knowledge or expertise also give rise to ethical authority to determine what the goals of treatment ought to be? For example, if there is disagreement about whether a seriously disabled infant should be kept alive or allowed to die, does the doctor's medical expertise give us any good reason for accepting his answer to the question? Of course, the doctor's expertise in diagnosing the condition and in providing a prognosis might be relevant in reaching a decision, but that is different from saying that the doctor is the one who should *make* the decision.[59]

Expert knowledge is instrumental knowledge. It can tell us how to achieve a particular goal; but it cannot, by itself, tell us what our goals ought to be. If I want my lettuces and tomatoes to thrive, I will do well to accept the advice of a gardener; if I want my leaking roof fixed, I will do well to listen to a roofer. Similarly with regard to medicine: if I want to find out whether I suffer from a particular disease, or what the medical prognosis of a disabled child just born to me is, I will do well to consult a doctor. If I want to find out what long-term care for my disabled child entails, I may be well advised to consult a nurse. Just as I would take seriously the advice of a plumber, gardener or electrician as to how best to overcome a particular problem or achieve a particular goal, I would take seriously the information provided by a doctor or a nurse.

Whether I should in the end have my roof fixed, spend the money on a holiday or send it to Community Aid Abroad is a different matter altogether. This is a question of goals or ends. Similarly when it comes to decision-making in health care. While a doctor can tell me that a series of operations will significantly increase my chances of living for another year or two, whereas I will certainly die now if I decline, he cannot – in his role as doctor – tell me whether this is the option I ought to choose. When it comes to ethical questions, to questions of moral values or ends, the doctor *qua* doctor has no particular expertise and hence no authority to tell others what to do.

The fundamental question is, of course, when and why a particular decision can be said to be morally sound. A related question is who should make that decision. The next chapter will attempt to give an answer to the first question, whereas the second is addressed in chapter 8. All we have established so far is that there is no direct link between the possession of professional expertise and the worth of an ethical judgement. This means that the mere fact that doctors are experts in medicine provides nurses with no good reason to accept the doctor's ethical judgements as superior to their own, and to accept a subservient role when ethical questions in health care are at issue.

Do Patients Need Subservient Mother Surrogates?

A different kind of argument is sometimes put to show that nurses should, for the sake of patients, adopt a subservient role to doctors. Only then, the argument asserts, will nurses be able to meet the emotional needs of patients. To examine that claim, we shall once again focus on an argument provided by Lisa H. Newton. In her defence of the traditional role of the nurse, Newton appeals to an argument based on the patient's needs. Because a patient may not be able to take care of himself, Newton points out,

> his entire self-concept of an independent human being may be threatened . . . He needs comfort, reassurance, someone to talk to. The person he really needs, who would be capable of taking care of all these problems, is obviously his mother, and the first job of the nurse is to be a mother surrogate.[60]

But, Newton continues her argument, mothers are not only figures of considerable authority; it is also ordinarily part of the mother's role to take control of various aspects of her dependent children's lives, and to make important decisions for them. Patients are, however, not children. Their autonomy must be protected from the threatening authority of the mother surrogate. This requires, Newton asserts, that

> the role of the nurse must be from the outset, as essentially as it is nurturant, unavailable for such attribution of authority. Not only must the role of the nurse not include authority; it must be incompatible with authority: essentially, a subservient role.[61]

This non-threatening caring function, performed by the nurse, would not only permit the patient 'to be cared for like a baby', but would also allow patients to unburden themselves and to express their doubts and resentments about doctors and the treatments prescribed by them. Patients, Newton notes, may sometimes be torn between the desire to discontinue treatment (to reassert control over their lives) and a desire to continue treatment (to reap its benefits). The nurse will be there as a sympathetic listener 'but in her subordinate position . . . can do absolutely nothing to change the course of treatment,' that is, both nurse and patient are subject to what she calls the 'sapiential authority' of the physician.[62]

The traditional subordinate role of the nurse is thus justified by the needs of patients. Patients, Newton holds, need the emotional support of a mother surrogate but, to protect the patient's autonomy and to ensure compliance with the medical treatment plan, the nurse must completely surrender her autonomy.

Should we accept this type of argument? The first point to be noted is this: Newton's claims about humiliating treatment, about strong emotional needs and about the threatened loss of the patient's self-concept as an independent human being, while undoubtedly correct in some cases, do not apply to all patients and in all circumstances. Many patients enter hospital for relatively minor treatments or observations and do not feel that their self-concept is threatened in any way by their status of patient. They do not need or want a mother surrogate. Rather, their needs are much more likely to be met by a nurse who not only provides them with professional nursing care, but who also refuses to surrender her professional intelligence and autonomy to the doctor to protect the patient from potential harm.

Then there are the patients who are seriously ill and whose self-concept may indeed be threatened by the medical treatment they are receiving or by their incapacitated state. Many of these patients will undoubtedly benefit from the presence of a caring and sympathetic nurse, who will listen to them with warmth and understanding. But would they want the subservient nurse Newton holds in store for them? Would their emotional needs really be satisfied by talking to a self-effacing health-care professional who, afraid of either posing a threat to the patient's autonomy or the 'sapiential authority' of the doctor, would be making sympathetic clucking noises, but would not engage with the patient in any meaningful way? I doubt it very much. By refusing to engage with patients in a meaningful way, she would be signalling to them that she does not take their concerns seriously, no more seriously than a well-meaning mother would take the incoherent babbling of her sick baby. This would not only be extremely upsetting to many patients, but would also enforce their sense of powerlessness, the feeling that they have lost control over their lives – as indeed they may have, if they find themselves in a situation similar to that faced by Mac.

As we noted above, Newton recognizes that a patient may wish to discontinue treatment so as to 'reassert control over his life'.[63] Would supporting the patient in this desire – assuming that it is a reasonable one – really threaten his autonomy? And is not the nurse's refusal ever to take the patient's desire seriously tantamount to abandoning him to another authority – the authority of the doctor? While we should not ignore the possibility that a powerful mother figure might pose a threat to the patient's autonomy, why should we assume that a powerful father figure – that of the doctor – might not pose a similar or a greater threat?

Newton simply assumes that the therapeutic success of treatment presupposes that the patient defer to the 'physician's sapiential authority'. What she does not explain, however, is why the physician's ends or goals – therapeutic success or prolongation of life, for example – should count for more than, say, the judgement of the patient or the nurse. In other words, we are not told where the doctor's moral authority comes from or why we should regard his decisions as sound.

I doubt that a totally subservient nurse could even meet the basic emotional needs of patients, or that she could meet them any better than an autonomous nurse could; and a subservient and self-effacing nurse certainly could not meet the perhaps even stronger needs of patients who want to retain or regain control of their lives and make treatment decisions for themselves.

The adoption by nurses of a subservient role of the kind envisaged by Newton would most likely harm patients more than it would benefit them; it would also be an utterly demoralizing role for many contemporary nurses, even if it would be compatible with some understanding of autonomy. Nurses would be required to stand by, doing nothing, while doctors make the occasional mistake, or provide treatment to unwilling but disempowered patients. To conclude, then, I can see no good reason why nurses should adopt a subservient mother surrogate role for the sake of patients. On the contrary, there are a number of strong reasons why nurses should reject it.

Conclusion

Social institutions are not natural phenomena. They operate in particular social and historical contexts. While it is true that existing structures and relationships will often appear so natural to us that it is difficult to imagine that they could be otherwise, they are none the less quite frequently the outcome of accidental, arbitrary and sometimes unjustified social arrangements, and bastions of the unequal distribution of power and privileges. Medicine and nursing are examples of this. They are examples not only of the unequal and somewhat arbitrary distribution of power and privilege, but also of the sexism that has, for a long time, shaped the relations between women and men.

Sexism refers to unjustified discrimination against women (and, sometimes, men), on the basis of their sex. It finds expression in a variety of social practices and beliefs, and has, as we have seen, shaped the relationship between medicine and nursing. Sexism is not dead. In the United States, for example, women constitute more than 80 per cent of paid health-care workers, but men hold almost all the positions of authority.[64] Moreover, as in the past, nursing is still widely regarded as 'women's work'.[65] As Margaret Thornton puts it,

> nursing is the paradigmatic example of a predominantly female occupation which is undervalued vis-à-vis predominantly male occupations which involve a comparable degree of skill, effort and responsibility.[66]

It is, of course, impossible to prove irrefutably that particular contemporary social arrangements or institutions have their source in something as all-embracing as sexism, but it is difficult to see the relationship between medicine and nursing, and between doctors and nurses, at least in large part, as anything other than a contemporary expression of sexism.[67] As Andrew Jameton has noted, once the very basis of the present division of labour is questioned, 'it is transparent that strong traditional gender expectations have had a profound effect on how the complex task of patient care is divided up.'[68]

And why, to return to our central question, is it still widely assumed that it is appropriate for doctors to make value-laden decisions and for nurses to carry them out? The reason is that ethics, like much else, has widely been regarded as the realm of men. As we shall see in chapter 5, many historical male thinkers, from Aristotle to Immanuel Kant and Arthur Schopenhauer to Sigmund Freud, have thought women lacking in ethical sense or reason.

Let us bring this chapter to a close. We have seen that there are no good reasons why nurses should play a subservient role to doctors and to medicine 'for the sake of patients'. While it will, particularly in situations characterized by urgency and by shared goals, be quite appropriate for nurses to accept the doctor's medical authority on a prima facie basis, this is not the same as adopting a subservient position. As we have seen, medical (or nursing) expertise as such does not give rise to ethical authority and cannot determine the rightness or wrongness of actions. But what can? To answer that question, we need to look at the nature of ethics.

4

Ethics

Should we inquire into the truth of a matter, or merely accept it on our own authority and that of others?

Socrates, in Plato's *Euthyphro* (*c*.400 BC)

Do unto others as you would have them do unto you.

Golden Rule

How do we know whether an action is right or wrong, good or bad?[1] Was Dr Cox performing a morally good or a morally bad action when he deliberately ended the life of his patient Lillian Boyes? How do we decide what our goals should be and what values or moral principles we should support – as private individuals, as citizens and as members of a particular profession or group? Should nurses, for example, support the 'right to die' or should they support the 'sanctity of life' view? How can we ever know that we have found the right answers, and how can we demonstrate their rightness or wrongness to others?

Questions such as these lead one quite naturally to inquire into the nature of ethics. What is ethics? What is an ethical judgement? How does the judgement 'It was wrong to resuscitate Mac' differ from the judgement 'I like chocolate ice cream best'?

This chapter is about ethics. The subject is vast. It covers not only some 2500 years of Western ethical thought, but also many other ethical approaches to the way in which we ought to lead our lives.[2] I shall be approaching the subject from within the Western tradition. Even with this limitation it would, however, be imposs-ible to cover so large a field adequately in a single chapter on eth-ics. Rather than attempt such an impossible task, I have decided to sketch – first negatively and then positively – what I take ethics to be. The view put forward here is a minimalist position, that is, even if the positive features identified by me do not constitute the whole of ethics, it is difficult to see how any plausible ethical theory can do without them. Ethical theories that reject them encounter, as we shall see in later chapters, some very serious problems on account of this rejection.[3]

The brevity of my discussion means that I cannot develop argu-ments fully, and my statements will, at times, be dogmatic. If I have occasionally allowed myself to succumb to what philosophers ordinarily regard as a vice, this is because I believe that good reasons and arguments exist in support of the views presented (some of the relevant references can be found in the notes to this chapter), and that it is important to make clear the central presuppositions on which much of our discussion in the remaining chapters of this book is based. None the less, I have not attempted to provide a neat account of 'the truth', that is, I have not attempted to defend one particular ethical theory as the one and only true and correct one to be endorsed. Different ethical theories have their particular strengths and weaknesses; and while I do believe that we have bet-ter reasons to accept some ethical theories than others, no attempt to formulate an ethical theory has as yet met with universal accept-ance. As in much of philosophy in general, there is no consensus in ethics – a fact that has, as we shall see, some important implica-tions for the formulation of an ethics for health-care professionals, such as nurses.

Ethics is Not . . .

. . . a matter of religion

In *The Brothers Karamazov*, Fyodor Dostoyevsky has Ivan Kara-mazov espouse the view that if there were no God, we would have to invent one. Without a belief in God and an afterlife, there would be no morality, no civilization, no love between people. If you were to destroy the belief in god, Ivan Karamazov says, 'every living force on which the continuation of all life in the world depended, would dry up at once . . . There would be nothing immoral then, everything would be permitted, even cannibalism.'[4]

For hundreds of years, religious teachings have provided a bulwark against the view that 'everything is permitted' and have kept ethical scepticism and nihilism in check. Religion did not only tell people what they should and should not do, how they ought to live, it also provided them with strong incentives to abide by the relevant teachings. Because a supreme authority – such as God – was thought to have determined what was good and bad, the content of morality could not easily be questioned. Nor was it prudent to do so: transgressors would be punished by the same authority that had laid down the moral laws. The theologian E. J. Carnell put it this way: 'God gives . . . content to the good . . . The good is what God rewards and the bad what he punishes.'[5]

In most Western societies, religion – and with it the belief that ethics consists in living in accordance with the will of God – is no longer as widely accepted as it once was. While many people in Western societies still subscribe to one of the various Christian beliefs, many others do not. They might be Muslims, Buddhists, Hindus or Jews; or they might be humanists or atheists, and reject all supernatural beliefs. This means that a particular faith-based ethics will have only a limited appeal. It will appeal only to those who subscribe to the particular religion and its metaphysical or revelationary presuppositions. A doctor's argument, for example, that a patient (and we might think here of the case of Mac) should be kept alive because doing otherwise is contrary to God's commands, or the teachings of a religious leader such as the Chief Rabbi or the Pope, will carry no weight with anyone who does not share that particular religious view.

The problem is not only that faith-based ethics have a rather narrow appeal; another difficulty also presents itself. To find out what a particular religious tradition, the Chief Rabbi, the Pope or some New Age guru says does not amount to establishing the truth of the matter. Religious leaders can be terribly mistaken in their views. The infamous Inquisition conducted by the Roman Catholic Church constituted the practical implementation of the recommendations of religious thinkers such as the great thirteenth-century Roman Catholic theologian St Thomas Aquinas, who held that unrepenting heretics should be removed from the face of the earth by death.[6] Nor was the Catholic Church alone in its zealous persecution of heretics. In 1526 the great Protestant reformer Huldreich Zwingli had all the Anabaptists (a religious and social movement believing in adult baptism and a kind of Christian communism) rounded up and decreed that they be drowned in the lake of Zurich; and thousands of women and young girls were burned in an unrelenting campaign waged by both Catholic and Protestant leaders against the devil's earthly representatives – witches.[7] A more recent reminder of the fact that religious belief is no protection against moral error is provided by what has become known as 'the Guyana Massacre'. In 1970 Jim Jones, the leader of the People's Temple, had lemonade laced with cyanide, which his followers were to give to their children and then drink themselves. Most of them followed Jones' command. Those who did not were shot.[8]

It might be said that the slayers of heretics were but children of their time, who – like many other religious leaders – had wrongly interpreted the true commandments of God, and that Jim Jones was an evil or mentally deranged person. But this response raises the obvious question of how we would go about establishing what the true commands of God or the relevant deity are, and how we would distinguish between correct and incorrect interpretations of her or his will. And even if we assume that this formidable problem could be overcome, a new one immediately presents itself.

The view that we should live according to the commands of a divine authority is often referred to as the 'Divine Command Theory'.[9] On this view, an action is morally good or right if the supreme being – God – approves of it, and an action is morally bad or wrong if the supreme being disapproves of it. Some 400 years before the birth of Christ, the great Greek philosopher Plato raised a profound difficulty for this view. In one of Plato's dialogues, the *Euthyphro*, the discussion between the philosopher Socrates and a scrupulously religious man by the name of Euthyphro revolves around the question of whether 'good' is synonymous with what the gods command.[10] In the course of this discussion Socrates asks what is often regarded as the most famous question in the history of philosophy and ethics: is an action good or right because the gods approve of it; or do the gods approve of it *because* it is good? This is not just a clever play on words. If 'good' meant simply 'commanded by the gods', then goodness would be entirely arbitrary. Had the gods been deemed to approve of cannibalism – to use Ivan Karamazov's example – or of torture, then cannibalism and torture would have been good. But to agree that these actions would have been good makes morality entirely arbitrary – just as arbitrary as Ivan Karamazov thought it would be without a god. On the other hand, if one wanted to deny that cannibalism or torture is good, this presupposes that there are standards of goodness or badness that are independent of the will, command or approval of gods.[11]

As the British philosopher Antony Flew has noted, 'one good test of a person's aptitude for philosophy' is to determine whether she can grasp the 'force and point' of Socrates' question.[12] The question forces those who want to base ethics on the commands of a supreme being to choose between two alternatives: to accept the arbitrariness of such an ethics and consequently of their own moral convictions, or to acknowledge that ethics is independent of the will of God.

Since the first alternative is clearly unpalatable, many contemporary religious thinkers have given up the claim that ethics has a religious basis; rather, they accept that the basic principles of ethics must be defensible on universal and non-religious grounds. In other words, they agree with secular philosophers that ethics, in distinction from a faith-based system of beliefs, must address a universal audience[13] and not merely one or other sub-group of society.

. . . a matter of obedience to authority

When Socrates asked Euthyphro whether an action is good because the gods approve of it or whether the gods approve of it *because* it is good, he had preceded it with another question: *Should we inquire into the truth of a matter, or merely accept it on our own authority and that of others?*[14] For Socrates, then, the question was not simply whether we should accept *religious* authority as the basis of truth, but more generally whether we can hope to find truth in authority as such.

In the development of Western ethical thinking, the appeal to authority has been widespread.[15] To find justification for their moral beliefs, people have appealed not only to religious teaching and to religious leaders, but also to secular leaders, to public opinion, to the law, to professional codes of conduct and the like. But just as ethics is not reducible to the commands of a divine authority, so it is not reducible to the commands of a secular authority.[16] To know what a professional code of conduct says is one thing. To determine that it is morally sound and should have our moral support is quite another.[17]

Similar problems are raised for the law. The law does not cover the whole of morality; in distinction from most plausible moral views, common law does not, for example, require us to help a stranger in need – even if we could do so at very little cost to ourselves. Moreover, we all know that laws, like professional codes of conduct and similar guides to social action, can be wrong and are subject to change. To hold, then, that social-action guides are synonymous with morality would have some very strange results. Slavery – to give just one example – would have been morally right before the abolition of the US slavery laws, and wrong once these laws were repealed. This would make ethics entirely arbitrary, just as arbitrary as it would be if we were to base it on the commands of a divine authority, and would raise the same or very similar problems to the ones already identified above.

To say that ethics is not reducible to the law or to some other socially sanctioned institution is not the same as saying that social institutions have *no* moral import. Not only will it generally be prudent to pay heed to the law, and to recognized institutions such as professional codes of conduct, but we may also have a prima facie moral obligation to act in accordance with some social institution. As the term prima facie suggests, these obligations are not absolute and can at times be overridden by other and stronger moral considerations. In other words, obedience or disobedience to a professional or legal code must be justified by *ethical* considerations rather than by appeal to the code itself.

. . . *what comes naturally*

If ethics is not a matter of divine or secular authority, can it be based on nature, or on what it is natural for human beings to do? For a long time, it was widely believed that there is a fabric of 'natural law' which would allow us to judge the rightness or wrongness of actions across cultures and times.

Natural law theory rests on the view that there exists a rational order, a value and purpose in nature itself. This applies also to human conduct. The basic and most general premise of natural law theory is thus that ethical beliefs have a rational basis, that is, the theory assumes that principles of right conduct can be ascertained by reason and that these principles reflect a determinate and rational human nature.[18] This view has played an important role in Western philosophical and legal thinking. There are, however, a number of difficulties with attempts that try to base ethics on nature, or on what it is natural for human beings to do.[19]

An initial difficulty with this approach is that to describe something as 'natural' is usually not to state a plain fact. What people at different times and places regard as 'natural' will, more often than not, be coloured by their particular cultural beliefs and values. Practices that coincide with accepted values and beliefs will typically be regarded as 'natural' and good; those that do not will be regarded as 'unnatural' and bad. This is often most clearly seen in the conflict of cultures. Tristram H. Engelhardt gives the following example: on one of his voyages, Captain James Cook, the great eighteenth-century English explorer, and his men were shocked to find that Hawaiians thought it quite natural and proper for unmarried men and women to sleep together; the Hawaiians, on the other hand, were shocked by the fact that the Europeans found it proper for women and men to eat together, something that the Hawaiians regarded as taboo.[20] As we can read in Cook's journal:

the women never on any account eat with the men, but always by themselves. What can be the reason for so unusual a custom, it is hard to say; especially as they are a people in every other instance, fond of Society and much so of their Women. They were often asked the reason, but they never gave no Answer, but that they did it because it was right, and expressed much dislike at the custom of Men and Women eating together of the same Victuals . . . more than one-half of the better sort of the inhabitants have entered into a resolution of enjoying free liberty in Love, without being troubled or disturbed by its consequences . . . both sexes express the most indecent ideas in conversation without the least emotion, and they delight in such conversations beyond any other. Chastity, indeed, is but little valued.[21]

The fact that different people regard as natural and good what others regard as unnatural and bad raises the question of how to distinguish between those acts that are 'truly natural' and good, and those that are a perversion of our natural proclivities.

This question presents itself not only when the customs of different cultures conflict, but also when practices within one cultural tradition are at issue. The moral theology of the Roman Catholic Church, for example, is based on natural law theory. Roman Catholic thinkers will thus typically appeal to natural law theory to back up their judgements on such matters as contraception, *in vitro* fertilization and other new reproductive technologies, masturbation, sex between partners of the same sex and so on. Masturbation and gay sex, for example, are often condemned as 'deviant' on account of their being 'contrary to nature'.

But when is a practice 'deviant' or unnatural? Is it a matter of statistical abnormality or one of deviation from a natural human end? Take masturbation. It is a well-known fact that masturbation, particularly among young unmarried males, is very common. In a statistical sense, this would make the practice 'natural'. Yet one of the great early proponents of natural law theory, St Thomas Aquinas, seems to have thought that masturbation was, all things considered, a greater sin than a naturally performed rape. The reason was that, on Aquinas' view, the natural purpose or end of sex is procreation. Because masturbation does not serve this purpose, it is unnatural or deviant in a way in which rape is not, and therefore morally worse.[22] This is hardly obvious. Masturbation does not harm anyone, and the mere fact that masturbation does not serve the end of procreation is not the same as showing that the practice is either morally wrong or that rape, which involves harm to another person, is less rather than more reprehensible than masturbation.

Contemporary natural law theorists, such as John Finnis, have somewhat revised the traditional approach. Finnis, for example, has developed a natural law theory based on the view that there is a range of basic 'human goods', such as life, knowledge, play, friendship and practical reasonableness.[23] While this list of human goods is not, on the face of it, an implausible one, it is far from clear how Finnis, a Roman Catholic himself, can derive from this list of basic human goods not only a general duty of beneficence, but also some specific moral injunctions about, for example, the wrongness of contraception and masturbation. It seems clear that Finnis has, as one commentator notes, brought his theory 'into line with Roman Catholic orthodoxy at the expense of its general plausibility'.[24]

Outside the Roman Catholic tradition, natural law theory does not have many supporters. Many philosophers reject it on the grounds that it involves an illegitimate conflation of 'is' and 'ought', or of facts and values. It may well be the case, for example, that the natural purpose of sex is procreation, but it does not follow from this fact that people ought to engage in sex for this purpose only, and that non-procreative sexual activities are morally wrong. It may also be natural for human beings, especially male human beings, to be aggressive. It does not follow from this fact that they ought to be aggressive.

. . . social practice

There is another cluster of views according to which ethics is neither a matter of religion nor of natural law, but can be iden tified with the customary practices of individual societies. In other words, ethics is thought to be relative rather than universal: what is right or wrong depends on where one happens to live.[25]

Most of us can give many examples to show that moral stand-ards differ from culture to culture: some Muslims practise poly-gamy, and the Nepalese polyandry; some ethnic groups engage in so-called female circumcision, whereas other societies regard the practice as wrong; the Jains will not eat meat; the Hopi were obli-vious to the suffering of animals and thought nothing of torturing them; the Netsilik Eskimo used to kill first-born female infants, and New Guinean tribes practised cannibalism. The recognition that moral standards can be so different has led people to believe that ethics is relative to culture and synonymous with group approval. As the sociologist W. G. Sumner put it at the beginning of this cen-tury: 'We shall find proof that "immoral" never means anything but contrary to the mores of the time and place . . . the "right" way is the way which the ancestors used and which has been handed down.'[26]

Marxist and Freudian theories have, it might seem, added weight to the relativists' claims. Both views have one thing in common: the claim that human beings are 'conditioned', that our moral responses are determined either by our place in the economic system or by familial relationships. If these claims are understood in a strong sense, that is, that we are simply the product of our background or upbringing, then ethics would be superfluous. It would be swallowed up by either the study of political economy or psychoanalysis.

This way of thinking has been quite influential. But is it correct? If our moral views were really determined by the economic system or by familial relationships, then it would be difficult to explain how the very proponents of such views can themselves raise questions about morality which put them outside the confines set by their respective frameworks.

Karl Marx himself is a good example. Although a member of a particularistic class society, he was able to advance a universalistic view of ethics and society. This, he thought, was possible because consciousness can, at times, be 'further advanced than contemporary empirical relationships'.[27] But if this is so, then it is difficult to see how consciousness could also have been *determined* by those very same empirical relationships. We may be conditioned by our social class and by our upbringing, but not inescapably so. We still can and do ask whether the practices of our society, class or family are good or bad, right or wrong.

And we can do the same regarding the moral codes of other societies. The fact that different societies have different moral codes proves nothing in itself. There is also disagreement between cultures regarding non-moral matters. Some people believed that the earth was a flat disc, others that it was a great ball resting on the back of a turtle, and some that looking at your mother-in-law caused disease.[28] If we do not, from such disagreements, draw the conclusion that there is no truth or falsity in geography or medicine, why conclude from ethical disagreement that there is no truth or falsity in ethics? Societies, like individuals, can be mistaken in their ethical judgements. To deny this would preclude us from ever morally condemning a practice accepted by society, such as slavery, racism or sexism.

. . . *just a matter of feelings*

Contemporary philosophers generally reject the claim that ethics is relative in the above sense of 'relative'. The claim does, however, survive in a different form. According to this view, which goes back to the eighteenth-century Scottish philosopher David Hume, ethical judgements do not belong to the class of statements called cognitive, which can be verified as true or false; ethical judgements are emotional expressions of approval or disapproval, or are merely prescriptions for action. In other words, when I say 'I think slavery is wrong' or 'I believe it is wrong not to ask a competent but terminally ill patient whether or not she wants to be resuscitated,' I am expressing my attitudes and preferences, and want to influence and manipulate the behavioural dispositions in my hearers. According to this view, we do this because we care about our feelings and attitudes and care about what people do.[29]

If we accept this view of ethics, often described as 'subjectivist', does this mean that one ethical judgement is as good as another? I think not. Even if ethics is subjective in this sense, that is, if there exists no separate realm of ethical facts and values independent of the attitudes and preferences we hold, it does not mean that this is the end of the matter.

The point is this: a moral argument must be supported by *reasons*. This makes a moral judgement different from the expression of a mere personal preference. If I say 'I think chocolate ice cream is best,' I need give no further reasons for my view – I may simply be making a statement about my taste. Moral judgements, on the other hand, need to be backed by reasons. As James Rachels notes, if there are no reasons, a moral judgement is not merely arbitrary, it lacks the necessary features of a moral judgement: 'One *must* have reasons, or else one is not making a moral judgement at all . . . To say "It would be morally wrong to do X, but there is no reason why it would be wrong" is a self-contradiction.'[30]

When we are required to back our arguments by reasons, we find that there is not only room for rational argument and debate, but also that some conclusions are more worthy of our support than others. This is not to say that we may not have strong feelings about some matters, that our emotions don't count, but ethics always requires us to reflect on these feelings.[31] After all, our feelings may be little more than the results of our upbringing, of shared prejudice or of selfishness. And once we start giving *reasons* for our moral judgements, our judgements can be criticized, shown to be adequate or inadequate on a number of grounds. Moral problems can be debated, and become amenable to solution by rational method.

Minimally Ethics is . . .

So far we have dealt largely with what is often referred to as 'meta-ethics', that is, we have asked questions about the nature of ethics and about the foundation of ethical judgements. I argued that there are good reasons for rejecting the view that ethical judgements can be founded on either religious or secular authority, on natural law, on social practice or on feelings alone. Ethics, I suggested, is essentially a matter of reason – a critical or reflective enterprise.

When it comes to giving reasons for our views, we are moving into the area of 'normative ethics'. We are no longer concerned with questions *about* ethics, but rather with questions of value and of action: what ethical principles and values should we adopt; what reasons count as *ethical* reasons; what actions should we perform; and why should we choose some principles or values over others? While there is some overlap between meta-ethics and normative ethics, normative ethics is primarily concerned with the justification of particular moral judgements.

In the preceding section, we defined ethics largely negatively, in terms of what it is not. The time has come to describe it in terms of its positive features, and to establish the nature of the link between ethics and reason.

. . . reflective

No society or group could survive without setting limits on some actions, while encouraging others. Even if different societies and cultures have different moral rules and ethical standards, these

differences should not be overestimated. The indiscriminate killing of members of one's own group, or murder, is the most universally condemned action, and care for the young the most widely
encouraged one. While there are differences between cultures and
groups in what they regard as justifiable exceptions to these rules,
there is agreement on the general point that members of the group
must neither kill each other indiscriminately nor neglect the care of
their young. If these two basic rules were not heeded, the group
would not survive. To enable the group to flourish, additional rules
and standards are needed. In short, then, wherever people are living
together, we will find that certain standards of behaviour are set and
that conduct is classified as 'right' or 'wrong', as 'good' or 'bad'.

There is, however, an important difference between customary or habitual morality and normative or critical ethical thinking. As we already noted briefly above, in our living together as
social beings we absorb many values, beliefs and rules – sometimes without ever questioning them throughout the whole of our
lives. Take the case (described at the beginning of chapter 3) of
the young midwife working in a Melbourne hospital in the 1920s,
who was asked to take a deformed baby to the pan room, to
allow it to die. While she felt uncomfortable about the order, she
did not question it. As she put it: 'it would never have occurred to
me then to question that order . . . you just did as you were told.'
Or take the Hawaiians encountered by Captain James Cook during one of his voyages. Cook recorded that the Hawaiians believed
it was improper for men and women to eat together. When asked
why this was so, the Hawaiians could apparently give no reason
for the prohibition other than to say that this was how it was.

When we simply follow a code, a practice or a rule, we may be
living according to some culturally approved moral standards,
but these standards are not our own because they lack the stamp
of our reflective approval: we are living in accordance with custom,
merely habitually. This is true even if we are living in accordance
with standards that we, in our society, regard as unquestionably
ethical standards, for example, that we should not lie, steal, cheat
and so on. If we do not lie or cheat *simply* because we have been
inculcated with the belief that we must not do so, then this is no
different from living in accordance with a mere taboo.

Living reflectively, according to an ethics or morality that we can rightly call 'our own', requires us to give reasons for our views, and to attend to the consequences of our actions and omissions. To say this is not, however, the same as saying that these reasons must be acceptable to everyone, or that any reason whatsoever will do. Many members of Captain Cook's generation, for example, believed that sexual intercourse between unmarried women and men was contrary to God's laws and therefore wrong. They might also have believed that it was prudent to obey God's laws, either because God would punish offenders, or because living in accordance with the laws of a benevolent God would promote the flourishing of the group. Now, we might want to reject these reasons as ultimately non-rational (because we might, for example, take the view defended above that ethics cannot be based on religion), but, to the extent that people are living according to standards which they believe can be defended and justified on universal grounds, they are living reflectively and in accordance with a moral code of behaviour that is 'their own'.

To give another example, take the Netsilik Eskimo who frequently exposed their first-born daughters. The Netsilik practised exposure because the survival of whole families depended on male hunters providing them with food. Having a female infant and suckling it for two or three years would prevent a woman from having another male child who could eventually take on the role of a future provider. At the beginning of the century, the Danish Arctic explorer Knud Rasmussen asked an older Netsilik Eskimo woman what she would do if her daughter gave birth to a female child: 'If my daughter Quertiliq had a girl child I would strangle it at once. If I did not, I would be a bad mother.' The woman thought that not strangling a female grandchild would make her a bad mother because allowing the infant to live would threaten her own daughter's and her family's survival, and might ultimately threaten the society's survival.[32]

Those who take the view that a human life must never deliberately be cut short will not agree with the Netsilik woman's judgement. To the extent that she was able to give reasons for her action, that she was able to defend it by pointing to the potentially devastating consequences of letting a first-born female infant live, she was not acting in accordance with a mere taboo, but was making a moral or ethical judgement.

. . . a social activity

Living according to ethical standards is thus tied up with giving reasons for what we do, with justifying and defending the way in which we live. This means that ethics is not primarily a privately reflective enterprise, but a social activity, a dialogue with others, conducted against the backdrop of a variety of shared assumptions, beliefs and institutions. In other words, as soon as we attempt to justify our actions to others (or try to persuade others that their actions are wrong), our ethical reflections take on a social dimension.[33] In our particular area of concern, such social dimensions exist as soon as nurses, doctors and patients engage in critical dialogue about such matters as truth-telling, not-for-resuscitation orders, voluntary euthanasia or the proper role of the nurse in ethical decision-making.

The cases of Roisin Hart and Barbara Huttmann, discussed in chapter 1, are two cases in point. What started as the private reflections of two nurses on what they should do took on a social dimension when Roisin Hart blew the whistle on Dr Cox, and when Barbara Huttmann publicly defended her decision to contravene orders and to allow her patient Mac to die.

. . . a matter of sound reasoning

But not every judgement will do in ethics. A number of necessary conditions must be met before we can accept a reasoned judgement as morally sound.

Facts: It is a fairly elementary point that one cannot engage in ethical reasoning, or in any other kind of reasoning, unless one has an accurate understanding of the relevant facts. When the facts are wrong, we are starting from faulty premises and cannot hope to reach valid conclusions.

Consistency: If getting the facts right is a basic requirement of sound reasoning of any kind, so is the logical requirement of consistency.

Inconsistency is a fatal flaw in any argument, including ethical argument. If we can detect an inconsistency in someone's view, we will often be justified in thinking that we have dealt it a mortal blow. If I were to argue that all nurses are women and that Jo is a nurse, I would contradict myself if I were then to go on to declare that Jo is a man. The three assertions I have made would be mutually inconsistent and would hence fail to affirm anything. The only conclusion we could draw would be that at least one of the claims must be false.

In a famous argument, David Hume, the Scottish philosopher we mentioned before, tried to uncover an inconsistency in the then prevalent objection to suicide. The objection to suicide was that God is the author of life and that we must not cut short our lives because by doing so we interfere with the course of nature, that is, usurp the prerogative of God to give and take life. But, Hume pointed out, if that is the objection to suicide, then surely it would also be wrong for us to deliberately lengthen our lives, for we interfere in the course of nature no less when we lengthen our lives, than we do when we shorten them. This is how Hume put it:

> If I turn aside a stone which is falling upon my head, I disturb the course of nature, and invade the peculiar province of the Almighty by lengthening out my life beyond the point which . . . he had assigned it.[34]

For Hume this meant that the objection to suicide must either be based on something other than the claim that it constitutes an invasion of 'the peculiar province of the Almighty' or, if it is not, then, he suggested, not only the shortening but also the lengthening of life must be objected to. We would, as it were, have to stand still and wait for the stone to hit us. Those who claim that we interfere in the 'course of nature' when we shorten life, but not when we lengthen it, are being inconsistent, Hume thought.

This argument has obvious relevance for medical end-of-life decisions, such as euthanasia or assisted suicide. If the argument against euthanasia is that we must not shorten a patient's life because this involves us in 'playing God' by interfering with the course of nature, are we then not also 'playing God' when we lengthen a patient's life by, for example, treating her infections with antibiotics or by attaching her to life-support systems, thereby interfering in the course of nature?

The above argument may be too swift. None the less, the example demonstrates how this type of reasoning may be employed in an attempt to render an opponent's views invalid. Once the charge of inconsistency has been raised, additional reasons must be provided by the person denying the charge to show that no inconsistency is involved. These reasons may then become the subject of further argument and debate, and may be accepted or rejected, as the case may be.

Concepts: Inconsistencies and confusions appear in many guises, even in the concepts we employ in our ethical arguments. This is why it is sometimes impossible to make progress in an ethical impasse until we have clarified the terms that are crucial to the debate. What, for example, does it mean to be 'terminally ill'? In one sense, we are all terminally ill. Life just *is* a terminal condition. We are born and eventually we must die. What reason could we give, for example, for saying that a person who has another six months to live is 'terminally ill', whereas another person who has seven or twelve months to live is not 'terminally ill'. And is a patient terminally ill if we could, in fact, sustain her life by various means for another year or two, but decide not to do so, knowing that she will die as a consequence?

Or take another term: 'human life'. What is 'a human life' or 'a living human being'? Do human cells and embryos constitute a human life? Is a patient in a persistent vegetative state a living human being? And if our answer is 'yes', in what sense is a brain-dead person 'dead' when her heart is beating, when she is pink and warm to the touch, and when it is possible to sustain her vital processes for long periods of time? Moreover, are all human lives the same and do they warrant morally equivalent treatment? Or is there, for example, a morally relevant difference between merely biological human life, such as a cell or an embryo, and the life of a thinking rational person?

Fuzzy and unanalysed broad concepts will often hinder rather than help ethical debate, for we may wrongly assume that finding out *what* something is, how it should be described, will also answer ethical questions. It may not do that. Much depends on why we think that members of a group covered by a concept, such as 'terminally ill' or 'human being' should be treated in certain ways.

This means that progress in a debate is often not possible until we have clarified the underlying considerations that constitute the basis for our judgements.

Take the concept of 'dog', and let us assume that a community has decided that it is impermissible for its members to keep dogs. The reason is that the residents are sensitive to noise and do not want barking dogs in their neighbourhood. One resident has now acquired a dingo, one of Australia's native animals, and wants to keep it. The community council meets to decide on the fate of the dingo. They come to the conclusion that the dingo is clearly a dog – *Canis dingo* – and that it is therefore impermissible for the owner to keep it. But now the owner points out that there is a significant difference between dingos and other dogs: dingos don't bark. Therefore, she might argue, the prohibition that applies to other dogs should not apply to dingos. She does not deny that dingos are dogs, but points out that the original prohibition covering the class of 'dogs' was too crude. The real issue, as far as the council is concerned, is not whether an animal is or is not a dog, but rather whether it belongs to a class of dogs that can or will bark.

The same kind of reasoning can sometimes be applied when bioethical questions are at issue. The mere fact that something can be classified as one thing, rather than as another, will often not settle the question of how it should be treated. If there is a relevant difference between two entities belonging to the same class of things, then it might be entirely justifiable to treat them differently. We may, for example, agree that both a human embryo and an adult person are human beings, but also take the view that there are morally relevant differences between these two kinds of human being, and reject the view that they must be treated equally.[35]

. . . impartial and universal

Impartiality – in one form or another – is at the heart of almost every traditional ethical theory. The basic idea is rather simple: it holds that an ethical principle or rule cannot be justified by reference to partial or purely personal considerations. To be acceptable as a *moral* principle or rule, the principle or rule must apply universally, that is, not just to me or to you, but to everyone in similar relevant circumstances.

Recently, the idea of impartiality has been challenged on a number of grounds and from a number of ethical perspectives – central among them the care approach to ethics. We will discuss these criticisms in subsequent chapters. Here I will merely state my views, without attempting to defend them against these charges.

Ethics eschews bias and arbitrariness and requires us to treat like cases alike. For example, I would not be thinking ethically if I weighed my own desires or interests – simply because they are my own – more heavily than the like interests or desires of others. The following example will illustrate the point.

Let us assume that I have long admired one of Arthur Boyd's paintings in the National Gallery of Victoria. I have the opportunity to steal it, I do so and then try to justify my action to you by saying that it has always been my desire to possess this painting. It is true, I say, that other people will now no longer be able to have the pleasure of being able to view the painting, but the fact that my desire has now been fulfilled gives me great satisfaction and, surely, I point out to you, this is a good thing.

Now, we noted above that an approach comes within the realm of the ethical if it is backed by *reasons*. My justification for stealing the painting is backed by a reason, but this reason is not acceptable from the moral point of view. To qualify as a morally acceptable reason, a justification must go beyond mere self-interest and be defensible on wider grounds. As David Hume put it: anyone seeking to justify his conduct ethically must 'depart from his private and particular situation and must choose a point of view common to him with others'.[36] In other words, conduct is ethical only if it is in some sense impartial, if it can be defended from a universal point of view.

The central idea that ethical conduct must in some sense be impartial has a long history, and is captured in the so-called Golden Rule: 'Do unto others as you would have them do unto you.' In the New Testament this idea is expressed positively as 'So whatever you wish that men would do to you, do so to them';[37] and in the *Apocryphal Books* negatively as: 'And what you hate, do not do to anyone.'[38] Jesus himself expressed the same idea positively as: 'You shall love your neighbour as yourself.'[39] The precept is not peculiar to Christianity. It is also found in the writings of two great Jewish scholars Hillel (first century BC) and Philo of Alexandria (first century BC and first century AD)[40] and, to give just one more example, in the teachings of Confucius: 'What you do not desire, do not effect on others.'[41]

The idea of impartiality is also at the heart of philosophical ethics. It finds expression in Immanuel Kant's famous Categorical Imperative, 'Act only according to that maxim by which you can at the same time will that it should become a universal law,'[42] and is captured in the utilitarian idea articulated by Jeremy Bentham, according to which: 'Everybody to count for one, nobody for more than one.'[43] It is basic to the universal prescriptivism of the former Oxford philosopher R. M. Hare,[44] to the approach advocated by the utilitarian Peter Singer,[45] the contractarian theory defended by John Rawls,[46] and is expressed by the contemporary American liberal philosopher Ronald Dworkin as the 'right to equal concern and respect'.[47]

Some of the British philosophers tried to capture the idea of a universal viewpoint, which goes beyond our personal and sometimes selfish concerns and weaknesses, in vivid images, such as that of an imaginary 'impartial spectator', an 'ideal observer' or an 'archangel'.[48]

There are important differences between the various ways in which the idea of impartiality has been understood, but these need not concern us here. What is important for us is to note that all the above approaches have one thing in common: they take it as given that ethics is incompatible with arbitrariness and partiality. Like cases must be treated alike, and the mere fact that 'I' rather than 'you', or my group rather than yours, will benefit from an action is not a sufficient reason in itself to make a difference to the way in which we should act.

Let us draw together the strands of our argument so far. We had initially noted that ethical judgements must be backed by reasons. We have now seen that not every reason will do. To be an acceptable reason, it must be defensible from a universal or impartialist point of view. This requirement has an important consequence for the nihilistic view expressed by Ivan Karamazov above. Even if we were to sever the link between religion and ethics, not everything would be permitted. Rather, ethics demands that we go beyond our individual standpoint, beyond that which benefits us, our family or group, and adopt an impartialist point of view.

The Minimum Conception of Ethics

The positive view of ethics I have outlined above is a minimum one. I have suggested that ethics always requires us to give reasons for our view, and that these reasons must be of a certain kind – they must in some sense meet the requirements of universality and impartiality.

Different impartialist ethical theories

To state this minimum position is one thing; to derive from it an ethical theory that can guide our actions is quite another. The point is this: quite different ethical theories are compatible with this formal view of ethics, and very different substantive judgements can be expressed in an impartialist way. To illustrate the point, let us look at two broad and in some ways diametrically opposed approaches to ethics: deontological ethical theories and consequentialist ethical theories. As commonly stated, both meet the formal requirements of impartiality, but they will at times support quite different practical judgements.

Consequentialist theories hold that the moral goodness or badness of actions is determined by their consequences.[49] Utilitarianism is probably the best known consequentialist ethical theory. Its basic tenet is that we should always act in such a way as to produce the best consequences.[50] In its 'classical form', as espoused by, for example, the eighteenth- and nineteenth-century utilitarian philosophers Jeremy Bentham and John Stuart Mill, the term 'best consequences' is generally thought to have been understood in terms of the maximization of pleasure and the minimization of pain.[51] Modern utilitarians, like R. M. Hare, understand it to mean what, on balance, best serves the preferences of all those affected by a decision.[52]

At the other end of the spectrum are strict deontological theories of ethics. The term 'deontological' is derived from the Greek *deon*, meaning duty. Put somewhat crudely, deontologists deny what is central for utilitarians: that the goodness or badness of actions is (solely) determined by their consequences. Rather, deontologists hold that we should act in accordance with certain fundamental duties, principles or rules.

Just as there are various consequentialist approaches to ethics, so there are many different deontological approaches.[53] A strict or absolute deontologist will deny that consequences should ever play a role in our ethical thinking.[54] But not many deontologists are absolutists. Rather, deontologists will generally grant that, even if consequentialist considerations are not constitutive of the whole of ethics, they must none the less play at least some limited role in our ethical thinking. What is common to all deontological theories is this: they hold that an agent's fundamental ethical task is to perform certain actions, the ethical nature of which cannot (solely) be dependent on the value of their consequences.

This view was most persuasively developed by the influential eighteenth-century German philosopher Immanuel Kant. In his *Groundwork of the Metaphysics of Morals* (1785), Kant argued that moral duties are identified by rational, free moral agents through reason, and that the moral law must be above personal considerations, that is, independent of the consequences, special feelings and circumstances of those involved.[55] This meant that ethics consisted, at least in part, of a number of absolute duties, including the duty never to tell a lie. Even if our telling a lie could save an innocent person from death, this would not release us from our moral duty to tell the truth.[56] Utilitarians, on the other hand, hold that lying is not wrong in itself and is permissible if our doing so is likely to prevent something very bad from happening.

Consequentialist and deontological ethical theories are not the only possible impartialist approaches to ethics. There are, for example, also virtue ethics approaches (which may be held in either consequentialist or deontological forms),[57] contractarian ethical theories and theories based on rights, as well as various hybrid or mixed ethical theories that, while accepting the requirement of impartiality, answer substantive questions about 'the good life' in a variety of ways. The reason is that the principle of impartiality is a *formal* rather than a *material* principle; it reminds us to act fairly and non-arbitrarily, but it does not tell us what we should be fair or impartial about. In short, it may be possible to defend, on impartialist grounds, views that take principles or values such as rights, interests, virtues, personal integrity, autonomy and so on as the fundamental building blocks of ethics, or to defend mixed theories, that is, theories that incorporate a range of different fundamental ethical principles or values.

The role of universal rules and principles

All impartialist ethical theories have one thing in common: at one level or another, they make use of universal principles and rules – principles and rules that apply universally to you, to me and to anyone else, whenever a certain set of circumstances prevails. These rules and principles not only allow us, as John Rawls puts it, to 'judge . . . without bias or prejudice',[58] but also to set standards for behaviour. In health care, for example, such standards might be set in terms of the duty adequately to inform patients, to protect their privacy and so on. Deontological theories are thus often described as rule or principle-based approaches, and the Ten Commandments – while not a product of a rational philosophical approach to ethics – are an example of a rule-based approach. They present a kind of answer to how we should behave to each other – an issue that is, of course, also at the heart of philosophical ethics.

At first glance, consequentialist theories seem to lack rules and any principles, other than the one principle to maximize the good. After all, if it can be right for a person to lie under one set of circumstances and wrong under another, this might suggests that consequentialists are unprincipled, do not have any moral rules and perhaps lack moral standards altogether. But this interpretation is too simple.

It is true that consequentialism does not start with rules but with goals, for example, that we should maximize pleasure and minimize pain. It does, however, recognize that rules and principles are necessary for the overall achievement of these goals. For this reason, it is often thought important that people have stable moral dispositions or virtues that accord with those goals, and that they internalize the corresponding rules and principles that should be followed. John Stuart Mill, for example, held that the 'object of virtue' is the 'multiplication of happiness'. For him, rules, principles and virtues were thus *instruments* of the good life – instruments that should be employed to help us achieve our moral goal.[59] The contemporary utilitarian R. M. Hare relies on a very similar approach. He holds that there are 'both practical and psychological reasons for having relatively simple principles of action if we are to learn to behave either morally or skilfully or with prudence'. In raising our children, for example, we want them above all to learn not merely to adopt principles but rather to possess 'firm dispositions of character' that accord with the principles.[60] We want them to have strong dispositions to do the right thing – not to steal, lie and cheat, and to treat others fairly – because to have these dispositions or virtues and to follow the relevant rules will be best, most of the time.[61] This means that there will often be considerable agreement, at the level of rules, principles and virtues, between, for example, consequentialist, deontological and virtue approaches to ethics.[62]

Consequentialists would not accept rules or principles as either absolute or as having intrinsic value. Rather, they would accept rules or principles on a prima facie basis only or, as Hare would put it, accept rules or principles on the intuitive, everyday level of moral thinking. These principles would always be only instruments for the good life, and their acceptance or rejection would ultimately have to be justified by appeal to the *critical* level of ethical thinking. Both a deontologist and a consequentialist could thus agree, for example, that we should not lie. While a deontologist might want to defend this rule or principle by appeal to the intrinsic wrongness of lying, a utilitarian would always want to defend it in terms of its consequences: for example, that lying will lead to distrust and will undermine relationships between people.

My own view is a broadly consequentialist one,[63] but I shall not attempt to defend any particular substantive view of ethics here. Rather, my aim is a much more modest one: to suggest that we accept, at least as a starting-point for our ethical reflections, what James Rachels has called 'The Mimimum Conception of Ethics'.[64] This conception is derived from the twin requirements that ethical judgements must be impartial and backed by reasons, and from our being prepared to take one additional though not entirely uncontroversial step. This step involves the acceptance of the notion of 'interests' as a central concept in ethics.

While not every ethical theory takes 'interests' as its starting-point, few, if any, would, I take it, want to deny the moral relevance of interests. There is, after all, a strong connection between the satisfaction of interests and the interest-holder's well-being. (Indeed, doctors and nurses generally regard it as their primary goal to act in the best interests of those for whom they care.) Given the close connection between interests and well-being, we have good reasons for wanting our interests satisfied and, if we think ethically, to give equal consideration to the interests of others. Peter Singer puts it well when he says:

> In accepting that ethical judgements must be made from a universal point of view, I am accepting that my own interests cannot, simply because they are my interests, count more than the interests of anyone else. Thus my very natural concern that my own interests be looked after must, when I think ethically, be extended to the interests of others.[65]

If we accept this line of reasoning, we should also accept Rachels' Minimum Conception of Ethics:

> *Morality is, at the very least, the effort to guide one's conduct by reason — that is, to do what there are the best reasons for doing — while giving equal weight to the interests of each individual who will be affected by one's conduct.*[66]

As James Rachels notes, the above view of ethics provides us, amongst other things, with a conception of what it means to be a conscientious moral agent:

> A conscientious moral agent is someone who is concerned impartially with the interests of everyone affected by what he or she does; who carefully sifts facts and examines their implications; who accepts principles of conduct only after scrutinizing them to make sure they are sound; who is willing to 'listen to reason' even when it means that his or her earlier convictions may have to be revised; and who, finally, is willing to act on the results of this deliberation.[67]

In one form or another, most ethical theories incorporate this central idea. If there is disagreement, this does not generally involve

a rejection of the minimum conception of ethics, but rather disagreement about the *completeness* of the approach – how it should
be expanded or modified, or whether the picture of the moral
agent as an impartial and in some sense detached adjudicator between interests is one we should accept.[68] Given this, one may
grant that the Minimum Conception of Ethics does not constitute
the *whole* of ethics and yet insist, as I want to do, that it is an
important part of it. As we shall see in later chapters, those who
reject it in favour of an ethics of care encounter some very serious
problems.

Conclusion

The above sketch of a Minimum Conception of Ethics has shown
that there may be, despite some fundamental differences between
various ethical theories, a common core to ethics. This common
core is the idea of impartiality and the acceptance of universal
rules and principles. When we turn from theoretical to practical or
applied ethics, we frequently find some agreement as well. People
subscribing to different moral or religious views may yet be able to
agree on common principles and rules, and reach satisfactory solutions to ethically complex practical problems. The near-universal
acceptance of brain death signifying the death of a person is an
example of this, as is the principle that competent and informed
patients should be able to accept or refuse treatment for themselves.
In light of this, it is important to guard against overestimating
differences at a practical level.[69] None the less, some differences –
and contemporary debates about voluntary euthanasia may be an
example of this – seem irreconcilable and different conceptions of
the 'good life' will lead people to arrive at different answers. This
raises the following question: what is the proper relation between
the moral views held by individual members of society, including
patients, doctors and nurses, and the health-care policies and laws
we should adopt if we live in pluralist and liberal societies, such
as, for example, Australia, Britain or the United States?[70]

I will not attempt to answer this complex question here, but will
sketch some answers in chapter 8. Here we should merely note
that our discussion of the nature of ethics has obvious implications

for what can count as an acceptable answer. We could not, for example, support public policies that, even if they served us well, would discriminate against others on morally irrelevant grounds, such as, for example, race, colour or sex.

Nor could we simply assume that religion, natural law or unexamined social values and beliefs are an appropriate basis for public policy, for all the reasons outlined above. Rather, public policy, like ethics, requires us to give reasons for our views – reasons that go beyond mere opinion, revelation or faith.

What implications does this have for health-care professionals, such as nurses? First, on an individual level this means that nurses – like all of us – ought to engage in systematic ethical thinking. Without such thinking, we may unwittingly and unjustifiably impose our own unexamined values on others. On a public policy level it means that we ought to develop public policies that will, at the very least, give equal consideration to the interests of all those affected by the policy or law.

5

Women and Ethics: Is Morality Gendered?

Over the past ten years, I have been listening to people talking about morality and about themselves . . . the women's voices sounded distinct.
Carol Gilligan, *In a Different Voice* (1982)

Women, I allow, may have different duties to fulfil; but they are human duties, and the principles that should regulate the discharge of them, I sturdily maintain, must be the same.
Mary Wollstonecraft, *A Vindication of the Rights of Woman* (1792)

One is not born, but rather becomes, a woman.
Simone de Beauvoir, *The Second Sex* (1949)

In the preceding chapter I argued that impartiality is central to ethics, and suggested that acceptance of that view will lead one to endorse the Minimum Conception of Ethics – the view that our own interests cannot, simply because they are our own, count for more than the like interests of others. Impartialist ethical theories have recently been challenged on various grounds and from various quarters. One of the charges, put by feminists, is that these theories are 'gendered', that is, that they provide an inadequate or even wrong-headed account of ethics. These 'principled approaches' to ethics, it is claimed, may capture the moral experiences of men, but they do not capture the moral experiences of women. The problem is not only that traditional 'male ethics' put excessive emphasis on such formal notions as impartiality and consistency, to the detriment of responsiveness and caring in human relationships,

but they also exclude women from moral discourse, thereby per-
petuating women's subordination to men.

These kinds of criticism have also been taken up by nurses in
their call for a new ethics – a (female) 'nursing ethics of care'. An
ethics which is appropriate for nurses and for nursing, it is now
frequently claimed, is different from traditional (male) medical
ethics; it is not concerned with impartial principles, rules or rights,
but with care and responsiveness in human relationships.

Claims such as these need careful unpacking, and the present
chapter and the next two are devoted to this task. Here we begin by
tackling the question: is morality gendered? The answer is important for our inquiry. After all, proponents of a female care approach
must explicitly or implicitly assume a positive answer to that question. If they did not, there would be no grounds for proposing
a separate woman-centred approach to ethics rather than a universal human approach. But is the assumption that ethics is gendered
correct? If it is, where does this difference have its origin? In our
female and male biology, or perhaps in our social institutions?

Female Virtues and Male Reason?

It is not self-evident that ethics should be gendered – at least not
to a feminist like myself who has always defended the view that
sex roles, and ways of looking at the world, are largely a matter
of socialization. If a female ethics is 'different from' or, as it is
sometimes thought, 'better than' traditional male ethics, what is
it that makes it different or better? Are women inherently more
moral than men, more inclined than men to do what is ethically
good and right? And why should this be so? Does their female
biology simply predispose women to one moral point of view,
whereas male biology predisposes men to another?

The idea that there are different moral virtues, standards of
behaviour and modes of moral reasoning for women and men is
not new. As we have already seen in chapter 2, in Victorian times
there was a strong belief that women possessed certain female virtues which made them eminently suitable for the task of nursing
the sick. The general view that morality is gendered is, however,
much older than that. The classical Greek philosopher Aristotle, for

example, was an early exponent of the idea that women's virtues differed from those of men. 'Clearly,' Aristotle maintained,

> moral virtue belongs to all . . . but the temperance of a man and of a woman, or the courage and justice of a man and of a woman, are not, as Socrates maintained, the same; the courage of a man is shown in commanding, of a woman in obeying . . . as the poet says of women, 'Silence is a woman's glory', but this is not equally the glory of man.[1]

Similar ideas about specifically male and female virtues, and a gender-specific natural order, can be found in various other philosophical writings as well,[2] including those of the eighteenth-century French philosopher Jean-Jacques Rousseau.[3] In his book *Emile*,[4] written some 30 years before women like Mary Wollstonecraft were beginning to assert that one morality and one set of moral virtues should be applicable to both women and men, Rousseau drew a sharp distinction between male and female virtues. 'Sophy,' to be educated as the 'helpmeet' for Emile, should, Rousseau wrote, 'be as truly a woman as Emile is a man, i.e., she must possess all those characters of her sex which are required to enable her to play her part in the physical and moral order.'[5]

Playing her part in the physical and moral order included the cultivation of distinct female traits or virtues. These virtues, Rousseau thought, could flourish only in the privacy of the home and the family, where women should be playing a dependent and subordinate role as wives and mothers. While Rousseau did not deny that women might be able to develop masculine traits, he was quite adamant that they should not. A woman, he argued, cannot be 'nurse today and warrior tomorrow'.[6] Such fudging of roles, he thought, would ensure everyone's misery, including that of the woman herself. 'A brilliant wife is a plague to her husband, her children, her friends, her valets, everyone.'[7] On the other hand, a woman who had developed her distinctively female traits (such as gentleness, tenderness, beneficence, compassion, nurturing, self-sacrifice, intuitiveness, mental passivity, and physical and emotional dependence), who declined the call of the world and devoted her energies to her husband and family, was only a 'little lower than the angels'.[8]

The so-called female virtues were often – as here by Rousseau – exalted and praised as somewhat 'higher' than the male virtues of courage, independence, assertiveness, ambition, rationality, fairness and emotional control. At the same time, however, the virtues possessed by these 'angels' or, as the poet Lord Tennyson called them a century later, 'interpreters between gods and men',[9] were often and paradoxically also regarded as wanting, as ultimately inferior to the qualities possessed by men. While distinctions were not always drawn between, for example, psychological traits (such as courage and timidity) and what we might today think of as moral virtues or moral dispositions (such as benevolence and fairness)[10] there was, for a long time, little doubt in most writers' minds that male traits and dispositions were the definitive standard against which female traits and dispositions were to be measured.

Hand in hand with this belief went the view that women lacked proper reason.[11] In his poem *Paradise Lost*, the seventeenth-century poet, John Milton, for example, told his fellow-men that reason or contemplation was their special gift, a gift that God had not granted women. Adam and Eve in Eden, Milton wrote, were

> Not equal, as their sex not equal seemed;
> For contemplation hee and valour formed,
> For softness shee and sweet attractive Grace:
> Hee for God only, shee for God in him.[12]

A century later, Immanuel Kant defended the view that there was a strong link between morality and reason. While women had, he suggested, 'just as much understanding as the male', it was not a '*deep understanding* [italics in original] . . . Her philosophy is not to reason but to sense [and . . . women] will need to know nothing more of the cosmos than is necessary to make the appearance of the heavens on a beautiful evening a stimulating sight to them.'[13]

Rousseau took a somewhat similar view. He granted women reason, but their reasoning was, he thought, complementary and ultimately subordinate to that of men. A woman's reason, Rousseau wrote, was practical, attuned to detail and basically unprincipled. A man's reason, on the other hand, was abstract, general and principled. This dichotomy in male and female reasoning, Rousseau thought, applied to ethical reasoning as well. This entailed that women's morality could only be of an 'experimental kind'; it required systematizing by men.

> The search for abstract and speculative truth, for principles and axioms of science, for all that tends to wide generalisation, is beyond a woman's grasp; their studies should be thoroughly practical. It is their business to apply the principles discovered by men, it is their place to make the observations which lead men to discover those principles . . . Woman should discover, so to speak, an experimental morality, man should reduce it to a system . . . woman observes, man reasons.[14]

Similarly 'the father' of psychoanalysis, Sigmund Freud, charged that 'for women the level of what is ethically normal is different from what it is in men.' Women, he wrote, 'show less sense of justice than men . . . are less ready to submit to the great exigencies of life . . . [and] are more often influenced in their judgements by feelings of affection or hostility.'[15]

In denying women a sense of justice, Freud echoed the nineteenth-century German philosopher Arthur Schopenhauer. Not known for his complimentary view of women, Schopenhauer had described women as 'intellectually short-sighted' and 'defective in the power of reasoning and deliberation'. Women, he thought, had an intuitive understanding of what lies close to them, but their reasoning power was weak. This is why 'present circumstances and those concrete things which lie directly before their eyes exercise a power which is seldom counteracted by abstract principles of thought, by fixed rules of conduct.' Accordingly, Schopenhauer thought, 'the fundamental fault of the female character is that it has *no sense of justice*.'[16]

While these misogynist views of women dominated the Western historical tradition, there was, Alison Jaggar reminds us, also a small but distinguished number of philosophers – Plato, John Stuart Mill and Karl Marx among them – who can be seen as early proponents of a contemporary feminist approach to ethics. Even though certain aspects of their views can clearly be criticized from a feminist point of view, these philosophers, Jaggar maintains, none the less challenged at least some aspects of the subordination of women by utilizing the philosophical resources available to them at the time.[17]

The dominant belief that there are distinct male and female virtues and modes of ethical thinking was shared by some – although by no means all – early feminists. There was frequently an important point of difference between these feminists and traditional male thinkers, such as Aristotle, Kant, Rousseau and Schopenhauer. While these male thinkers had little doubt that the male approach to morality was the definitive and morally superior one, some of the early feminists strongly disagreed. They thought the world would become a better place if women were to bring some of the traditional female virtues to bear on it. These virtues were not only seen as different or complementary to those possessed by men, but frequently also as somewhat 'higher' and more 'noble'. A nineteenth-century writer, Theresa Harris, who had quite unblushingly entitled her book *Women: The Angel in the Home and the Saviour of the World*, thus wrote, in the florid style characteristic of the period:

> Like the sweet soft odour of white roses transfusing through the atmosphere an influence of natural beauty, so should the character of women blend with the sterner and more practical nature of man, and so speak to him of a higher life, a nobler existence than that of the busy commercial world in which he daily toils and strives for progress.[18]

A similar separatist ideology was expressed by the feminists Margaret Fuller (in her tract *Woman in the Nineteenth Century*)[19] and Elizabeth Cady Stanton. Stanton had no doubt that man 'is infinitely woman's inferior in every moral quality'. While she believed that much of this was due to the false education of men, underlying this socialization process, there was also a 'female element' that determined the 'goodness' of women and a 'male element' that determined the 'badness' of men:

> The male element is a destructive force, stern, selfish, aggrandising, loving war, violence, conquest, acquisition, breeding in the material and moral world alike discord, disorder, disease and death. See what a record of blood and cruelty the pages of history reveal . . . The male element has held high carnival so far, it has fairly run riot

from the beginning, overpowering the feminine element everywhere . . . The need of this hour is not territory, gold mines, railroads . . . but a new evangel of womanhood, to exalt purity, virtue, morality, true religion, to lift man up into the higher realms of thought and action.[20]

In less effusive language, some feminists today still give expression to their belief that a 'female ethics' is needed to save the world from the consequences of human activities that have their basis in a male ethos of domination, conquest and aggression on the one hand, and in men's adherence to abstract and rigid moral principles on the other.[21] Wars, environmental degradation, overpopulation and the ills of modern medicine, it is frequently thought, are closely linked to the nature of 'masculinity'. One modern feminist, Helen Bequaert Holmes, thus recently adapted Virginia Woolf's statement about science to medicine: 'Medicine is not sexless; she is a man, a father, and infected too.' Women ought to try and 'heal' or 'disinfect' medicine because, Bequaert Holmes writes, women might have an 'epistemic privilege in "caring"'.[22]

The view that women have a special moral role to play in health care is reflected in some contemporary perceptions of the nurse's role. Whereas (male) doctors are often seen as overly aggressive in their use of medical technology as principled and hard-nosed technicians, nurses are frequently portrayed as gentle carers, as 'angels of mercy' and the saviours of patients.[23]

While the idea of distinct 'female virtues' has been attractive to many women, others are and have been deeply suspicious of it. Take Mary Wollstonecraft. While Jean-Jacques Rousseau had been busy telling the world that women ought to display the virtues specific to their sex,[24] Mary Wollstonecraft was admonishing women that they needed to develop some of the positive male virtues, such as assertiveness, reasonableness and emotional detachment, before they could hope to be regarded as full human beings. Infuriated by Rousseau's and some other contemporary writers' conception of the role and capacities of women, she referred to these writers as 'specious reasoners' and 'moralists', who, she said, never failed to give women 'all the "submissive charms"', who consistently recommended '[g]entleness, docility and a spaniel-like affection . . . as the cardinal virtues of the sex',[25] but who ultimately regarded women as 'gentle, domestic brutes', incapable of the kind of reason or the creativity which distinguishes human beings from the beasts.[26]

Mary Wollstonecraft not only saw a direct link between the 'feminine virtues' of gentleness and docility and the subjection of women; she also held that 'the nature of reason must be the same in all, if it be an emanation of divinity, the tie that connects the creature with the Creator.'[27] In distinction from many of her contemporaries, she viewed the various female traits as socially constructed and reached the conclusion that women had to change if they wanted to achieve full human status.

Many modern feminists share Wollstonecraft's concerns. They fear that the perpetuation of the idea of 'women's virtues' or of a 'female morality' may tie women to a 'familiar ghetto', rather than provide them with a liberated space.[28] Beverley Harrison thus argues that, even though gender inequality is now almost universally condemned, none the less it still receives implicit support from those who believe that different moral norms should govern the lives of women and men:

> Many philosophers and theologians, although decrying gender inequality, still unconsciously assume that women's lives should express a different moral norm than men's, that women should exemplify moral purity and self-sacrifice, whereas men may live by the more minimal rational standards of moral obligation.[29]

On the one hand, Harrison notes, women have been exhorted to be passive; on the other, they are expected to be more giving, more caring than men, and more responsible than men for meeting the needs of others. 'We live in a world where many, perhaps most, of the voluntary sacrifices on behalf of human well-being are made by women' but, Harrison charges, 'the assumption of a special obligation to self-giving or sacrifice . . . is male-generated ideology.'[30]

Feminists such as Beverley Harrison and Mary Wollstonecraft before her thus reject the notion that differences in the moral approaches of women and men have their source in the 'maleness' or 'femaleness' of the subjects, that is, they are critical of the idea that women and men have gender-distinct and largely monolithic psychological or moral natures. Rather, critics of what has been described as 'essentialism' or 'biologism' see 'the nature' of women and men – and their social roles and moral virtues – as socially and historically constructed, as malleable and changeable, rather than as immutably given.[31] Women, as we observe them, may think and behave differently to men, but this, these critics would want to say, tells us little if anything about 'natural' women and 'natural' men; rather, all we can conclude is that women and men will – under certain social and historical conditions – think and act in certain ways.

We will return to this point below, after considering the empirical debate. Is there any evidence for the prevailing belief that women and men do, as a matter of fact, approach ethics from two distinct moral perspectives? In her famous book *In a Different Voice*, Carol Gilligan claims to have provided some evidence for this view.[32] The book and subsequent publications by Gilligan and her critics have become an important focal point of ethical and feminist discussions.[33] In the next section, we shall take a brief look at that debate.

Carol Gilligan and the Ethics of Care

Until the late 1960s, philosophers in the Anglo-American tradition had little, if anything, to contribute to the debate about the relationship between gender and philosophy and ethics. The implicit assumption seems to have been that sex and gender are irrelevant to fundamental philosophical issues, such as truth, beauty or the nature of ethics.

The resurgence of feminism coincided with a renewed interest in practical ethics, that is, in issues raised in the context of contemporary social life. Questions such as contraception and abortion, the idea of equality, racism, war, animal rights, environmental issues, pornography and rape were now being discussed by feminist and mainstream philosophers. Other feminist philosophers turned their attention to traditional ethical theory to discover, as we have already seen above, that these theories often portrayed women as lacking reason. While women were endowed with certain female virtues, these were of a lesser kind than male virtues.

Women had, to put it somewhat crudely, good hearts, but they lacked a sense of justice – the ability to approach ethical issues from a universal and impartial point of view.

By the late 1970s doubts were being expressed by feminist philosophers about the feasibility of addressing 'women's issues' – central among them the issue of abortion – in terms of traditional ethical theories. These theories, it was said, had a male bias and failed to capture the female point of view. It was then, out of the convergence of critical feminist work in applied ethics and in ethical theory, that 'feminist ethics' was born – the attempt to articulate a theoretical approach to ethics that would capture the moral experiences of women.[34]

The philosophical project of mapping a feminist approach to ethics was much encouraged by the work of the psychologist Carol Gilligan. In her book, *In a Different Voice*, published in 1982, Gilligan draws on the work of another psychologist, Nancy Chodorow, on objects-relation theory as the basis for the reproduction of sex differences[35] to explain the discrepancy between women's and men's moral perspectives.[36] Gilligan asserts that her research has shown that there are two different moral 'languages' – a language of impartiality or 'justice' and a relational language of 'care' to, as she puts it, 'encode disparate experiences of self and social relationships'. The 'different voice', that of care, her research had found, was mostly associated with women.

On page 2 of *In a Different Voice*, Gilligan makes clear that she is not speaking about an absolute link between gender and moral orientation:

> The different voice I describe is characterized not by gender but theme. Its association with women is an empirical observation and it is primarily through women's voices that I trace its development. But this association is not absolute, and the contrasts between male and female voices are presented here to highlight a distinction between two modes of thought . . . rather than to represent a generalization about either sex.[37]

Both the justice and the care perspective, she says, are open to women and men, and both are equally valid approaches.[38] But, Gilligan holds, her research has shown that the vast majority of males rely primarily on the justice perspective. When it comes to women, on the other hand, about one-third of all females rely primarily on the care approach, while another third rely primarily on a justice-based morality. In other words, while a considerable number of women approach ethics from the justice perspective, almost no men approach ethics from a perspective of care.[39]

The story of the genesis of Gilligan's research is, by now, fairly familiar. It is briefly recounted here to tease out the points that are of particular importance to us. Gilligan's research took as its starting-point the work of her former mentor and associate, Lawrence Kohlberg, a prominent researcher in the field of moral development. Building on the psychological theories advanced by Jean Piaget, Kohlberg claims that children go through a definite sequence of stages of moral thinking. Broadly speaking, development proceeds from an egoistic level, at which morality is seen as a matter of authority and of reward or punishment, through a second level where the individual conforms to expected stereotypical roles and conventional social standards, to a third level, where moral principles are based on neither self-interest nor on conventional standards of right or wrong, but rather on universal and impartial principles of justice.

On Kohlberg's view, there is a progression in logical reasoning between these levels – an expansion in the categories of those to whom our moral concerns apply – with each subsequent level having a higher logical structure. For example, to go beyond the egoistical level, it is necessary to step outside oneself and to identify with others, until, at the third level, one applies impartial principles of justice. This entails that a universal and impartial mode of reasoning is a necessary condition for an individual to reach that level.

Kohlberg's theory of moral development had its empirical basis in a study of 84 boys, whose development he had followed for more than 20 years.[40] When gender differences first appeared in studies based on Kohlberg's research, it seemed that women did not, on average, achieve as high a standard of moral reasoning as men. In other words, women were, on average, found to be less morally mature than men.[41]

The standard assumption at the time was that single-sex research of this kind had universal validity, that is, it was applicable to both men *and* women. It is this assumption that was challenged by Gilligan. Drawing on the conceptions of her largely female research subjects, Gilligan claims that there is an alternative female ethics. While Kohlberg's research may have provided an account of *male* moral development, it has not provided an account of *female* moral development. Men and women, she suggests, approach ethics differently and follow different paths towards moral maturity. The 'different voice' used predominantly by women is not based on impartial principles of justice, but on care and responsibility within personal relationships.[42] In short, Gilligan accepts that there are higher and lower levels of moral reasoning, but she questions that there is only one path – the impartialist 'justice approach' – to moral maturity. Women's approach to morality is not, she holds, an immature form of male moral development; rather, women's moral reasoning is *different* from that of men.

Let us take a closer look at one of the examples Gilligan gives in support of her theory. She describes an interview with two 11-year-old children – 'Jake' and 'Amy'. The dilemma these children were asked to resolve was one in a series of hypothetical moral dilemmas devised by Kohlberg. It involves a conflict between moral principles or norms, where the Kohlbergian researcher would determine levels of moral reasoning by looking at the way in which this conflict is resolved.

Jake and Amy were presented with the following dilemma: a man named Heinz considers whether or not to steal a drug which might save his ailing wife's life. The drug is extremely expensive, Heinz cannot afford to buy it, and the druggist is unwilling to lower the price of the drug. The question is: should Heinz steal the drug?[43]

For Jake, the answer was clear from the start: Heinz should steal the drug. According to Gilligan, Jake constructed the dilemma as a conflict between property and life, and justified his answer by ranking life more highly than property:

JAKE: For one thing, a human life is worth more than
          money, and if the druggist only makes $1000, he
          is still going to live, but if Heinz doesn't steal the
          drug, his wife is going to die.

QUESTION: Why is life worth more than money?

JAKE: Because the druggist can get a thousand dollars
                 later from rich people with cancer, but Heinz can't
                 get his wife again.
QUESTION: Why not?
JAKE: Because people are all different and so you couldn't
                 get Heinz's wife again.[44]

Gilligan describes this 11-year-old boy as being 'fascinated by the power of logic' and as 'locating truth in math' which, according to him, is 'the only thing that is totally logical'. A moral dilemma, Jake says, is 'sort of like a math problem with humans'. As Gilligan notes, Jake sets the dilemma up as one would a mathematical equation and then proceeds to work out the answer. Moreover, since this solution is rationally derived, Jake assumes that anybody else who thinks rationally about this question would arrive at the same conclusion.[45]

Amy's response to the dilemma is, according to Gilligan, very different. She fails to give an answer that fits the Kohlbergian ethical framework. Rather than viewing the dilemma as 'a math problem with humans', Amy sees it – in Gilligan's words – as 'a narrative of relationships that extends over time'.[46] For anyone who puts great value on logical reasoning and decisiveness, Amy's response may, Gilligan notes, give the impression that her development is stunted 'by a failure of logic and inability to think for herself'.[47] Asked whether Heinz should steal the drug, she replies:

> AMY: Well, I don't think so. I think there might be other ways besides stealing it, like if he could borrow the money or make a loan or something, but he really shouldn't steal the drug – but his wife shouldn't die either.

Amy does not rank the conflicting moral norms in the way Jake had done, but rather looks at the way in which stealing the drug might affect the ongoing relationship between Heinz and his wife. Hence, when asked why Heinz should not steal the drug, she answers:

> AMY: If he stole the drug, he might save his wife then, but if he did, he might have to go to jail, and then his wife might get sick

again, and he couldn't get more of the drug and it might not be good. So, they should really just talk it out and find some other way to make the money.[48]

For Amy, Gilligan holds, people do not stand alone; rather, they live in a world that is determined by human connections and not by system of abstract and impersonal rules. Thus it is puzzling for Amy that the druggist does not respond to the wife's predicament; for her this suggests that he does not fully recognize the consequences of his refusal. Were he to see the consequences of his refusal to lower the price, he would realize that 'he should just give it to the wife and then have the husband pay the money back later.'[49]

Amy's world, Gilligan suggests, is a different one from the one portrayed in Kohlberg's construction of the Heinz dilemma. 'Her world is a world of relationships and psychological truths where the awareness of the connection between people gives rise to a recognition of responsibility for one another, a perception of the need for response.' While Amy scored lower on Kohlberg's moral development scale than Jake, this is so because she adopted a different moral approach. Amy's approach, Gilligan suggests, is based on the recognition of relationships, her belief in communication as the mode of conflict resolution, and her conviction that the solution to the dilemma will follow from its compelling representation. Rather than being immature or naive, Gilligan concludes, 'Amy's judgement contains the insights central to an ethics of care, just as Jake's judgements reflect the logic of the justice approach.'[50]

Gilligan's thesis is not, of course, simply that she has discovered differences in the ethical reasoning of a male and a female 11-year old child, but rather that several empirical studies, including interviews with 29 women who were faced with the decision of whether they should have an abortion,[51] suggest that there are common or typical differences in the moral reasoning of women and men.[52] These differences need not, Gilligan keeps emphasizing, be understood in terms of a 'higher' or 'lower' level of moral reasoning, but rather in terms of different, but equally valid, moral perspectives.[53]

Gilligan's research raises two separate issues: first, whether Gilligan and others are right when they claim that the 'care approach' constitutes an *alternative* to the impartialist justice approach; second, whether this alternative moral approach is correctly characterized as a *female* approach. We will discuss the second question below, and the first in chapters 6 and 7.

Do Women Speak in a Different Voice?

The results of any empirical study into gender-specific approaches to ethics will be subject to debate. This is also true of Gilligan's research. Can we, for example, be sure that Amy's response to the Heinz dilemma is correctly categorized as a 'care' approach, and that of Jake as an impartial 'justice' approach? This is doubted by some writers.[54] Might it not be said that Amy put a universal principle of justice (the principle that we should not steal what rightfully belongs to another) above care for a particular person, whereas Jake discarded principled thinking for the sake of care?[55] And how would we classify the responses of Nigel Cox and Roisin Hart, when the first deliberately ended the life of his patient Lillian Boyes, and the second blew the whistle on Dr Cox? Who acted from a perspective of justice and who from a perspective of care? Can we be entirely confident about the answer we might want to give?

But let us assume that we have indeed identified two different moral approaches. Does this mean we can be sure that these two moral approaches constitute a male and a female approach respectively? Some writers have argued that Gilligan's own interviews do not corroborate her conclusion that the moral approaches of her research subjects can be distinguished by gender.[56] Other commentators have granted that Gilligan may well have identified a difference between the moral approaches of her male and female research subjects, but they have claimed that the same differences can be found between members of different socio-economic groups and between white and ethnic minorities.[57]

Some other empirical studies appear to show differences in moral reasoning between male and female research subjects,[58] but a critical 1984 survey of a large number of empirical studies conducted by Lawrence Walker purports to show that the 'the moral reasoning of men and women is remarkably similar' and that differences in moral orientation are better analysed in terms of differences in education and occupation.[59] Following a more recent survey of the relevant literature, Joan C. Tronto reached the conclusion that '[e]mpirically, Gilligan's argument offers little reason to accept it as a definitive description of who engages in an ethics of care.'[60]

The literature on the Kohlberg/Gilligan debate is vast, and the issue of the presence or absence of empirical differences in the moral reasoning of women and men has not been resolved, despite more than a decade of research and debate. This might lead one to dismiss the whole debate as unresolvable, and to assign Gilligan's works to the archives. This response, however, would be too swift. The point is this: even if there are some serious doubts about Gilligan's research, and acknowledging that the empirical question about gender differences in moral reasoning has not been resolved, the fact remains that the association of women with care has not only a long history but also a strong continuing appeal. By 1989, *In a Different Voice* had sold 360,000 copies,[61] and female readers of the book report that the gender differences postulated by Gilligan 'resonate . . . thoroughly with their own experience'.[62] Every academic discipline touched by feminist thought, from women's studies to public policy and law, from literary theory to environmental and veterinary science, from philosophy to bioethics and nursing, has regarded Gilligan's work as of fundamental importance. This requires an explanation. Even if the presence of the 'different voice' cannot incontrovertibly be established, it is none the less the case that women and men have, for a very long time, lived in ways that seemed to express gender-distinct moralities or virtues, and the gender differences postulated by Gilligan still 'resonate' with the moral experiences of so many of the female readers of her book. How might this be explained?

Nature or Nurture?

Let us assume that Carol Gilligan has, in fact, identified some relevant differences in the moral approaches of women and men. What would this show? As we have seen above, only about one-third of the women in Gilligan's research were said to favour the care approach. This entails that Gilligan's research (and any other research that merely establishes an *association*, rather than an absolute link, between gender and moral approach) would not allow us to draw inferences about 'all women' and 'all men'. It would also suggest that the association between gender and moral approach is merely a contingent one, that is, that the reason why there are statistically significant differences in the moral reasoning of women and men may not lie in women's biology, but rather in some other social or historical fact.

The problem is that there are dangers in highlighting *biological* categories, to the relevant or total neglect of possible *social* factors, in explanatory models of human behaviour.[63] Gilligan herself is aware of the dangers of such 'biological determinism',[64] and, as we have seen above, wants to characterize the distinction between the 'care' and the 'justice' approach, not in terms of gender, but in terms of 'two different modes of thought'. She states emphatically that she makes

[no] claims . . . about the origins of the differences described . . . Clearly, these differences arise in a social context where factors of social status and power combine with reproductive biology to shape the experiences of males and females and the relations between the sexes.[65]

Despite Gilligan's disclaimers, her writings are more often than not understood as describing not only a different moral voice, but a different *female* voice – a trend probably unwittingly encouraged by Gilligan herself, in her frequent identification of the voice of care with that of women.[66] Moreover, despite Gilligan's overt disclaimers, in at least one instance she seems to edge uncomfortably close to biological determinism.[67]

In a 1987 article by Carol Gilligan and Grant Wiggins, the authors state:

stereotypes of males as aggressive and females as nurturant, however distorting and however limited, have some empirical claim. The overwhelmingly male composition of the prison population and the extent to which women take care of young children cannot readily be dismissed as irrelevant to theories of morality or excluded from accounts of moral development. If there are no sex differences in empathy or moral reasoning, why are there sex differences in moral and immoral behaviour?[68]

In this passage Gilligan and Wiggins use an association between gender and empirical data to draw some, admittedly tentative, conclusions about the link between gender and moral development. But even this, Moody-Adams argues, has its dangers. After all, if it is thought that women are more moral then men, because proportionally more men populate our prisons, would it not also follow from this that American whites are more moral than blacks, because a higher percentage of American blacks than whites occupy a place in US prisons?[69]

This is a legitimate question. Merely associative empirical evidence between a biological category, such as sex or race, and a person's moral approach cannot tell us whether it was the biological factor or some other factor that 'caused' the phenomenon in question. In short, research that regards a biological category as central may, wittingly or unwittingly, divert attention away from other possible factors that might equally well or better explain the empirical phenomenon. The explanation for the disproportionately high number of blacks in American prisons, for example, might have its source in the unequal social conditions in which black and white Americans find themselves, rather than in some racial distinction between the two groups.[70]

There is a danger, then, that empirical evidence, when analysed in terms of biological categories, such as sex or race, will be understood as 'biologically determined', with the result that it might render us blind to the real social cause or causes. More than that: there is also a real danger that ultimately irrelevant differences between people, such as colour or sex, will be regarded as morally significant characteristics: whites are seen as inherently more moral or less crime-prone than blacks; and women are seen (in Gilligan's and Wiggins' example) as inherently more moral than men. The result is stereotyping and, often, unjustified discrimination, subjection and domination.[71]

And indeed, attempts have been made to harness research which purports to show that there are differences in the moral reasoning of women and men to bolster the stereotypical conceptions of the traditional subordinate role of women. One well-known opponent of feminism, Michael Levin, for example, has attempted to utilize Gilligan's research in support of the Freudian idea of women's somewhat defective psychic development; and Nicholas Davidson, in his 1988 book *The Failure of Feminism*, refers to Gilligan's work and then pointedly asks whether it was really necessary 'to pass through all the storm and stress of the Feminist Era in order to arrive at ideas that were generally available forty years ago'.[72]

Gilligan objects to such representations of her work and has voiced her concerns in the feminist journal *Signs*, where she writes: 'I am well aware that reports of sex differences can be used to rationalize oppression, and I deplore any use of my work for that purpose.'[73] Moreover, as Susan Faludi notes, Gilligan now also privately states 'that if she had to do it again, she would cast some of her ideas differently; in particular, she would refine her argument "so that Jake and Amy wouldn't be presented so starkly 'male' and 'female'." '[74]

There are some feminists, however, who take the view that there is, in some sense, a biological explanation for women's different moral approach and that men are not, because they are men, capable in principle of the experiential and moral sensibilities that women allegedly share. Some of these writers emphasize the moral and epistemological significance of such distinctively female experiences as menstruation, intercourse, pregnancy, birth and lactation; while others – often referred to as 'cultural feminists' – see women's liberation as linked to 'the development and preservation of a female counter culture', and their commitment to the preservation of distinctively female traits and gender differences.[75]

I regard any essentialist claims with a large degree of scepticism. Not only would essentialism seem to entail that a feminist ethics, including, of course, a female nursing ethics of care, would be inaccessible to men and male nurses; it would also seem to presuppose an essentialist notion of 'woman', that is, to assume a substantial degree of sameness where there are important differences.[76] Women without children, and especially those who do not wish to have any children, have pointed out that the emphasis in contemporary feminist ethics on motherhood does not correspond with their moral experiences. In addition to that, one would expect that women's moral sensibilities will vary considerably from culture to culture, and even within cultures. I very much doubt, for example, that the epistemological and moral experiences of intercourse are the same for lesbian and heterosexual women. Reflections such as these would lead one to the view that even distinctly female experiences are always mediated by culture, and have meaning only in the context of particular systems of beliefs and values.[77]

If essentialist explanations of empirical evidence purporting to show statistically different moral orientations in women and men must thus be treated with great caution,[78] how else might one try to explain any perceived differences in male and female approaches to ethics?

As already briefly noted, Carol Gilligan draws on the objects-relation theory expounded by Nancy Chodorow. According to this view, the 'self' *becomes* a self through relations with others. As Gilligan explains it, for boys, separation from the child-rearer – the mother – becomes critically important for gender identity and the development of masculinity. For girls, on the other hand, 'issues of feminity or feminine identity do not depend on the achievement of separation from the mother.'[79] While this appears to be a promising approach, it is not without problems,[80] and elements of essentialism remain: attachment behaviour might ultimately, for Gilligan, be a biological rather than a relational function.[81]

Other writers – Nel Noddings, in her book *Caring: A Feminine Approach to Ethics and Moral Education*, and Sara Ruddick, in *Maternal Thinking: Towards a Politics of Peace*, for example – take a different view. They hold that child-rearing encourages certain moral sensibilities which might, in light of the fact that child-rearing is mostly performed by women, quite appropriately be called 'feminine'.[82] Similarly, Caroline Whitbeck and Virginia Held suggest that women's central role as mothers and carers is conducive to a relationship-based ethics, which is governed by norms or standards that are very different from those that are appropriate to govern the more public life of men.[83]

The general suggestion is that there is a link between the work or functions typically performed by women and women's different moral voice. Women have, for example, largely functioned in the 'private sphere', that is, they have traditionally tended the home, nurtured children, supported husbands and, more generally, provided physical and emotional care for 'concrete others'.

Their activities formed the backdrop to the more 'public' activities of men – their work outside the home, their involvement in business, church, government and various other social institutions.

The public activities of men, in distinction from the more private activities of women, did not primarily involve care for 'concrete others', but rather dealings with strangers. The suggestion is that different moral approaches might well be appropriate for these two spheres of activities – a 'care approach' in the private realm and an impartialist 'justice approach' in the public realm.[84]

To the extent, then, that particular spheres of activity, and the roles and functions performed within them, give rise to particular kinds of moral experiences and to specific visions of 'the good', it is quite conceivable that women and men will develop different concerns and priorities, and regard varying characteristics – necessary for the achievement of the respective goods – as 'virtues'.[85] This might also be the case with regard to nurses and doctors. To the extent that nurses are more intimately involved in delivering ongoing care to particular others than hospital-based doctors are, the two professions might have developed different visions of the good.

This view does, of course, receive some backing from those empirical studies that purport to show that differences in moral reasoning are better analysed in terms of occupation and/or education than in terms of sex or gender, and it has led writers such as Alison Jaggar to the conclusion that

> if women indeed show more concern than men for so-called personal relationships, this difference is less likely to be the consequence of some innate predisposition than to be the result of women's culturally assigned confinement to and/or responsibility for the one area of life and their relative exclusion from the other.[86]

While this type of analysis cannot irrefutably be shown to be correct, it has, with some qualifications,[87] considerable persuasive force.[88] It would explain why previous generations of women might indeed have approached ethics from a care perspective. It does not, however, explain why the belief that ethics is gendered lingers and is, or so we are told, reflected in the moral experiences of many contemporary women. Many women today are occupying roles in the so-called public sphere, while some contemporary men have taken over the traditional caring role. Why, then, has this not closed the gap between the moral approaches of women and men?

It is true that many women today are occupying roles in the public sphere. It is, however, also true that women are still the primary care-givers, not only when it comes to the delivery of care in the private sphere of the family, but also in public life. Nursing is, of course, an example of this. We should not be surprised, then, to find that empirical studies, such as Gilligan's, might indeed continue to detect statistically significant differences between the moral approaches of women and men. In addition to that we must not overlook the power of lingering 'moralistic' conceptions of what being a virtuous woman, or a man, entails. As Marilyn Friedman suggests, it may well be the case that genders are 'moralized' in distinctive ways. Moral standards and norms about appropriate conduct, gender-characteristic virtues and vices, she argues, become part of our conceptions of femininity and masculinity, of what being a man or a woman entails, morally speaking. The result is, Friedman suggests, 'a dichotomy that exemplifies what can be called a "division of labour" between the genders'. Women are associated with 'care', men with 'justice'.[89]

The above account provides a plausible – even if by no means watertight – sketch of why the 'care approach' has traditionally been associated with women, and why many contemporary women continue to hear and speak with a 'different voice'. After all, if women and men have internalized traditional gender-specific virtues, this can explain why these perceptions linger on, and will, as a matter of fact, reflect the 'lived moral experiences' of many contemporary women.

In short, then, even if Gilligan may not have identified a voice that is female in any deep or biological sense, she may still have identified significant gender-linked differences in the moral experiences of (white, middle-class) North American women and men, and in the moral norms and values that have traditionally been associated with, and shaped, the moral perceptions and experiences of each gender.

Conclusion

How, then, should we answer the question posed in the title of this chapter: 'Is morality gendered?' My answer would be 'yes' and 'no'. Morality may well be gendered in a superficial sense, without also being gendered in a deeper sense. Let me explain.

It seems entirely plausible that Carol Gilligan has, in fact, identified statistically significant empirical differences in the way in which contemporary men and women respond to particular moral issues. In that superficial sense, then, ethics would be gendered. It would be gendered in so far as particular women and men interpret the moral world, and their role in it, in terms of gender-specific values and norms. This does not, however, show that morality is gendered in a deeper sense, that is, that a person's moral approach is 'determined' by her gender, rather than by internalized cultural norms and beliefs, derived, at least in part, from women's and men's historical engagements and activities in the public and private spheres of social life respectively.

This would also explain why the moral experiences of a considerable number of contemporary women would be captured by Gilligan's 'care approach', and why more men appeal in their moral thinking to the 'justice approach'.

But is the care approach a proper alternative ethics to the so-called justice approach? And is it an appropriate ethics for nurses and for nursing? The next two chapters will attempt to give some answers.

6

Care versus Justice: An Old Debate in New Clothes?

Hypothetical dilemmas, in the abstraction of their presentation, divest moral actors from the history and psychology of their individual lives and separate the moral problem from the social contingencies of its possible occurrence.

Carol Gilligan, *In a Different Voice* (1982)

Indeed, I shall reject ethics of principle as ambiguous and unstable. Wherever there is principle, there is implied exception and, too often, principles function to separate us from each other.

Nel Noddings, *Caring* (1984)

Caring may lead us to focus on particular cases. Concern for particulars is an admirable antidote to the lifeless, overly broad strokes to which we have been so often subjected by moral philosophers. But I think we must beware of any corresponding tendency to devalue principles excessively.

Laura Purdy, 'Feminist Healing Ethics' (1989)

The last chapter focused on the question of whether ethics is gendered. My answer was that there may well be an empirical association between gender and moral approach, but that this association is unlikely to have its source in any female 'essence', but rather in historical and cultural conditions, including the physical and moral division of labour between the sexes.

For most of the present chapter, we shall set the question of gender aside (returning to it briefly towards the end of the chapter) and focus on a different but related issue. The publication of Carol

Gilligan's *In a Different Voice*[1] not only spawned debates about whether ethics is gendered; it also gave further encouragement to already existing debates within feminist and mainstream philosophical ethics about the nature of ethics itself. Here the question was not, or not only, whether traditional ethical theories express male ethical thinking, but also whether these theories provide an adequate map of the moral domain. Central among the issues raised was the question of whether the traditional emphasis on impartiality – the element identified in chapter 4 as a necessary component of a minimally adequate ethics – should be rejected or modified, on the grounds that it provides an incorrect picture of the moral agent as an impartial and somewhat detached adjudicator between competing interests, rather than as a relational being, who is attached to others by bonds of love, affection or care.

The debate on these issues is not always as clear as one might wish. One reason is that there are great differences in the way in which individual authors understand the ethics of care, the ethics of justice and the differences between the two perspectives. On both sides of the debate, there is a tendency to generalize and even to caricature the other side, with proponents of the care approach not always distinguishing adequately between different traditional ethical approaches that accept the idea of impartiality. While the ethical theories advanced by, for example, Immanuel Kant, John Stuart Mill and John Rawls are all impartialist, there are also some very important differences between them. Debates about the similarities and/or differences between these theories and, of course, between various other traditional theories as well, fill volumes and, in some cases, span centuries. Quite wrongly, it is thus sometimes assumed that all traditional ethical theories share the features identified by Carol Gilligan in her debate with Lawrence Kohlberg as characterizing what she calls the 'justice tradition'. While ethics in the so-called justice tradition are part of traditional ethics (in so far as they accept the idea of impartiality), not all traditional ethics share the central features characteristic of Kohlberg's ethics of justice.

In light of this, it is important that I should make clear my own understanding of the terms 'ethics of care' and 'ethics of justice'.[2] My understanding of the care approach takes Carol Gilligan's[3] characterization as its starting-point and then relies primarily on

Nel Noddings'[4] explication of an ethics of care. Gilligan's empirical work and reflections have, of course, played a central role in stimulating the care/justice debate, while Noddings has attempted to provided an ethical theory that has care at its centre.

I understand ethics in the 'justice tradition' as ethical theories that correspond with Kohlberg's view of ethics, that is, as a broadly Kantian or deontological approach to ethics.[5] I shall, however, at times also follow what has become commonplace in the literature and use the term 'justice' to identify a cluster of ideas that are common to a range of traditional ethical theories – central among them the idea of impartiality. To avoid confusion, I shall – whenever possible – refer directly to the underlying concern, rather than using the labels 'justice' or 'justice approach'.

Deontological approaches to ethics are, of course, only one of a number of traditional ethical approaches, such as consequentialism, virtue ethics and contractarian ethical theories. Given, then, that ethics in the so-called justice tradition have come under very serious criticism by proponents of the care approach, this raises the following question: Do these criticisms apply equally to all traditional ethical theories or perhaps only to a subset of traditional ethical theories, namely to ethics that might be described as broadly deontological?

Consequentialist ethics, such as utilitarianism, are impartialist and thus clearly part of traditional ethics. They are also the best-known rivals to a deontological approach to ethics. This makes consequentialist ethics an appropriate touchstone for testing the question of whether all traditional ethics are flawed in the way in which care proponents allege ethics in the justice tradition are flawed. Consequently, I will often contrast the deontological justice tradition with consequentialist ethics.

The literature on the justice/care debate is now vast and touches on many different aspects of philosophical ethics. For the purposes of this chapter, we will concentrate on only one central theme in this debate: the status of impartiality and of universal principles in ethical thinking. The status of impartiality and of universal principles is not only of direct relevance to the validity of the Minimum Conception of Ethics advanced in chapter 4, but also, as we shall see, to the fashioning of a minimally adequate nursing ethics.

Are proponents of the care approach right when they suggest

that we should treat universal principles, rules and norms with complete or at least a considerable degree of disdain? And are they right when they suggest that care for particular others – not impartiality – should be the centre-piece of our ethical approach?

The main part of this chapter is devoted to answering these questions by allowing consequentialists to enter the debate, and to respond to the criticisms levelled by proponents of the care approach against ethics in the justice tradition. As we shall see, there are a number of areas relating to the role principles and rules play in ethical thinking where consequentialists would agree with proponents of the care approach that they have identified areas of concern. Indeed, these types of concern have long been central points of debate between proponents of consequentialist and deontological approaches to ethics.

When it comes to the care critique of impartialism, however, this critique is clearly directed against consequentialism as well. Consequentialist ethical theories, such as utilitarianism, are impartialist; the care approach is inherently partialist. While proponents of the care approach have once again highlighted a central area of concern within ethics, we shall find that these concerns echo another (and much older) debate between partialist and impartialist ethics, which has been conducted within (predominantly male) philosophical ethics for some time.

The Care Critique of Traditional Ethics

During the last decade or so, a number of moral philosophers – not all of them feminists – have criticized, and tried to find alternatives to traditional ethics.[6] Martha Nussbaum sums up this general trend as follows:

> Anglo-American moral philosophy is turning from an ethics based on enlightenment ideals of universality to an ethics based on tradition and particularity; from an ethics based on principles to an ethics based on virtue; from an ethics dedicated to the elaboration of systematic theoretical justification to an ethics suspicious of theory and respectful of local wisdom; from an ethics based on the isolated individual to an ethics based on affiliation and care; from an ahistorical detached ethics to an ethics rooted in concreteness and history.[7]

The recent care approach is part of this contemporary trend. It sees itself, as we have already briefly noted in chapter 5, as having its basis in care and responsibility in personal relationships, rather than in universal ethical principles and impartial reasoning. As the philosopher Rita Manning puts it, the moral voice of care 'is not located in the heady realm of abstraction, but is centered in the . . . emotion-infused world of human interaction'.[8] A similar point is made by the nursing theorist Jean Watson, when she contrasts 'the traditional rationalist' approach of medical ethics, with a care approach that is 'rooted in receptivity, intersubjective relatedness, and human responsiveness'.[9]

Gilligan explains the contrast between a care and a justice approach in the following way: from a justice perspective, the individual moral agent stands 'against a ground of social relationships, judging the conflicting claims of self and others against a standard of equality or equal respect (the Categorical Imperative, the Golden Rule)'. From a care perspective, on the other hand, the relationship defines the self and others. Within the context of relationship, the self as a moral agent perceives and responds to the perception of need. This shift in moral perspective is manifest by a change in the moral question from 'What is just?' to 'How to respond?'[10] Indeed, as Gilligan points out, '[t]he metaphor of voice itself carries the terms of the care perspective.'[11] After all, voices are inter-relational and social; they characterize the interaction of physical and embodied beings, not the solitary and rational perspective of an 'ideal observer' or 'impartial spectator'.

Along with the rejection of the perspective of the detached and socially unencumbered 'impartial spectator' goes the rejection of such universal principles as Immanuel Kant's Categorical Imperative ('Act only according to that maxim by which you can at the same time will that it should become a universal law') and Jeremy Bentham's 'Everybody to count for one, nobody for more than one.' Universal and impartial moral principles in general are seen as wrong-headed, often irrelevant and not conducive to the moral life. In other words, an ethics of care rejects a model of moral deliberation that requires us to adopt the detached and rational perspective of an impartial spectator which in turn requires us to strip away, or abstract, certain contextual details from complex and emotion-infused actual situations, until they can be subsumed under general and rationally derived principles or norms. Rather, the care perspective identifies as constitutive of the moral life the elements of mutual interdependence, of emotional response, and the particularity of individual situations, people and circumstances.

This has led proponents of the care approach to criticize the idea of impartiality and the usefulness of universal principles and rules. Universal principles and rules, they say, cannot, and should not, guide our action.[12] We begin by examining the care critique of principles and rules.

The Critique of Principles and Rules

Beauchamp and Childress give the following example, derived from a report by a doctor, Timothy Quill, and a nurse, Penelope Townsend, of a discussion with a young woman who has just been told that she is infected with HIV:

PATIENT: Oh God. Oh Lord have mercy . . . Please don't do it again. Please don't tell me that. Oh my God. Oh my children. Oh Lord have mercy. Oh God, why did He do this to me? . . .

DR QUILL: The first thing we have to do is learn as much as we can about it, because right now you are okay.

PATIENT: I don't even have a future. Everything I know is that you gonna die anytime. What is there to do? What if I'm a walking time bomb? People will be scared to even touch me or say anything to me.

DR QUILL: No, that's not so.

PATIENT: Yes, they will, 'cause I feel that way . . .

DR QUILL: There is a future for you . . .

PATIENT: Okay, alright. I'm so scared. I don't want to die. I don't want to die, Dr Quill, not yet. I know I got to die, but I don't want to die.

DR QUILL: We've got to think about a couple of things.[13]

As Beauchamp and Childress note, Quill and Townsend have moral responsibilities to this and other similarly situated patients, but it seems difficult to capture these responsibilities in universal principles and rules.[14] Each patient and each situation is different and requires a finely tuned response. Abstract principles and rules, however, are universal – they are instruments of impartiality and seem to require simplification. They are guides to conduct, where the right action or the right attitude is the one that accords with the relevant principle, rule or norm. This, proponents of a care approach suggest, is where a rule or principle-based approach goes wrong: it takes insufficient account of the complexity and particularity of each situation, and of the individuality of those involved.

The cases of Mac and Lillian Boyes, described in chapter 1, may serve as another practical example. How, it might be asked, can we have general principles and rules – for example, a principle that affirms the sanctity of life and regards the intentional shortening of life as absolutely wrong – when there are cases like those of Mac and Lillian Boyes? While it will often, and probably usually, be a good thing for doctors and nurses to prolong rather than shorten their patients' lives, there are clearly cases where a principle affirming the sanctity of life would either not be very helpful or even suggest a course of action that is incompatible with care.

The critique of abstraction

In her book, *Caring: A Feminine Approach to Ethics and Moral Education*, Noddings provides an extensive critique of principle- and rule-based approaches to ethics.[15] She distinguishes that approach – Noddings calls it the 'approach of the father' – from an ethics of care – the 'approach of the mother'. The following passage is illustrative of the principal charge brought by proponents of the care approach against a principled ethical approach: that it is 'abstract', rather than 'concrete', and fails to respond to the specific ethical context in which an event takes place:

> The first ['the approach of the father'] moves immediately to abstraction where . . . thinking can take place clearly and logically in isolation from the complicating factors of particular persons, places, and circumstances; the second moves to concretization where . . . feelings can be modified by the introduction of facts, the feelings of others, and personal histories.[16]

But what do we mean when we speak of 'abstraction'? Sara Ruddick provides us with a useful starting-point: abstraction, she says, 'refers to a cluster of interrelated dispositions to simplify, dissociate, generalise and sharply define'. Its opposite, which she calls 'concreteness', 'respects complexity, connection, particularity and ambiguity'.[17]

Now abstraction, as care proponents correctly point out, can sometimes be undesirable, as it would be if a rule or principle required us to ignore or 'abstract' a salient feature of a situation, to make it 'fit' the rule in question. If one takes the view, for example, that it is a morally relevant feature of a situation whether a competent and terminally ill patient wishes to live or die, then we will, other things being equal, reject as inadequate a simple rule or principle that requires us to always prolong life. But not all abstraction can, or should be, avoided. Rather, it is necessary to distinguish between benign (and necessary) and some more dubious forms of abstraction.

Why we can't do without some abstraction

In the passage from Noddings quoted above, the contrast between 'abstraction' and 'concretization' seems to rest, at least in part, on the distinction between 'thinking in isolation from complicating factors' and 'thinking modified by the introduction of facts'. Here it is important to recognize that ethical thinking can *never* proceed in isolation from concrete facts and particular circumstances. Even Immanuel Kant, who rigidly held that one must never lie, even to a would-be murderer who asks about the whereabouts of his intended victim, needs to refer to concrete facts in order to judge whether the statement 'I don't know where he is' is to count as a lie.[18] Without reference to such facts, it would be impossible to determine whether a relevant act infringes the principle or rule in question.[19]

The converse also holds: those who take Noddings' 'mother approach' will have to abstract some details from the infinite number that form the backdrop to a given situation. We might, for example, agree with Noddings that 'feelings' and 'personal histories' may well be morally significant and ought to be considered in our moral deliberations. Indeed, we may agree that they are centrally important in cases where a patient has, for example, been identified as HIV positive, and in cases relating to death and dying.

But such reference to 'feelings' and 'personal histories' is, of course, already an abstraction of particular aspects of the situation: it obviously leaves out such things as a person's height, hair colour or the size of her feet. And even if we were to focus on 'feelings' and 'personal histories' as the morally salient features of the situation, further abstractions will need to be made: it is simply not possible to take all the feelings or each aspect of every personal history into account. In short, then, *any* moral response must regard *some* factors as morally relevant, while ignoring other factors as morally irrelevant. This means that the central question is not *whether* context is relevant, but rather *which* elements of a particular context ought to be 'abstracted' from the overall context as significant for ethical decision-making.[20]

This is a question that must be answered by any ethical approach, regardless of whether it is a so-called justice approach, a care approach, or a consequentialist approach. Whatever the answer will be, it involves 'abstraction' – focusing on some elements of a context, of a person or of a relationship, while ignoring others. These 'abstractions' are the stuff that moral principles are made of.

What *should we abstract?*

A closer look at the writings of those who take a care approach bears this out. Proponents of an ethics of care are not generally advocating an entirely non-principled approach to ethics, even if they frequently sound as if they do. Rather than rejecting a principled approach to ethics, these writers seem to be objecting to the *kinds* of principles advocated by traditional theorists who approach ethics from outside that perspective. As Claudia Card observes with regard to Noddings' objection to a principled approach to ethics: 'What Nel Noddings finds objectionable about acting on principle may have more to do with *the content of particular principles* than with the idea of abstraction.'[21]

As we have noted above, there are some common themes discernible in the care approach to ethics: that it should be sensitive to context, to relationships, and to care and responsibility to particular others. These principles may not have been at the forefront of traditional ethical thinking, but as Laura Purdy correctly points out, they are principles none the less. They are meant to guide the ethical thinking of those who use them, and to make it consistent.[22]

But if proponents of the care approach are proposing that we select principles, factors or aspects different from those regarded as relevant by proponents of other ethical approaches, they are not doing anything very different from what other traditional moral philosophers have been doing for a very long time: raising questions about the adequacy and appropriateness of the criteria thought relevant by rival ethical theories. The very reason why there is a diversity of ethical theories is that those who propose them have different conceptions of 'the good life', and of the different principles, factors and aspects that are central to it.

The importance of context

There is, however, also another way in which the critique of abstraction can be understood. A proponent of the care approach may not wish to dispute that it is always necessary to select from a particular context some features before a decision can be made. Rather, what she may wish to deny is that these features can be selected 'in the abstract', without taking the concrete circumstances of each particular situation into account – the particular persons involved, their social and historical circumstances and the like. This means that it will not, on this view, be possible to apply general rules or principles, for to attempt to apply a rule or principle would require us to 'abstract', that is, to ignore or discount those features of the situation that make it what it is. Because each situation is different, it requires a finely tuned response, a response that cannot be brought under a general principle or rule.

This is connected with the rejection, by proponents of the care approach, of hypothetical dilemmas. As Gilligan puts it in her objection to Kohlberg's use of abstract rather than real-life moral dilemmas in his research:

> Hypothetical dilemmas, in the abstraction of their presentation, divest moral actors from the history and psychology of their individual lives and separate the moral problem from the social contingencies of its possible occurrence. In so doing, these dilemmas are useful for the distillation and refinement of objective principles of

justice and for measuring the formal logic of equality and reciprocity. However, the reconstruction of the dilemma in its contextual particularity allows the understanding of cause and consequence which engages the compassion and tolerance repeatedly noted to distinguish the moral judgement of women.[23]

There is indeed something unsatisfactory about the bare-bone dilemmas sometimes found in the medical ethics literature: 'A donor heart has become available. Should it be given to the 21-year-old college student or to the 65-year-old Nobel prize winner?' Such dilemmas will leave many of us bewildered, because few people make moral decisions by applying broad principles or simple rules, such as always tell the truth, always treat the younger/older patient first and so on. As Nel Noddings correctly observes: 'Faced with a hypothetical dilemma, women [and I would add, many men] often ask for more information. We want to know more, I think, in order to form a picture more nearly resembling real moral situations.'[24] Take the principle: 'If resources are limited and we must choose between the lives of two people, we ought to attempt to save the younger person.' Many people will find such a rule persuasive – but only 'in the abstract', that is, as a prima facie principle or rule. When assenting to it, they will implicitly insert an 'other things being equal' clause. They would abandon the principle if, say, the college student had only a 5 per cent chance of long-term survival, whereas the Nobel prize winner had a 60 per cent chance; or if the college student was in a persistent vegetative state and the Nobel prize winner was not; or perhaps, if the college student, despite her youth, already had a long criminal record, and the Nobel prize winner was on the verge of a breakthrough that might be instrumental in the fight against cancer.

Henry Sidgwick, a nineteenth-century utilitarian, has illustrated the importance of context in the application of a relatively simple rule, such as 'Promises ought to be kept':

If we ask (e.g.) how far our promise is binding if it was made in consequence of false statements, on which, however, it was not understood to be conditional; or if important circumstances were concealed, or we were in any way led to believe that the consequences of keeping the promise would be different from what they turn out to be; or if the promise were given under compulsion; or if circumstances have materially altered since it was given, and we find that the results of fulfilling it will be different from what we foresaw when we promised; or even if it be only our knowledge of consequences which has altered, and we now see that fulfilment will entail on us a sacrifice out of proportion to the benefit received by the promisee; or perhaps see that it will even be injurious to him though he may not think so . . . [T]he mere discussion of these points seems to make it plain that the confidence with which the 'unsophisticated conscience' asserts unreservedly 'that promises ought to be kept,' is due to inadvertence and that when the qualifications to which we referred are fairly considered, this confidence inevitably changes into hesitation and perplexity.[25]

For many people, knowing more about a situation will determine the answer they would want to give to a moral dilemma. Of course, if a person believes that ethics is a system of rigid rules or principles, she is less likely to be sensitive to context than a person who believes that the rightness of her action is determined by its consequences. For a utilitarian, for example, sensitivity to context must always be of the utmost importance for, as we have seen in chapter 4, from the utilitarian perspective the rightness of an action depends solely on its consequences; and the consequences of a particular action will, of course, depend on the contextual features of each individual situation. Whereas Immanuel Kant, for example, thought that lying was never justified, even if it would save a person's life, utilitarians would say that lying is right in some situations and wrong in others.

This means that proponents of the care approach are not alone in emphasizing the importance of sensitivity to context. While some traditional ethical thinkers have ignored context, other thinkers – utilitarians foremost among them – have always insisted that attention to context, that is, to the particularities of people and of situations, is a precondition for an adequate moral response.

The critique of universalizability

It might be said, however, that impartialism presupposes a degree of sameness: that you and I have similar interests, duties or rights. Without such assumptions of similarity we would not be able to arrive at any judgements that are universalizable, i.e. that apply to different individuals who find themselves in like circumstances. But, proponents of an ethics of care have argued, we cannot make such assumptions of sameness. As Nel Noddings has summed it up: 'Conditions are rarely "sufficiently similar" for me to declare that you must do what I must do.'[26]

As the discussion above has shown, utilitarians agree with proponents of an ethics of care that context, including the particularity of the persons involved, is of the utmost importance. They would also agree that 'responsiveness to other persons in their wholeness and their particularity is of singular importance'[27] and that we should always try to adopt 'the standpoint of the concrete other'.[28] But, proponents of an ethics of care may say, this is not all. We must also take account of the *relationships* holding between different individuals – individuals who have different histories, beliefs and ideals, who are interacting with and are tied to other equally unique individuals in various ways. It is because of this, proponents of an ethics of care say, that relationships can give rise to special duties and responsibilities and that it will be difficult, if not impossible, to apply impartial and universally applicable judgements to different situations.

We might thus understand Noddings as holding that personal relationships are so specific as to make it near impossible to bring them under a universalizable principle or rule – that I have duties to my mother, husband or lover that I do not have to anybody else's mother, husband or lover, no matter how similar the situations might be. Moral duties, Noddings might say, are linked to particular individuals and this particularity – 'the duty owed by Tom to his mother' or 'the promise made by Mary' – will impugn the universalizability of moral judgements.

But is this understanding of relational duties incompatible with the principle of universalizability, as Noddings thinks it is? The answer is no. Noddings' rejection of universalizability appears to rest on a confusion between particular individuals having duties and the universality of such duties. The principle that a son has an obligation to do certain things for his mother, or that someone who has made a promise should keep it, is not specific to a particular individual; rather, it holds for all individuals who find themselves in the relevant circumstances or relationships.[29]

But, a proponent of an ethics of care might press on, underlying the above rejoinder there is an as yet unjustified assumption of sameness: that the people who find themselves in the relevant relationships or circumstances are in some sense the same – that sons, daughters and mothers, for example, have similar duties, interests or preferences, are the holders of similar rights and the like. It is only because of this assumption of sameness, of seeing people as the holders of rights or interest or the bearers of promises, rather than as unique individuals, that universal principles can gain a foothold.[30]

Now it might be the case that universalizability in the context of an ethics such as Kant's requires an assumption of sameness, where an individual must be flensed down 'to the bare bones of abstract personhood'[31] before a universal principle or rule can be applied, but it cannot reasonably be directed against the principle of universalization as such. Utilitarians, for example, accept the idea of universalizability, but also insist that in my application of this principle, I use my imagination in order to put myself in the position of all those affected by my action – to imagine that I am the other, with her history, preferences, values and beliefs. This means that I am also required, whenever this is possible, to regard the other as a *particular* other with a unique history, particular interests, with personal ideals, preferences and the like, and as an individual who is embedded in particular personal relationships and is linked to others by promises, friendship or love.

If this is correct, it means that Noddings' critique of universalizability is wrong-headed. Universality is not the same as generality.[32] Indeed, universalizable principles can be so finely tuned that they allow us to take account of all the morally relevant nuances of a situation. While Noddings' criticism may justifiably be applied to some ethics that do not allow for contextual sensitivity, they cannot be applied to all traditional ethics that make use of the idea of universalizability.

The critique of a multiple principles approach

In her discussion of ethics based on rules and principles, Nel Noddings raises another criticism. She points out that when principles clash – as they inevitably will when an ethical theory advocates more than one fundamental principle – the agent must decide on some hierarchical ordering or balancing of these principles or rules. This, she says, gives ethical problem-solving a 'mathematical appearance', and 'moves discussion beyond the sphere of actual human activity', as if it were 'governed by the logical necessity characteristic of geometry'.[33] Moral decisions are, however, Nodding holds, 'qualitatively different from the solution of geometry problems'.[34] A similar point is made by Gilligan when she says that women do not see in Kohlberg's moral dilemmas 'a maths problem with humans but a narrative of relationships that extends over time'.[35]

This criticism can be understood in various ways. Here we shall deal with one possible interpretation: that a theory that takes a number of principles or rules to be basic is flawed, because it requires us hierarchically to rank or balance principles, rules or norms, as if we were solving a mathematical problem rather than a problem in ethics.

This is an important objection. But, as we shall see, it has long been a commonplace in, for example, consequentialist criticisms of those ethical approaches that take a number of ethical principles to be basic.

Critics of the justice approach do not generally draw a distinction between ethical theories that take one or a number of principles to be basic. Such a distinction is, however, very important. As we have already noted, proponents of an ethics of care are not proposing an entirely unprincipled approach. Rather, they are proposing principled approaches that are qualitatively different from those proposed by traditional ethical theorists. This is also true of Noddings. According to Noddings, a decision is 'right or wrong according to how faithfully it was rooted in caring – that is, in a genuine response to the perceived needs of others'.[36] It suggests that Noddings takes one principle, caring, to be basic[37] – for the rightness or wrongness of an action is determined by how faithfully it meets the perceived needs of others.

Utilitarians, too, take only one principle to be basic – the principle that we should maximize the good. On this view, an action is right or wrong depending on whether or not it maximizes the good.

For ethical theories that take only one principle to be basic, there can, of course, be no conflict or clash between different ethical principles or rules. While proponents of a single-principle approach, including proponents of care[38] and of utilitarianism,[39] may well accept various principles and rules on a prima facie basis or as rules of thumb, any conflict between these non-basic principles or rules can, on the face of it, be settled by appealing to the one basic principle – the principle of care, the principle of utility or whatever other principle an ethical theory takes to be basic.

Many ethical theories, including theories in the justice tradition, take a number of different ethical principles as basic. If one bases one's moral approach on a number of ethical principles – for example, on the much-discussed principles of autonomy, beneficence, non-maleficence and justice – then one must find a non-arbitrary method of settling conflict when clashes between these principles occur.[40]

Take the Heinz example, discussed in chapter 5, where the question was whether, and if so why, it would be morally permissible for Heinz to steal the drug for his dying wife. What Kohlberg would score as a higher stage moral response is one that would justify stealing, on the grounds that 'life' is more important than 'property', and that would rank impartialist duties more highly than duties arising out of particular relationships. Kohlberg provides an example of this sort of reasoning by a post-conventional thinker named Bill,

> BILL: It is the husband's duty to save his wife. The fact that her life is in danger transcends every other standard you might use to judge his action. Life is more important than property.

> *Suppose it were a friend, not his wife?*

> BILL: I don't think that would be much different from the moral point of view. It's still a human being in danger.

> *What is this [moral point of view]?*

> BILL: I think every individual has a right to live and if there is a way of saving an individual, he should be saved.[41]

Noddings, who takes only one principle to be basic, does not think that morality is either a matter of impartialist ethical thinking or of the hierarchical ranking of principles, rules or norms. On this point, utilitarians would agree with her. Ranking 'life' more highly than 'property', while intuitively plausible, will often not be very helpful in practice, where the context may call for a revision of that principle. The life in question may, for example, be that of a terminally ill patient who wishes to die; the property in question may be needed to support a deserted wife, caring for a number of young children; and so on. Such contextual details, Marilyn Friedman points out, can be very complex – some swaying us in one direction, some in another. Very soon, 'we will need principles for the *ordering* of our principles.'[42] However, and this is the crucial point, there is no predetermined hierarchy of finely tuned principles, nor is there a master principle to which proponents of a multi-principle approach can turn to tell them how to justify their rankings.

Lawrence Kohlberg thinks that close attention to contextual detail will help us to puzzle out which principle to apply.[43] But this suggestion is, of course, not very helpful. If the ranking of principles depends on context, then we cannot turn to context to tell us how to rank our principles.[44]

Utilitarians, who recognize only one principle as basic, have usually objected to ethical theories that take several principles as basic, on the grounds that these principles are prone to come into conflict with each other. This, utilitarians argue, makes such pluralist theories not only difficult to apply in practice, but also raises problems for the ultimate theoretical justification of complex ethical judgements.

The point is forcefully brought home by the contemporary utilitarian philosopher R. M. Hare. Hare argues that a multi-principle approach will land one squarely on the horns of a dilemma, where one would either have no determinate procedure for settling moral conflicts or one would have principles of ever-increasing complexity, which will not be much use in practice.

In order to demonstrate this point briefly, Hare employs a formal approach, using letters for the features of situations which figure in the conflicting principles. Starting with a set of relatively simple principles, such as 'One ought never to do an act which is

F' and 'One ought never to do an act which is G' (where 'F' and 'G' stand for two different actions, one of which may, for example, be promise-breaking), an agent who finds herself in a situation where she cannot avoid doing either F or G may initially attempt to solve the problem by ranking F as morally worse than G. 'But,' Hare argues,

> by the time we have been in, or even considered without actually being in them, a few such dilemmas, we shall be getting very long principles indeed. Very early on we shall get principles like: 'One ought never to do an act which is G, except that one may when it is necessary in order to avoid an act which is F, and the act is also H, but if the act is not H, one may not.'

Eventually, Hare finishes up with a 49-word principle.[45] Having considered some other ways of avoiding the dilemma, Hare concludes

> It is . . . obvious that any attempt to set up what is called a hierarchy of principles, telling us which is to override which, and when, will, if it is to do justice to the moral judgements which we actually make in cases of conflict, soon become extremely complicated; for the instructions for operating the hierarchy will mostly be in the form of the 49-word principle just mentioned.[46]

Moreover, Hare notes, that is not all. We might also want to change the order of priority of the principles just listed.

> [S]hall we not want to say that we ought to tell lies to avoid giving pain in *some* circumstances, but that we ought to give pain in order to avoid telling lies in *other* circumstances (for example when the pain is not great)?[47]

Hare's conclusion, like that of other utilitarians, is that we ought to reject an approach to ethics which sees the resolution of moral conflict as lying in the hierarchical ordering of principles or rules. Such ranking is not only cumbersome, and therefore difficult to apply consistently in practice; those who propose multiple basic principles are also hard-pushed to justify their particular rankings because there is no master principle to which they can turn.[48]

When it comes to criticisms of ethical approaches that take a number of hierarchically ranked principles to be basic, there are thus once again some central common themes in the criticisms advanced by proponents of a care and a utilitarian approach to ethics. But now we must turn to the fundamental point of difference between an ethics of care and traditional ethical theories in general: the debate over impartialism.

The Critique of Impartialism

Proponents of the care approach to ethics may accept that they share some common ground with utilitarians in their criticisms of some principles-based approaches to ethics. There is, however, a further important criticism that affects utilitarianism no less than it does other traditional ethical theories. This is the charge that it is 'impersonal' or 'impartialist', emphasizing universal obligations to all those affected by our actions, rather than obligations to those for whom we care in a personal way. The feminist philosopher Susan Sherwin, for example, agrees that utilitarianism is in many ways 'an antidote' to rigid ethics in the Kantian tradition. None the less, she holds, it cannot meet the requirements of an ethics of care because it evaluates actions 'in abstraction from the relationships holding between the participants performing them and those affected by them'.[49]

As we have seen in chapter 4, the requirement that ethical judgements must, in some sense, be universal and impartial has a long history. Indeed, impartialism in ethics can be seen as the common ground shared by both deontological and utilitarian approaches to ethics. Lawrence Blum describes this common ground as follows:

> Both views identify morality with a perspective of impartiality, impersonality, objectivity and universality. Both views imply the ubiquity of impartiality – that our commitments and projects derive their legitimacy only by reference to this impartial perspective.[50]

To be considered an *ethical* judgement at all it must, on these views, be impartial: the justification of our projects and commitments cannot be in terms of a particular person, section or group.

Rather, an ethical judgement must go beyond personal or sectional interests, that is, apply impartially to everyone, under relevant similar circumstances. As we have seen in chapter 4, this has usually been understood to mean not only that I cannot justify a particular moral judgement by the special advantages it would bring me, but also that I must not give special preference to those near and dear to me – for example, my family and friends or, if I am a nurse, my patients – because they are *my* family or friends or *my* patients.

Perhaps the most famous – or infamous? – example of impartialism is the argument of the eighteenth-century philosopher William Godwin, a utilitarian and an anarchist. In his book *Political Justice*, first published in 1793, he held that if one had to choose between saving two people from a fire, and one was Archbishop Fénelon, a person whose writings were bringing happiness to millions, while the other was one's chambermaid, then one ought to save the Archbishop. And Godwin went on:

> Suppose the chambermaid had been my wife, my mother or my benefactor. This would not alter the truth of the proposition . . . What magic is there in the pronoun 'my' to overturn the decision of everlasting truth?[51]

Impartialism has recently been attacked by various philosophers, not all of whom think of themselves as writing from a feminist perspective or from a perspective of care. Thus, it has been alleged that the demands of an impartialist morality interfere with an individual's pursuit of her own ends, with her commitment to deeply cherished beliefs, and commitment to particular people, groups and traditions.[52] As Bernard Williams has noted, such ethics require us to 'treat friends as strangers'.[53] The critique of impartialism by proponents of an ethics of care, while not necessarily at odds with the first two kinds of criticism, falls broadly into the third. It holds that impartialist ethics are flawed because they do not allow us to pay sufficient attention to special relational and motivational concerns and obligations. Rita Manning asks us to imagine the reaction of a woman who has just been rescued by her husband. Upon asking him 'What took you so long?' her husband tells her: 'I was trying to see if I could justify rescuing you rather than the stranger drowning with you. When I realized that I could apply an impartial rule impartially and still save you, I immediately proceeded to do so.'[54] Might it not be said that the husband asked 'one question too many'?

The partialist critique of impartialism

The central issue for proponents of an ethics of care is the potential conflict between the demands of impartialist moral concerns and those arising out of our partialist attachments to particular others. What kind of a world would it be, one might take proponents of care to be asking, where husbands are morally required to allow their wives to drown, where mothers might be required to sacrifice their own children's well-being for the sake of the greater good of others, and where we would 'treat friends as strangers'?

It would appear to be a bleak and inhuman world indeed. Instead of advocating impartiality, we should thus, proponents of the care approach say, recognize that we have special attachments and responsibilities to 'proximate others' that we do not have to those more distant from us. In other words, if the choice is between saving Fénelon (a stranger) and, say, your husband, then you ought to save your husband — even if you could achieve better overall consequences by saving the stranger.

Reasoning and moral motivation

The traditional view that ethical thinking must be impartialist is echoed in Kohlberg's method of scoring responses, where respondents are expected to eschew partialist concerns. Earlier on, we looked at Kohlberg's example of the post-conventional thinker Bill. Bill did well on Kohlberg's test because he adopted an impartialist mode of reasoning. Bill did not think that Heinz should steal the drug simply because this might save his wife's life; rather, he expressed 'the moral point of view' in impartialist form: '[E]very individual has a right to live and if there is a way of saving an individual, he should be saved.'[55]

Noddings, like other proponents of the care approach, would disagree with Bill. For her, acting morally is not a matter of impartialist thinking; rather, it involves a caring response, arising out of an 'affective-receptive . . . feeling [mode]'. This, she says, is 'qualitatively different from the analytic-objective mode in which we impose structure on the world'.[56] While '[w]omen can and do give reasons' for why they act in the way they do, 'these reasons often point to feelings, needs, impressions.'[57] For Noddings, ethics has its source not in impartialist reason, but rather in an 'acceptive-receptive' mode of the one-caring. As Noddings describes it:

> We enter a feeling mode, but it is not necessarily an emotional mode. In such a mode, we receive what-is-there as nearly as possible without evaluation or assessment . . . An affective-receptive mode of this kind . . . is clearly, qualitatively different from the analytic-objective mode in which we impose structure on the world. It is a precreative mode characterized by outer quietude and inner voices and images, by absorption and sensory concentration. The one so engrossed is listening, looking, feeling.[58]

Noddings is not alone in emphasizing the importance of affective receptivity and of engrossment. Both deontologists and consequentialists may well agree with her on this point, and we will return to the significance of affective receptivity (I shall call it 'dispositional care') in chapter 7. In the present section, we shall restrict our attention to the difference between what Noddings calls the 'analytic-objective mode' and the 'affective mode' – the distinction between acting on the basis of reason and acting on the basis of feeling.

According to Kant, a morally worthy action is a matter of reason, not of feeling, and must be done for the sake of duty. We know what our duty is because we are reasoning beings, and the Categorical Imperative is an imperative of reason. To the degree that an action is solely motivated by a feeling or emotion, it lacks moral worth. This entails that doing one's duty is not always easy: the requirements of the moral law may be in opposition to one's natural inclinations and feelings and may give rise to what Michael Stocker has called 'moral schizophrenia'.[59]

Not every traditional philosopher agrees with Kant that morality has its source in reason, and the eighteenth-century Scottish philosopher David Hume, sometimes called the 'women's philosopher', is a well-known exception. Proponents of a consequentialist approach to ethics are not committed to either side. They may hold, as the nineteenth-century utilitarian Henry Sidgwick did, that consequentialism is based on rational intuitions that will be self-evident to any rational being that reflects on them in a calm and clear-minded manner; or they may hold, as the contemporary utilitarian J. J. C. Smart does, that consequentialism has its source in a subjective feeling of general benevolence, and is not something capable of defence by reasoning or argument.[60] None the less, to the extent that utilitarianism is an impartialist ethical theory, it too may be susceptible to a kind of 'moral schizophrenia'. After all, if morality requires us to live according to such maxims as 'Everybody to count for one, nobody for more than one' and to act always in ways that will produce the best overall consequences, then our own feelings, desires and emotions will play a relatively small role in determining what we ought to do. Rather, morality may require us to act contrary to our affections and what we most care about.[61]

Those who follow Noddings' care approach do not experience a similar kind of tension between the dictates of their morality and their moral motivation. Rather, to the extent that caring is an 'affective-responsive' mode that has its source in what Noddings calls our 'longing for caring', caring actions more readily coincide with our natural inclinations.[62]

Here, then, it seems, we have identified a significant difference between the care approach and traditional impartialist approaches. Any traditional moral theory that requires us to give equal consideration to the interests of all those affected by our actions will potentially be at odds with our natural inclinations and may lead to the kind of 'moral schizophrenia' referred to above.

Can an impartialist ethics accommodate partialist concerns?

But might it be possible to reconcile partialism and impartialism and for an impartialist ethics, such as utilitarianism, to accommodate partialist concerns? As we have already noted, impartialism – and here utilitarianism is a particular target – is frequently criticized by proponents of an ethics of care on the grounds that it does not allow us to give special weight to responsibilities and duties we are usually thought to have towards those near and dear to us, and to ties of love and affection that bind us to them but not to the rest of humanity. As Godwin's opponents asserted, if impartialism demands that we save Fénelon, rather than our mother, then so much the worse for impartialism.

But does impartialism require us to save Fénelon and leave our mother, our husband or wife to burn? There seems to be no doubt that, given the way human beings are constituted, love, close family relationships and friendship are of great importance to a full and satisfying human life. So utilitarians will think that these concerns ought to be accorded a protected place in one's ethical theory. Even Godwin (who had a sadly brief relationship with the early feminist Mary Wollstonecraft – she died when giving birth to their first child) subsequently argued that:

> True wisdom will recommend to us individual attachments . . . True virtue will sanction this recommendation; since it is the object of virtue to produce happiness; and since the man who lives in the midst of domestic relations will have many opportunities of conferring pleasure, minute in the detail, yet not trivial in the amount.[63]

In addition to that, there are good consequentialist reasons why we ought, for example, to encourage parents to look after *their* children, and children to reciprocate when they are older. There are also good reasons why nurses and doctors should show particular concerns for 'their' patients, rather than for all the patients in the world. If parents were to care equally about all the children in the world, and nurses equally about patients in general, it is unlikely that children or patients as a whole would be as well looked after as they are now. The dispersion of care and responsibility would be self-defeating.

This general point was memorably encapsulated in Charles Dickens' portrayal of the impartialist Mrs Jellyby, who 'could see nothing nearer than Africa', neglecting her own children so that she could care better for those in foreign lands.[64]

The fact that impartialist concerns may require the neglect of those close to us means that an impartialist such as a utilitarian can, on utilitarian grounds, accept that there are some partialist personal attachments and ties of affection, professional loyalties, virtues and duties and responsibilities that ought to be fostered and cultivated. If one takes this view, it may, however, be necessary to distinguish between different levels or modes of ethical think-ing – as, for example, defended by R. M. Hare.[65] Hare distin-guishes between an intuitive and a critical level of ethical thinking. This distinction, already briefly touched on in chapter 4, comes roughly to this: the kinds of motivations or dispositions we ought to develop for acting in fairly time-pressured circumstances, and the kind of thinking we ought to engage in during periods of unpressured reflection, when we can decide what sort of intuitive responses we should have.[66] This distinction explains, of course, why some of our prima facie judgements in favour of our loved ones can be explained as the correct intuitive response, where thinking at the critical level has told us that they are correct in so far as they serve broader impartialist interests. This means that a utilitarian might well support the cultivation of virtues that would lead a husband or a wife quickly to save their partner from drown-ing, rather than engage in the lengthy calculations often assumed to be an inherent feature of a utilitarian approach.[67]

Why Partialism Cannot Replace Impartialism

Now, one may well agree that personal relationships are an im-portant part of our lives and ought to find a protected space within our moral thinking. But does it follow from this, as proponents of a care approach have assumed, that a partialist ethics should replace impartialism?[68] It seems clear that the answer must be 'no'.

The reason why a personal or partialist ethics cannot totally *replace* an impartialist ethics is obvious. Not all our actions affect individuals with whom we stand in personal relationships. This is the case, for example, when a hospital administrator determines the criteria for admission to the hospital's dialysis programme; or when a government decides to allocate resources to a heart trans-plant unit, rather than to, say, a programme of preventative care. And, to give just one more example, it is also the case when our generation, by exploiting and polluting the environment, leaves an impoverished and hazardous world to those who come after us. This means that unless exponents of a personal ethics of care wanted to take the hard-nosed view that we never have any moral duties and responsibilities to those with whom we have no personal relationships, they would still need to devise and defend some ethical principles to govern our relationship with strangers.[69] After all, it would not be obvious that a health-care minister contemplating the allocation of health-care resources should, for example, choose a heart transplant programme simply because her husband requires a transplant, even though the alternative preventative programme would save more lives for a similar expenditure of funds. This means that a partialist ethics of care can never account for the whole of ethics. An adequate ethics needs impartiality as well as care.

Care versus Justice – Not a Matter of Gender

As we have already noted in passing, not all contemporary critics of ethics in the justice tradition and of impartialism in general are either feminists or women. Rather, various criticisms of 'traditional male ethics' now advanced as 'feminine' concerns by proponents of an ethics of care have long been part of mainstream philosophical debates.[70] The debate over partialism and impartialism, in particular, has a long history,[71] and men and women have taken varying sides in the debate.

If Charles Dickens' portrayal of Mrs Jellyby,[72] for example, puts him on the side of Noddings and of partialism, Charlotte Perkins Gilman, a prominent early twentieth-century American feminist, must be seen as taking the side of impartialism. In a short story entitled 'The Unnatural Mother', Gilman considers the actions of Esther Greenwood, an unconventional young mother. Esther Greenwood noticed that a dam above the village in which she lived was about to burst. She ran past her own house, in which her baby was asleep, in order to rouse the village and send word to two other villages further down the valley. She then ran back to her own house to save the baby. But it was too late. While the baby miraculously survived, Esther Greenwood lost her own life.

The story contains the following exchange between two older village women – Mrs Briggs, mother of 13, and Miss Jacobs, a well-to-do old maid, and Maria Amelia, a daughter of Mrs Briggs:

'Don't tell me!' said old Mis' Briggs, with a forbidding shake of her head. 'No mother that was a mother would desert her own child for anything on earth!' 'And leaving it a care on the town, too!' put in Susannah Jacobs. 'As if we hadn't enough to do to look after our own!' . . .

The youngest Briggs girl, still unmarried at thirty-six, and in her mother's eyes a most tender infant, now ventured to make a remark.

'You don't any of you seem to think what she did for all of us – if she hadn't left hers we should all have lost ours, sure.'

'You are no judge, Maria 'Melia,' her mother hastened to reply. 'You've no children of your own, and you can't judge of a mother's duty. No mother ought to leave her child, whatever happens . . .'

'Well, now, Mother,' said Maria Amelia Briggs. 'It does seem to me that she did her duty. You know yourself that if she hadn't given warning all three of the villages would 'a been cleaned out – a matter of fifteen hundred people. And if she'd stopped to lug that child, she couldn't have got here in time. Don't you think she was thinkin' of those mill hand's children?'

'Maria 'Melia, I am ashamed of you!' said old Mis' Briggs. 'But you ain't married and ain't a mother. A mother's duty is to her own child! She neglected her own to look after other folks' – the Lord never gave her them other children to care for!'

'Yes,' said Miss Jacobs, 'and here's her child, a burden on the town! She was an unnatural mother.'[73]

We need not doubt that Esther Greenwood, or any parent finding herself in a similar situation, would have experienced heart-rending conflict between her natural inclinations to save her own child and her impartialist concerns towards others. When there are such conflicting obligations, we are often pulled in different directions. In a situation such as this, a two-level ethical approach, such as that defended by R. M. Hare and Peter Railton[74] is, perhaps, the best we can hope for. While the tension may not ultimately be resolvable, drawing a distinction between the objective rightness of an action and blameworthiness can somewhat ameliorate it. Few will blame me if I save my child or friend, rather than a stranger. Nor should others be so disposed, for I might be said to have my heart in the right place. This would be another way of saying that I have developed the kinds of motivation that may well serve us best, over time.[75]

The fact that there is a deep and, in some sense, irresolvable conflict between partialist and impartialist concerns, has little to do with debates concerning gender. While it may be true, for all the reasons outlined in chapter 5, that more women than men give priority to partialist concerns, this empirical fact alone does not give us any reason for rejecting all impartialist ethical theories on the ground that they have been developed by men and are 'masculine' in their approach. The centrally important issue is not whether an ethical theory is 'masculine' or 'feminine', but rather, as Alison Jaggar correctly notes, whether it is male-biased. Any such bias cannot merely be asserted, but needs to be *shown* to exist through detailed arguments which demonstrate that *particular* claims or assumptions, evident in *particular* texts, 'function ideologically to delegitimate women's interests, or subordinate them to men's'. In light of reflections such as these, Jaggar concludes:

> I believe that if feminist ethics focuses on male bias rather than on masculinity and femininity, it will be more likely to produce results that are not only textually defensible but also philosophically interesting and politically significant.[76]

Conclusion

It seems to me that Jaggar is right on this point. Even though some ethical theories devised by men may have functioned to legitimize the disenfranchisement of women, this is not the same as saying that all impartialist ethical theories are *inherently* male-biased. Rather, I regard impartialism as an essential element of *any* adequate ethical approach and, as I will argue in subsequent chapters, a valuable tool in feminist critiques of some traditional (male) assumptions. Impartiality is not, of course, the same as gender-blindness. While gender-blindness will frequently discriminate against women,[77] impartiality – like the idea of universalizability – allows and calls for the recognition of difference. Only like cases may be treated alike. If there is a morally relevant difference between cases, then that difference must be taken into account.

While impartiality thus has a central role to play in ethics, this does not mean that we can do without some partialist concerns – a point already well recognized by William Godwin some two centuries ago. In this sense, then, the debate over partialism and impartialism is not new. We may, however, see recent philosophical debates as a reaction to a modern emphasis on impartiality to the relative neglect of partialist concerns. That these criticisms should often, although not exclusively, come from women should not surprise us. False impartiality has not always served women well[78] and, as we have seen in chapter 5, there is a cluster of reasons that would explain why more women than men identify with a care approach.

Annette Baier has made the following observation: 'Women moral theorists . . . have this very great advantage over the men whose theories theirs supplant, that they can stand on the shoulders of men moral theorists.'[79] The idea of impartiality, it seems to me, can quite properly be seen as 'the shoulders of men'. Women theorists can stand on it, build on it, but should not reject it. Exclusive focus on partialist concerns, and on the virtues associated with it, can harbour serious dangers for women. Uncritical defences of partiality are often blind to social structures and 'provide no critical evaluation of the social roles that they take to warrant partiality'.[80] An adequate ethics, an ethics suitable for combating injustices, an ethics suitable for nurses and for nursing, needs impartiality as well as care. The next chapter will illustrate this point.

7

'Yes' to Caring – But 'No' to a Nursing Ethics of Care[1]

Our identity has suffered greatly because we have not fully studied our history.

Jo Ann Ashley, *Hospitals, Paternalism and the Role of the Nurse* (1976)

[T]he feminine is not the feminist.

Alison M. Jaggar, 'Feminist Ethics: Projects/Problems/Prospects' (1991)

And just when they seem engaged in revolutionising themselves and things, in creating something that has never yet existed, precisely in such periods . . . they anxiously conjure up the spirits of the past . . . in order to present the new scene of world history in this time-honoured disguise and this borrowed language.

Karl Marx, *The Eighteenth Brumaire of Louis Bonaparte* (1852)

Nursing is one of the caring professions. Indeed, many nurses believe that care is, in some sense, central and foundational to nursing:[2] it is seen as 'the essence'[3] or 'ontological substance'[4] of nursing, as its 'moral ideal',[5] 'the human (and also ethical) mode of being',[6] and the 'foundational value' on which any theory of nursing ethics must be built.[7]

There are some parallels in the discussions that are now occupying nurses and those that have been at the centre of feminist attempts to develop a woman-centred approach to ethics. For many nurses, as for feminist philosophers, an ethics appropriate for nurses 'was not simply a matter of adding [nurses] and stirring them into existing theory'.[8] Rather, an ethics that is appropriate for nursing must capture the moral sensibilities of nurses, rather than those of (male) doctors. As the Dean of a major American nursing school put it:

> We are not interested in *medical* ethics; there is virtually nothing there that is pertinent to nursing. Nursing has its own issues, problems and principles, and they're quite different from, and often opposed to, those of medicine.[9]

As we have already noted, contemporary discussions about a 'women's ethics' have been occupying feminist philosophers since the late 1960s. Nurses were, however, relatively late in entering these debates. They were continuing to appeal to traditional ethical theories and principles in their discussions of bioethical questions.[10] Debates regarding the nurse's role as patient advocate, for example, were still heavily premised on standard and soon to be scorned notions of rights and autonomy. It was only after the publication of Carol Gilligan's *In a Different Voice*[11] that this began to change: nurses were beginning to take a closer look at the ethical foundation of their profession.[12]

While nursing had, for some time, sought to establish an identity separate from that of medicine, Gilligan's articulation of a care approach had, it seemed, finally given nurses a theoretical perspective that would allow them to define themselves as members of a profession that was different from but not inferior to that of medicine – not by appeal to any functionalist accounts of medicine and nursing, but by the different ethical or philosophical approaches that were thought to define the two professions. While medical ethics was premised on impartialist rules and principles, an ethics appropriate for nurses and for nursing, it was thought, had its source in concrete relationships and care.

This general trend received further encouragement through the publication in 1984 of Nel Noddings' book *Caring: A Feminine Approach to Ethics and Moral Education*.[13] As we have seen, Noddings rejects 'masculine' impartialist and principle-based approaches to ethics in favour of what she calls a 'feminine' care approach. To put matters very simply – and in some ways, no doubt, too simply – while Gilligan seemed to have assured nurses that the care approach was not inferior to the justice approach, Nel Noddings seemed to tell them that 'caring' was all that was necessary for a nursing ethics of care. As long as nurses cared, there was no need for universal principles and rules, no need for concern with the traditional ideas of impartiality and justice.

Noddings has *not* been ignored by nurses. On the contrary, Noddings' description of the moral nature of care is, as Ann Bradshaw notes, 'widely reflected in the writings of contemporary nurses' and 'is similar to the ethical approach adopted by the nurse writer Patricia Benner, whose views are having a profound effect on nursing today'.[14] A similarly positive view of Noddings' import for nursing is taken by Sara Fry, an American nurse-philosopher, who is herself engaged in the project of fashioning a nursing ethics of care.[15] According to Fry, Noddings' work provides 'a viable theoretical framework that realistically represents the nature of the nurse–patient relationship'.[16]

For the purposes of this chapter, we will set aside the difficulties identified in chapter 3, regarding the absence of any clear demarcation between nursing and medicine, to examine whether Noddings' ethics of care (and other approaches that share the central features of her approach) are, first, an appropriate basis for the nurse–patient relationship and, second, able to provide a theoretical basis for an ethics that is adequate for nurses and for nursing. My answer to both questions will be no. In addition to that, I will attempt to show that there is a real danger that nurses who decide to conduct their professional lives in accordance with the care approach are likely to find themselves in a position where they, like generations of nurses and women before them, may be praised for their caring feminine traits and dispositions, but will be unable to assert their moral claims or to speak on behalf of those for whom they care.

We will begin by looking at the complex and slippery notion of 'care'. While I will argue that there are a number of reasons why we should reject Noddings' notions of relational care, there is, as we have already noted in chapter 6, value in the recent focus by Noddings and others on context and on the particularities of situations and individuals. In the present chapter we will look at the related notion of attentiveness – which Noddings calls 'engrossment' and 'affective receptivity' – and what I want to refer to as 'dispositional care'. Dispositional care is, I shall suggest, a necessary but not a sufficient condition for an ethics that will serve patients and nurses well. An adequate ethics needs impartiality or justice as well as care.

Care

Warren Thomas Reich has recently provided a rich account of the history of the notion of care. While the concept 'care' has never played a prominent role in mainstream Western ethics – in the way in which, for example, freedom, justice and love have done – it has a long history in philosophy, religion and in literature, figuring centrally in some existentialist and phenomenological approaches, such as those of the nineteenth-century Danish philosopher and religious thinker Søren Kierkegaard, and the twentieth-century German philosopher Martin Heidegger.[17]

Care, in one sense or another, is central to human life. It is, however, a complex and elusive idea. From its very beginnings in mythology and antiquity, *cura* (care) had at least two fundamentally different sets of connotations: on the one hand, it had connotations of worry, trouble, anxiety and personal inclination – an emotional response; on the other, it had connotations of providing for – of doing for – the other. These two sets of connotations still have currency today and are, as we shall see, at the heart of contemporary attempts to formulate a nursing ethics of care.

Today, caring not only has connotations of concern, compassion, worry, anxiety and burden; there are also strong connotations of inclination, fondness and affection; of commitment to a person, an ideal or a cause; connotations of carefulness, that is, of attention to detail, of responding sensitively to the situation of the other; and there are connotations of looking after or providing for the other.[18]

During the last 20 years or so, nurses have written much on care and caring, and have explored more extensively than any other group the role of caring in the delivery of health care to patients or clients.[19] While they have done important work in attempting to understand the meaning and moral significance of caring (reminding themselves and others that health care is not only about technical competence and expertise, but also about caring for patients as particular individuals), the project of fashioning a coherent care approach is no further advanced today than it was in 1988 when Madeleine Leininger wrote: 'Caring is yet to be explicated and systematically studied as a scientific and humanistic knowledge base of nursing.'[20]

One of the problems is that different nurses understand the term 'caring' in different ways. There appears to be some agreement that caring signifies a feeling, sentiment or disposition that characterizes the nurse–patient encounter. Johnstone speaks of it as a 'sentiment' akin to compassion, sympathy and empathy.[21] Another writer in the field, E. O. Bevis, speaks of nurse-caring as 'a feeling of dedication to the extent that it motivates and energizes action to influence life constructively and positively by increasing intimacy and mutual self-actualization.'[22]

These notions of caring often appear to involve relationships between nurses and patients of great depth and intimacy. One prominent nurse theorist, Jean Watson, thus holds that 'true transpersonal caring' entails that 'the nurse is able to form a union with the other person on a level that transcends the physical . . . [where] there is a freeing of both persons from their separation and isolation.'[23]

Other writers understand 'caring' as 'a committed, involved stance';[24] an 'interactive process', which is achieved by 'a conscious and intuitive opening of self to another, by purposeful trusting and sharing of energy, experiences, ideas, techniques and knowledge'[25] and as 'the creative, intuitive or cognitive helping process for individuals and groups based upon philosophic, phenomenologic, and objective and subjective experiential feelings and acts of assisting others';[26] while at other times 'caring' is described more soberly as 'cognitively learned humanistic scientific modes of helping and enabling'[27] or as 'seeing to the needs of X'.[28]

This suggests that there are at least two primary senses in which 'care' is generally understood by nurses, the two senses already mentioned above. The first sense involves an emotional response – concern for the other, emphasis on relationship, on attachment, openness, and on attentiveness and responsiveness to the needs of the cared-for.[29] The second sense suggests looking after or providing for the needs of the other.

That nurses engaged in direct patient care should 'look after' or 'provide for the needs' of patients is fairly uncontroversial. It is what nurses have been doing all along. It is 'caring' in the first sense that is central to attempts to fashion a nursing ethics of care. 'Caring' in this sense is not primarily concerned with tasks or processes, but is a mode of being, a virtue, or a stance or attitude towards the object of one's attention.[30] In other words, in attempting to articulate an ethics of care, writers are not so much trying to answer the traditional ethical question of right action: 'What should I do?' but rather the question: 'How should I, the carer, meet the cared-for.' As Jean Watson puts it:

> In nursing and caring we are not concerned primarily with justification through ethical principles and laws *in general* . . . Caring is held as a moral ideal that entails a commitment to a particular end. That end is the protection and enhancement of human dignity and preservation of humanity . . . An ethics of moral caring and curing calls out for nursing ethics that favor subjective thinking.[31]

This raises a number of questions, including the following two. First, what understanding of care is an appropriate basis for the nurse–patient relationship? Second, can the idea of an ethics of care be spelled out adequately without reliance on some principles, rules or norms, that is, without a prior defence of the values or principles we should be caring about? We will examine the first question in the following two sections and the second in the one after these.

What Kind of Nurse–Patient Relationship?

Verena Tschudin has subtitled her book on nursing ethics 'The Caring Relationship'.[32] This alerts us to the fact that caring is a *relational* concept.[33] This will come as no great surprise, of course. After all, caring necessarily involves an object – caring *about* something or someone. In the nurse–patient encounter this 'object' is the patient, for whom the nurse cares. But what should this caring relationship be like?

As we have already noted, Nel Noddings is one of a rather limited set of primary theoretical sources usually referred to by proponents of a care approach to nursing to explain the relational aspect of the nurse–patient encounter. The other two most prominent ones are Milton Mayeroff[34] and Martin Buber,[35] on whom Noddings draws. But, as Stan van Hooft has convincingly argued, the caring relationship Mayeroff and Buber have in mind is of greater depth and intimacy than would be appropriate in the nurse–patient encounter.[36] Milton Mayeroff speaks of the other 'for whom I care' as 'completion of my own being' and holds that the special features of caring for a person require that 'I must be able to understand him and his world as if I were inside it.'[37] Similarly, Martin Buber distinguishes between an 'I–It' and 'I–Thou' relationship, treating the latter as a very special encounter with something mysterious, awe-inspiring and transcendental. While there can be privileged moments in human relationships (for example, when people are in love), most human relationships are of a much more mundane kind, and it would be quite unrealistic to suggest – as many nurse theorists do – that the nurse–patient relationship ought to be of the 'I–Thou' kind. While Buber himself, in an afterword to the third edition of his book, has noted that the 'I–Thou' relationship is not, in his view, an appropriate model for the nurse–patient encounter, this has not prevented contemporary nurses from continuing to base their analyses on his work.[38]

Related questions can be raised about Nel Noddings' account of caring. Noddings believes that 'caring' requires 'engrossment' – a putting aside of self, of receptivity and responsiveness to the experiences of the other. Writing about relationships between teachers and students, Noddings draws on Buber and Mayeroff and, while denying that engrossment necessarily requires the stance of the lover,[39] notes that her notion of caring may indeed require personal relationships of the 'I–Thou' kind. She is aware that such relationships have been criticized in the literature as implausible and undesirable in a pedagogical context; none the less, Noddings insists, caring in this sense 'is exactly the kind of caring ideally required of teachers'. It is not necessary, she says:

> to establish a deep, lasting, time-consuming personal relationship with every student. What I must do is to be totally nonselectively

present to the student – to each student – as he addresses me. The time interval may be brief but the encounter is total.[40]

Setting aside the question as to whether care in this sense is an appropriate basis for the teacher–student relationship, is it an appropriate basis for the nurse–patient encounter? Those who follow Noddings have generally assumed that the answer is yes. There is, however, a great danger in requiring that every nurse–patient encounter be a 'total encounter' and in thus setting the ideal of caring in nursing too high. Take Jean Watson's comment: 'Human care can *begin* when the nurse enters into the life space of the phenomenal field of the other.'[41] Many a nurse who aspires to such ideals will think that she has failed when she finds it impossible to enter into the 'life space' of (most of) the patients for whom she cares, or is not able 'to form a union with the other person on a level that transcends the physical'.[42] To exhort nurses to strive for such often unattainable goals is not only to imbue them with a sense of failure; it is also to make them ask themselves why their professional nursing skills – that is, careful and skilled attention to the health-care needs of the patient – should count for so little.[43]

Moreover, I cannot help but wonder whether those who are advancing these lofty nursing ideals have ever paused to ask themselves whether this is what *patients*, the subjects of the nurses' ministrations, would want. It seems highly unlikely that every patient who enters hospital with a particular medical problem – say, to have her appendix or her varicose veins removed – would *want* the many different nurses who look after her during her hospitalization to make serious efforts to 'enter into her life space' or to form an engrossing relationship of the 'I–Thou' kind. Rather, what such patients are much more likely to want is to have their health-care needs competently and professionally attended to by a responsive and sympathetic nurse. A small-scale 1991 American survey lends some support to these views, and confirms a number of earlier studies that reached similar conclusions. The study found that 'nurses have a tendency to consider comfort and trusting relationship items as most important while patients perceive behaviors associated with physical care as most important.'[44]

Of course, attending to the health-care needs of patients will frequently involve more than administering procedures and attending to the physical needs of the patients. Patients will typically experience various degrees of anxiety, uncertainty, pain and frustration as the result of their illness, and it is entirely appropriate for a nurse sensitively to respond to such problems. If this requires her to enter into the life space of the patient, it would, however, be a limited entry – an entry into the health-related life space only. The nurse would care, as a nurse, about the patient's health status in the wide sense, but not ordinarily about his unhappy love affair, or the fact that the horse he backed came last.

What *no* patient would want, of course, is that she be treated as merely an 'object' or as 'the appendectomy in Ward 3'. Indeed, it is very salutary that nurse theorists have come to emphasize the uniqueness of persons and the importance of caring for patients as *individuals*, that is, of health-care professionals attempting to understand how the patient sees illness, disability and pain, and of responding sensitively to what Nel Noddings calls 'the reality of the other'.

The Importance of Dispositional Care

If we understand 'care' broadly in the sense of a willingness and openness to apprehend the health-related reality of the other, then, it seems to me, we have captured what I want to call a 'dispositional notion of care'. Such an understanding of care does not exhort nurses to aspire to a near-unattainable goal of achieving some kind of transcendental union with the patients for whom they care; instead it emphasizes the importance of receptivity and responsiveness, of what Rita Manning calls 'a willingness to give the lucid attention required to appropriately fill the needs of others',[45] as well as the uniqueness of particular persons and situations. Health-care professionals who are 'dispositional carers' in this sense are more likely to be receptive to the needs of patients, where these patients are recognized as *particular others*, that is, as individuals with special needs, beliefs, desires and wants, rather than a malfunctioning organism. This entails that dispositional care is not only an appropriate part of nursing ethics, but of medical ethics as well.

Lawrence Blum gives an example to illustrate the importance of what he calls 'particularized, caring understanding', even in principled approaches to ethics. Two adults are watching children playing in a park:

> One adult viewing [the] scene . . . may simply not see that one child is being too rough with another and is in danger of harming the other child; whereas another adult, more attentive to the situation, and more sensitive about children's interaction, may see the potential danger and thus the need for intervention and protection.[46]

On account of her greater attentiveness and sensitivity to the particulars of the situation, the second adult would be able to act on the principle 'protect children from harm,' whereas the first adult would not. Such 'particularized, caring understanding' would be part of what I have termed the 'dispositional notion of care', and would be – even if often ignored by traditional ethical theorists – a proper and necessary part of a two-level utilitarian approach and of other impartialist ethical approaches as well.[47] After all, any well-rounded ethical theory must concern itself not only with the principles or values we ought to pursue, but also with the character-laden or dispositional aspects that will help us to realize those goals.

A recently published observational study reporting on the interaction of nurses with dying patients lends some empirical support to the view that dispositional care – involving both a willingness to receive others and attention to particularity – is of great importance in the delivery of health care.[48] The non-participant observer reports a number of cases where nurses seem to have failed in 'particularized, caring understanding'. In one case, for example, nurses failed to notice that a dying patient was thirsty, that the patient could not reach the drink that was placed on the table before her, and that she could not sit up unaided and would fall back when no support was provided. While many factors other than the lack of dispositional care could also explain why this patient's needs were not met, the case description suggests that the nurses, rather than simply being overworked or callous, were not receptive and sensitive enough to recognize that this particular patient needed additional help to do what other patients could do unaided.

They seemed to have lacked in 'willingness to receive others, a willingness to give the lucid attention required to appropriately fill the needs of others',[49] in dispositional care.[50]

Care in this sense – as a disposition, a moral stance or a virtue[51] – is an indispensable element of good patient care and can and should be embraced by traditional impartialist ethical theories as well, regardless of whether these favour, say, a deontological or a consequentialist approach. Without dispositional care we may, while embracing the principles, values or goals entailed by our ethical approach, simply not be able to 'see' what is required of us in a particular situation. If this is correct, care is a necessary condition for the delivery of good patient care. But can it also serve as the basis for a minimally adequate ethics?

Care is Not Sufficient: A Critique of Noddings

Nel Noddings assumes a positive answer to the question.[52] As we have seen in chapter 6, Noddings rejects what she calls a 'masculine' approach to ethics – an approach that focuses on reason, on universal principles, rules and rights – and replaces it with a 'feminine' caring approach which, she says, has its source in affect and emotion. 'The very wellspring of ethical behaviour,' Noddings writes, is 'human affective response.'[53] Dismissing 'ethics of principle as inherently unstable',[54] and holding that 'one who attempts to ignore or climb above the human affect of the heart of ethicality, may well be guilty of romantic rationalism,'[55] she stipulates that, from a care perspective, relation is 'ontologically basic and the caring relationship . . . ethically basic'.[56] In other words, care – as expressed in the relationship between the carer and the cared-for – captures not only what Noddings sees as a feminine mode of being, but also what she regards as the ethical ideal or 'the good'. For Noddings an action is right or wrong not because it conforms, or fails to conform, to some universal or impartialist principle or rule; rather it is right or wrong 'according to how faithfully it was rooted in caring.'[57]

Various questions can be raised with regard to Noddings' ethical approach. A very fundamental one is this: can we be sure that all caring is intrinsically good?

Not all caring is good

For Noddings, the 'ethical ideal' of caring has its source in the 'natural caring' we experienced when we were young.[58] But, as we have already seen in chapter 4, not everything that is natural is good. By the same token, we cannot simply assume that all natural caring is good: the care we received when we were young may, for example, have been oppressive or stifling;[59] it may have been good or bad. Moreover, even if we did assume that natural responses in relationships are 'the good', this would not show that *care*, rather than some other natural response, ought to be regarded as the basic building block of our moral approach. Hate and jealousy, for example, are also natural phenomena in relationships. This means that the choice of care as the foundation of ethics, rather than, say, revenge, requires defence.[60] But such a defence has not been provided by Noddings in her articulation of an ethics of care. We are not told when and why care is good, and what we should be caring about.

The point is basic. Everyone cares about something or someone. As Peter Allmark has noted, even a torturer 'cares about' the object of his torture; Hitler cared about Aryans, and his mother may well have cared about her son Adolf.[61] This means that the mere directive to care is not enough; we must also be told what we should be caring *about*. Without such directives, the concept of 'care' remains empty and fails to distinguish between the 'goodness' of, say, a torturer and that of a human-rights activist.

Will it help to say that we should care about the maintenance of relationships? Hardly. The point is not only that the carer will sometimes pursue ideals and care about goals and objectives that are morally dubious at best; it is also that traditional caring relationships may themselves perpetuate patterns of domination, submission and exploitation.[62] The relationship between women and men and between doctors and nurses may be a case in point.

All this has obvious relevance for the nurse–patient relationship too. Given that nurses should care for patients, what should they be caring about? Should they, for example, care about the patients' health-care interests, or should they (also?) care about the patients' moral rights? Whatever the answer ought to be, it cannot be found in the notion of relational care alone, and to say, as some proponents of a nursing ethics of care sometimes will, that nurses ought to care for patients as 'whole persons' or so as to protect patients 'from being reduced to the status of objects',[63] is only to replace one slippery notion – that of caring – by other equally slippery notions, such as the notion of 'whole person'. Until and unless we are told what it means to be treated as a 'whole person', this notion has little more content than the notion of care.

To return to Nel Noddings' approach: she has not provided us with any good reason why relational care (in what sense?) should form the basis of ethics. To the extent, however, that ethics requires us to back our views by good reasons, this makes it doubtful that Noddings' care approach meets the requirements of a minimally adequate ethics. Further doubts are raised by Noddings' rejection of universal principles, rules and norms.[64] We have already touched on this point briefly in chapter 6; we shall now develop it more fully by drawing on Peter Allmark's discussion of three of Nel Noddings' own examples.[65] As we shall see, without a substantive notion of the good, and universal principles to guide us towards that good, relational care is not only blind – unable to tell us what we should be caring about – but also unable to provide non-arbitrary reasons for our actions.

Caring is arbitrary

First example: Noddings' first example involves a mother and a son. The son attends a school that allows absence only on the grounds of illness or bereavement. The mother gives her son permission to stay home from school 'in order to do something that both of us consider worthwhile':

> If I do not say that he was ill, he will be punished with detention . . . I prefer to say that he was because not saying it will cause my son to be punished. So I may choose to lie regularly in order to meet my son as one-caring [Noddings' term for someone who cares in a relational sense for another, 'the-cared-for'] rather than as one conforming to principle. I do not attempt to justify my behaviour on the grounds that the absence rule is foolish and unfair, because my behaviour is not primarily constrained by rules. I do

not need that excuse. One who does argue thus is obliged, I think, to fight the rule – to get it changed – or to live in some deceit. I do not have this problem. I can brush off the whole debate as foolishness and remain faithful to the ideal of one-caring.[66]

This example, presented by Noddings to illustrate how an ethics of care will put the ideal of care over impartial rule or principle, raises a number of problems. One is that it is frighteningly narrow and parochial. One-caring cares about the-cared-for, but not, apparently, about the fate of other children who are likely to suffer under the continued existence of what Noddings calls a 'foolish and unfair' rule. The mother's action, however, is not only frighteningly narrow and parochial, it is also ultimately arbitrary and capricious.

The next example – Noddings' version of a standard example repeatedly used in critiques of utilitarianism – will sharpen the point.

Second example:

> You are the leader of a team of ten explorers, and you are all captured by a fierce tribe that places the highest value on ruthless decision making. The chief announces that you will all be killed unless you, the leader, can prove by your ruthlessness that your tribe is worthy to be spared. He requires that you demonstrate your worthiness by picking one of your group and killing him. As usual in such problems, you must accept as given that there is no escape, no possibility of persuasion, etc. Kill one or all will die. What should you do?[67]

Noddings acknowledges that it would be better if nine people were saved.

> If I simply seize one of my party and kill him swiftly, mercifully . . . I can save the rest. Should I not do this? How shall I choose? . . . My eye falls on A. He is sick and probably will not live through the arduous trip home . . . But as I reach toward him, I feel the life, and fear, and trust, and hope, and whatever else is emanating from him. My long practice in receiving holds me back . . . So we all die.[68]

The question raised by Allmark is this: how can Noddings' mode of acting be justified from a *perspective of care*?[69] If the reason for not killing the one person is the 'life, and fear, and trust, and hope . . . emanating from him', why is the one-caring not equally, or more, swayed by the fear, hope and so on, that is presumably emanating from the eight others? To the extent that Noddings cannot provide a justification for her approach, any response she may want to give must ultimately be regarded as arbitrary and capricious.

A final example is this one.

Third example: Noddings recounts the experience of 'Ms A', a graduate student in the late sixties, at the height of the civil rights movement.

> A problem concerning the rights and education of blacks arose, and the only black student in class spoke eloquently of the prevailing injustice and inhumanity against blacks, of his growing despair. He spoke of 'going to the barricade.' Ms A was nearly moved to tears. He was clearly right in condemning the treatment of his people and in demanding something better . . . [Ms A said she] 'could not – ever – oppose my bigoted old father or my hysterical Aunt Phoebe! . . . Oh, she is wrong, and my father is wrong. But there are years of personal kindness. They must count for something . . . I know I could not fight – really fight on the other side. And what now of the black man, Jim, who is, after all, 'right'? If my sights picked him out . . . I would note that it was Jim and pass on to some other target.[70]

Is this thinking not deplorable? Noddings asks. After all, Ms A acknowledges that she would favour two bigoted persons over principle. 'No,' as Nel Noddings answers to her own question: 'To the one-caring, this is not diminution but agonized fulfilment.' Pressing the point, Nel Noddings asks again, what if a loved one decided to set up a concentration camp – Auschwitz – should we still side with him? Here, Nel Noddings thinks the answer would be 'no'. The question is, however, 'why'? What is the basis for the judgement? Why should we care up to a point and then no more? We are not told. As Nel Noddings herself notes, '[t]he one-caring displays a characteristic variability in her actions – she acts in a nonrulebound fashion.'[71]

Now, to refuse to be excessively rule-bound is one thing. To be utterly unprincipled is quite another. If we reject all universal ethical principles and norms, and eschew consistency, then we are left with only arbitrariness and caprice – and the above three cases are, of course, examples of the ultimate arbitrariness and capriciousness of Noddings' care approach.

The Object of Nursing Care

There are a number of reasons why nurses, like the rest of us, cannot do without inquiring into the nature of 'the good', and why nursing – like other morally significant social endeavours – cannot do without universal ethical principles, rules and norms. While those approaching ethics from a perspective of care have done much to highlight the importance of dispositional care, the importance of context and the uniqueness of persons, 'care' in this sense can always constitute only a necessary, not a sufficient component of ethics. It does not and cannot constitute the whole of ethics. We need to be able to identify the nature of the good we are pursuing, and we need universalizable principles and rules to counter arbitrariness and caprice.

But what is 'the good' or the 'object' of care? This question becomes particularly important in clinical encounters, where there is frequent moral disagreement about the rightness or wrongness of actions: whether a dying patient should, for example, be kept alive or allowed to die; told the truth or be protected from it for her own good. The case described by Barbara Huttmann in chapter 1 illustrates the point. The question was whether Mac, a terminally ill patient who wanted to die, should continue to be resuscitated (the doctor's view) or allowed to die (the nurse's view). Appeal to 'care' alone could not have settled the question. Both the nurse and the doctor could have appealed to care in an attempt to justify their respective courses of actions, the nurse by saying that care required allowing the patient to die; the doctor by arguing that care, as he understood it, required keeping the patient alive. If this conflict could have been settled, it could have been settled only by the nurse or the doctor providing further reasons for the view that 'keeping alive' or 'letting die' was or was not the appropriate caring action.

We saw in chapter 4 that moral judgements must always be backed by reasons. If we do not give reasons for our views, we are not making a *moral* judgement. Such reasons, however, cannot be found in a caring attitude or in a caring relationship alone. Care needs an 'object'. Only once the 'object' of care is identified and defended on the grounds of ethics are we entering the realm of ethics.

Here it might be tempting to say that the 'object' of nursing care, or of health care in general, is quite clearly the patient, that nurses ought to meet the health-related needs of patients. But this answer is too simple. At the beginning of this chapter we distinguished between two different senses of 'caring' that are of particular relevance in the nursing context: 'care' understood as concern, compassion or empathy for the individual patient, and 'care' in the sense of 'helping or enabling' or 'seeing to the needs' of the patient. Take the case of a patient who has experienced end-stage renal failure, who is incompetent, close to death, who has already suffered cardiac arrest and severe internal haemorrhaging during dialysis, and who appears severely distressed. In continuing dialysis, a nurse is seeing to the needs of the patient and thereby enables him to survive. And yet, in a situation such as this (and here the much-discussed US case of Corinne Warthen is a case in point)[72] the nurse might feel that she is not doing what she ought to be doing. Is she caring for the patient? 'Yes,' in the sense that she is competently attending to (caring for) the patient's medical problems and physiological needs; but 'no,' in that what she is doing – keeping a dying, incompetent, distressed patient alive as long as possible – she shows lack of compassion or care.

This entails that an ethical approach that simply exhorts nurses to 'care' cannot give practical direction. The problem is not merely lack of precision in our use of the term. Rather, it is a matter of deciding whether 'care' in the sense of attending to a patient's physiological or metabolic needs also constitutes 'care' in the sense of caring for the patient as a 'whole person', that is, in a morally appropriate way. In other words, while it is clearly an ordinary part of the nurse's role to attend to a patient's physical needs and to maintain and/or restore bodily functioning, the substantive question is when and why caring in this sense may sometimes cease in order to allow a nurse to care for a patient in the second sense – where caring may entail allowing or helping a patient to die. This question cannot be answered until the value or object of care has been made explicit and defended on moral grounds.

We are, however, unlikely to see the articulation of such values by proponents of a care approach, as long as they are misguided by the belief that care is not only necessary but also sufficient for ethics and does, in fact, constitute 'the good'.

Care Knows No Limits, No Fairness and Equality

As we have noted above, Noddings sees the caring relationship as ethically basic. She would therefore deny that care needs an object, over and above the maintenance of the caring relationship itself. The object of care *is* the relationship. It is *its* maintenance that is of basic moral significance.

But this is, of course, precisely where the problem lies. If care is its own object, it entails that care cannot know any limits. This is illustrated by Noddings' first and third examples. Care takes precedence over all other values and norms. This is not merely a matter of telling a lie and of not challenging a relatively trivial 'foolish and unfair' rule, as was the case in the first example, it is also to place care above such values as racial equality (example 3). Care would require us to give at least implicit support to bigotry and racism, and to leave unchallenged practices and beliefs that we, like 'Ms A.', regard as morally wrong.

What would a notion of unlimited relational care entail for health care and for nursing? Would it require a carer not only to lie, but also to act contrary to hospital policy, her code of conduct and the law (in the way in which Barbara Huttmann and Nigel Cox did, when they helped their patients to die) without regard for the further consequences of their actions, either for themselves or for others outside what Noddings calls 'a set of ordered pairs' – the carer and the cared-for?[73] It seems the answer must be 'Yes'. It must be 'Yes' because care cannot find within itself any limits, over and above the maintenance of the caring relationship itself.

If this is one enormous problem, here is another. Clinical nurses care not only for *one* patient, but for many patients. This raises the question of balancing the various patient interests involved. How should nurses allocate their time and energy between different patients? How could relational care itself provide direction for a nurse? She cares, or should care, for all patients. Does this not mean that she ought to care for all patients equally and impartially?[74]

If anything, the problem becomes more pronounced in other contexts. Take a 'triage nurse', working in a dialysis unit, who must decide which of a number of patients will be offered dialysis treatment. As Noddings' second example so clearly illustrates, care itself cannot provide a satisfactory answer to these kinds of dilemma. To escape caprice, arbitrariness and personal whim, we need to be able to give consistent and impartialist reasons for choosing one patient over another, or for selecting a defensible method of allocating dialysis treatment.

So far our discussion has largely focused on nurses engaged in direct patient encounters in, for example, the hospital setting. But not all nurses work in such settings. As we saw in chapter 3, nurses work in many different settings and occupy many different roles. Some of these roles require a broader point of view, where the focus is not on individual and known patients, but rather on patients or potential patients as a whole. This would be the case in, for example, public health, where a nurse may have to decide between different programmes of preventative care that will affect as yet unidentified and unidentifiable individuals. For example, how could a notion of *relational* care as developed by Noddings, and as it underpins many discussions in nursing, possibly help her reach a morally defensible decision? The answer is it could not help at all. The same would be true if a hospital were to decide to develop fair and equitable policy guidelines for admission to its limited dialysis programme. Here it would probably be very desirable that there be some input from the very people who care for dialysis patients on a sustained basis – nurses. While nurses would be able to draw on their experiences in direct patient care, they would not – from a relational care perspective alone – be able to join the debate on broader questions of equity and justice. The point is this: a relational ethics of care as explicated by Noddings is inherently contentless and parochial and does not have within itself the resources to deal with wider questions of equity and justice. It could not, for example, criticize existing arrangements and structures as 'unjust' or 'unfair', for it is devoid of a moral standpoint outside itself from which such a critique could proceed.

Silenced by Care

Let us think for a moment what would follow from a consistent rejection of the idea of impartiality and of universal ethical principles and norms. What would our ethical discourse be like? Could we even engage in ethical debate, or would we be trapped in what Jean Watson calls our 'own subjective thinking'?[75]

Some nurses *have* followed Noddings in their rejection of principled thinking. One such nurse is Randy Spreen Parker. She took the rejection of principles to its logical conclusion.[76] Parker was a 'seasoned critical care nurse', who had abandoned '[t]he language of rights, duties and obligations' (which she experienced as 'alien' and 'detached from the experience' of nursing) to 'learn the lines of a different script − a script that was written in a universal, relational language' − the language of care.

Parker was caring for an aphasic patient, Mike, who had difficulties in speaking and understanding. Mike was a diabetic and suffered from poor blood-circulation. This led to a hip disarticulation − a radical amputation of the leg at the hip. He was left with a deteriorating 'gaping cavernous wound that extended from his rib cage to his pelvis'. The wound needed dressing changes every three hours. This was excruciatingly painful, since Mike, who also had a lung problem, could not be given adequate pain medication. When it became clear to both patient and nurse that 'further medical interventions served no meaningful purpose', Parker spoke to the attending physician and head nurse and told them that she 'did not feel' that Mike (who had difficulty speaking coherently) wanted to continue life-sustaining treatment. Parker asked to remain Mike's primary nurse and to care for him, but, she explained, she could not participate in any further dressing changes or resuscitation measures.

> I tried to explain my rationale but found myself fumbling for the right words. How could I translate my own moral experience into traditional moral language? The scripts were different. After several meetings with the attending physician and other nurse managers, I was removed from intensive care and placed on a medical-surgical unit.

Over the next week, Mike was resuscitated several times, before he died 'in pain, frightened and alone'.[77]

Parker's realization that her 'moral experience' of caring and 'traditional moral language' have radically different scripts is of course quite correct. Moral experience is private, traditional moral language is not. One person's raw moral experience holds no persuasive powers for others, and should also be regarded critically by the person herself. After all, at times our feelings and experiences may seriously mislead us. They need testing against some standard that lies outside the experience itself.

When it comes to the justification of particular actions, we need to give reasoned arguments for our views. In the clinical context, such arguments might rely on certain universal principles, such as respect for autonomy or a health-care professional's prima facie duty to act in the patient's best interests. While such a principled approach will not be able to avoid all ethical dilemmas, it can provide us with a common moral language and hence a method for seeking solutions. To eschew all moral principles is to withdraw from moral discourse and to retreat into an essentially dumb world of one's own.

Conclusion: The Same Old Tune, Sung Upside Down?[78]

Moral experiences have a role to play in ethics. They have, in the case of nurses, highlighted the importance of caring for each person as a distinct individual rather than as an embodied medical condition, and have shown that sensitivity, responsiveness and attentiveness are necessary elements in patient care. We should certainly take the moral experiences of women and nurses seriously as the raw data for our moral approach, but we must not be tempted to confuse the fact that people have certain moral experiences with the much more fundamental question of whether these moral experiences are soundly based, that is, have their genesis in the pursuit of morally sound goals, and in personal and social relationships that deserve our moral support.

There are various ways in which the appropriation of an ethics of care by women can be used oppressively or can obscure from view relationships based on exploitation and domination. Jean Grimshaw, for example, has convincingly argued that the amorphous concept of 'care' makes it only too easy for women to be accused of failure to care – because they go to work (rather than stay at home), have an abortion, insist on a holiday alone, away from their elderly parents, 'try to seize a bit of space, time or privacy for themselves' and so on.[79] Women are much more vulnerable to accusations of failure to care than men, not only because they have traditionally been defined by their caring role, but also because their very moral goodness is called into question by the accusation that they fail to care.

It is also very common, Jean Grimshaw continues, for debates about industrial action by nurses, for example, to be framed in terms of an implied opposition of self-interest and caring.[80] Given the history of nursing, this is not surprising. After all, how can nurses 'who are doubly defined as "caring", both by being female and by the nature of their work, possibly entertain the idea of causing inconvenience, let alone suffering to others, by selfishly striking for some rudimentary form of social justice when all other means fail?'[81]

On the occasion of a historic nursing strike in the Australian state of Victoria in 1986, nurses were told by one commentator that their action was the antithesis of 'feminine behaviour'.[82] As we saw in chapter 2, in 1903 the *Una Journal of Nursing* expressed rather similar sentiments. Nurses who lacked the spirit of self-surrender and were interested in monetary rewards were not only bad nurses, but also 'poor specimens of womanhood'.[83]

Examples such as these suggest that appeals to 'care' may often hide more than they reveal: they may hide not only moral double standards, but also injustices and structural or relational forms of oppression.[84] This is facilitated by a distinctive moral language, a moral language that is part of the tradition that celebrates women as natural carers. It is also the language of maternalism, which has traditionally defined women's and nurses' virtues in terms of motherly care and boundless self-giving. As Janice Raymond notes,

[t]his language also encases women's activities in mothering metaphors, framing many of the creative endeavors women undertake. Motherhood becomes an inspirational metaphor or symbol

for caring, the nurturing, the sensitivity that women bring to a world ravaged by conflict.[85]

This will recall our discussions in chapter 2, where I suggested that a number of metaphors – that of the nurse as mother substitute, as nun or saint, domestic servant, obedient soldier, or as handmaiden to the physician – played a significant role in interpreting the nurse's role in a subservient way. These perceptions of subservience, I argued, were reinforced and supported by one overarching metaphor, which asserted that a good nurse equals a good woman, and the historical context in which women were seen not only as natural carers, but also as naturally inferior and subservient to men.

This is why the 'new' metaphors buried in some of the contemporary care discourse – a good woman = a caring woman (and/ or mother); a good nurse = a caring nurse (and/or a good woman and/or mother) – are so dangerous. They breathe new life into traditional – and I would have hoped by now moribund – perceptions of the limited role women and nurses can and should play in social life. The point is not, of course, that such metaphors are dangerous in themselves; it is rather that they create and recreate patterns of thought, and shape expectations as far as other aspects of the role of nurses and women are concerned. This includes shaping our vision of the scope of ethics. Metaphors and the role-perceptions embedded in them may thus reinforce what Marilyn Friedman has called the 'division of [moral] labour' between the genders[86] (see chapter 5) and between nurses and doctors.

The metaphors of the nurse as carer shape and reinforce this 'division of moral labour', where nurses are often seen, and see themselves, as merely dispositional carers whose focus is, and ought to be, restricted to that which is close at hand – care for particular patients. As admirable and necessary as this focus on the particularities of situations, on relationship and care for concrete others, may be, it can always be only a necessary – not a sufficient – condition for an adequate nursing ethics. An adequate ethics needs to be able to reflect on the 'division of moral labour' itself, to see whether it is soundly based, and will not unjustifiably prevent women and nurses from playing a role in some areas of social life.

As Catharine MacKinnon has noted,

For women to affirm difference, when difference means dominance, as it does with gender, means to affirm the qualities and character- istics of powerlessness . . . So I am critical of affirming what we have been, which necessarily is what we have been permitted.[87]

The point is not whether care should play a role in women's and nurses' ethical thinking; it should play a role in the lives of women *and* men, and of nurses *and* doctors. It is rather that the appropri- ation by women of an ethics of care cannot be abstracted from the gender-unequal moral and cultural values and structures that have traditionally shaped the lives of women and men.[88] In our present cultural and intellectual circumstances, it is more than likely that an ethics that ignores questions of impartiality and of justice, and fails to reflect on the historical circumstances of the relations between women and men, and nurses and doctors, will, wittingly or unwittingly, contribute to women's and nurse's con- tinued subordination. After all, as Alison Jaggar notes, 'the fem- inine is not the feminist.'[89]

More than two centuries ago, Jean-Jacques Rousseau held that '[i]t is [women's] place to make the observations which lead men to discover . . . principles . . . It is their business to apply the prin- ciples discovered by men.'[90] Contemporary nursing approaches to care that eschew impartiality and universal ethical principles will perpetuate this division of moral labour. Nurses will con- tinue to care for individual patients, but they will be doing so in the context of social structures and in accordance with institu- tional rules and principles that are not of their own making. They may well 'feel', as Randy Spreen Parker did, that Mike ought to be allowed to die, and that it was wrong to treat him against his will. Merely knowing what one takes the right answer to be will not, however, as Barbara Huttmann realized, be enough. If nurses want to ensure that patients are receiving morally appropriate care, they must also ensure that their moral insights are captured and defended, in the context of a universally accessible moral lan- guage of principles, rights or rules and, at times, legislation. As Barbara Huttmann put it when reflecting on the case of Mac, 'Until there is legislation making it a criminal act to code a patient who has requested to die, we will all of us risk the same fate as Mac.'

If nurses eschew all universal principles and norms, they will not be able to participate in ethical discourse. They will not be able to speak on behalf of the patients for whom they care, nor will they be able to defend their own legitimate claims – and the motto of the first Canadian school of nursing, 'I see and I am silent,' will have continuing relevance for nurses.[91]

8

Just Caring at the End of Life

The preservation of life must be the sole principle guiding medical practice, including the treatment of the hopeless cancer patient. The principle cannot be tampered with or interpreted loosely.
> C. S. Cameron, *The Truth About Cancer* (1956)

Nothing keeps an act from having two effects, one of which is in the scope of intention while the other falls outside that scope. Now moral actions are characterized by what is intended.
> Thomas Aquinas, *Summa Theologiae* (1265–73)

If I was in the position where the illness was terminal and incurable, I would wish that I had the opportunity of active euthanasia. Therefore patients in the same situation should be able to make that decision.
> Anonymous Nurse in 'Voluntary Euthanasia and the Nurse' (1993)

Many feminists agree that justice and care are both necessary constituents of any adequate ethical approach, and some of the most interesting contemporary work in feminist philosophical ethics concerns the question of how the dichotomy between justice and care might be transcended or bridged.[1] As we have seen, there has been a tendency among nurses to endorse somewhat uncritically a feminine ethics of care, but there are some dissenting voices as well. Contemporary articulations of nursing ethics of care, these critics hold, are seriously flawed on a number of grounds, central among them those identified in our discussions in chapters 6 and 7.[2]

A question does, however, remain. We might, for example, agree that Nel Noddings' feminine ethics of care is inadequate or wrong-headed, but is the care approach necessarily an *incorrect* approach? In other words, *could* there be an adequate (nursing) ethics of care?

Ann Bradshaw, a Lecturer in Palliative Care at the National Institute for Nursing in Oxford, England, argues that there can be, and indeed is, an adequate nursing ethics of care. While Bradshaw agrees that Noddings' approach is 'left with nothing but the shifting sands of emotion', the Judaeo-Christian understanding of care as *agape,* that is, as altruistic and universal love, she suggests, offers a more solid foundation.[3]

On the face of it, Bradshaw would seem to be right. Not only does the approach sketched by her recognize the moral significance of caring in a dispositional sense, it also meets the requirements of the Minimum View of Ethics developed in chapter 4: it asks us to show equal concern for the needs, wants or interests of others, irrespective of our personal attachments and like or dislike for them.[4]

This means that Bradshaw's ethical approach would, indeed, seem to qualify as a minimally adequate ethics of care. But what would follow if we were to accept that an ethics characterized by the features identified by Bradshaw constitutes an ethics of care? The implication would be that many other traditional ethical approaches would qualify for the description 'ethics of care' as well. All well-rounded views of ethics are in some sense impartialist, provide a vision of the good (of *what* we should be caring about) and will have something to say on the character-laden or dispositional aspects – the *how* – of caring.[5]

In short, then, nothing much would be gained by calling Bradshaw's favoured approach an ethics of care. That term would then have to be applied to a whole range of other traditional ethical theories as well. Hence, if we define 'care' narrowly and leave it without content (as Noddings has done) then we are, at best, left with an inadequate ethical approach; if we provide content by stipulating what we should be caring about and insist on impartiality, we have entered the arena of traditional ethics and need to justify and defend our particular vision of 'the good' against other competing visions – all or nearly all of which could claim to be 'ethics of care' as well.

To the extent that Bradshaw's approach is tied to a particular religious tradition, it cannot speak to everyone and is unable to serve as the basis for a universal health-care approach. A universal approach must be based on principles and values that are accessible to everyone – to people who subscribe to a variety of religious beliefs or to no religious beliefs at all.

In what follows, I will sketch such an approach. I will focus on health-care decisions for competent patients at the end of life – the kinds of decision that arose in the cases of Lillian Boyes and Mac, described in chapter 1. The approach sketched by me starts with dispositional care, but does not end with it. It tests the insights derived from care against the Minimum Conception of Ethics and demonstrates that there need not be a conflict between the demands of justice and care. Rather, in one area of health care at least – that of end-of-life decisions – impartialist reasoning will underpin the insights derived from care.

Our inquiry will challenge some deeply held traditional principles, rules and norms. And this is how it should be. If work in feminism and ethics has achieved nothing else, it has at least taught us this much: first, that the greatest danger for women and other marginalized groups lies in the acceptance of principles and norms that are so deeply entrenched as to make bias invisible;[6] second, that those intent on challenging traditional principles and norms need universal principles of their own. As Laura Purdy notes, without principles we are unable to press even the most basic ethical claims. This means that any insights derived from a perspective of care are defensible against possible alternatives only if we 'conceive of ethics as a social institution whose chief function should be to justly promote the well being of all'.[7]

This chapter should be seen as a practical application of these two assumptions.

Caring at the End of Life

As will be recalled, there was no doubt in Barbara Huttmann's mind that it was wrong to keep Mac alive. Mac was terminally ill, experiencing intolerable suffering, and wanted to die. Barbara Huttmann thought he should not have been resuscitated, over and over again. Mac's doctor did, however, believe that 'we must extend life as long as we have the means and knowledge to do it.'[8]

Disagreement between medical and nursing staff over medical end-of-life decisions is frequent and raises great moral concern among nurses.[9] Most typically, disagreement arises because the nurse believes that the doctor's decision to sustain a patient's life (and, occasionally, the doctor's failure to do so) is not in the patient's best interest, does not respect the patient's wishes or the patient's 'right to die'. In other words, nurses may often feel that doctors act from principle, whereas nurses respond from a perspective of care. Indeed, the case of Mac may initially be read in this way. On this reading, the doctor acted on the basis of 'vitalism' – the principle that life must always be sustained as long as possible – whereas Barbara Huttmann rejected principled ethical thinking and acted from a perspective of dispositional care: on the basis of what she thought was best for this patient, from his particular point of view.

But, as we have seen, the distinction between acting from principle and acting from care is often wrong-headed. If we take a closer look, we find that Barbara Huttmann's approach was far from unprincipled. Rather, what Barbara Huttmann was objecting to was the *kind* of principle employed by Mac's doctor – the principle that life must always be sustained, regardless of the circumstances. The principle supported by Barbara Huttmann was the 'right to die'. As she put it, 'Until there is legislation making it a criminal act to code a patient who has requested the right to die, we will all risk the same fate as Mac.' Not only was Barbara Huttmann's approach far from unprincipled, she also recognized that generally accepted principles, rules and laws can often play an important role in safeguarding the rights and interests of those who are vulnerable and in need of protection.

But which principles, rules, norms or laws deserve our support? In what follows, I take the view that we should start our ethical thinking from a perspective of dispositional care, that is, by focusing on the needs or interests of particular others, and that we should structure our health-care approach in accordance with the insights thus derived – unless, that is, there are good reasons for taking a contrary approach. A good reason, from the vantage point of the Minimum Conception of Ethics, would be one where acting in the patient's best interests would be contrary to the impartial consideration of the interests of others. Expressed in the language of the justice/care debate: care should trump principle and rule – unless the principle or rule is necessary justly to promote or protect the well-being of all.

My approach is thus a critical one: the mere fact that some principle or rule has a long history and is widely accepted is not in itself a sufficient reason for retaining it. If an accepted standard, rule, norm or law conflicts with good patient care, the presumption must be that it ought to be rejected. If we are to retain it, we need to be provided with good reasons for doing so.

The moral bases of patient care: well-being and self-determination

No other health-care issue has captured the public imagination more than medical decisions at the end of life. In many countries, the issue has also been the subject of intense professional debate, court cases, government inquiries and legislative responses.

At the most fundamental level, this debate revolves around 'the good' of health care. What are the values or goals that health care ought to pursue? We already have at least a partial answer. In chapter 4 we developed the view that a minimally adequate ethics should, at the very least, give equal consideration to the interests or well-being of all those affected by our actions. In other words, well-being is at least one of the values we ought to pursue or care about. Put into the context of health-care, doctors and nurses ought to preserve and promote the health-related well-being of those for whom they care.

Traditionally, the goals of medicine were understood in terms of the preservation of life and the promotion of health. While these would seem to be admirable goals, there are, however, some problems. Take the notion 'preservation of life'. Modern developments in medicine have taught us that attempts to prolong life will not always foster well-being. Rather than promote well-being, they can cause harm – as might be the case if a patient's life is prolonged in the face of great suffering, when there is no hope of ever restoring her to an acceptable level of well-being.

A somewhat similar problem is raised with regard to the notion of health. It is tempting to understand 'health' in an objective sense, as something that can be defined by the medical or biological sciences, irrespective of the standpoint of the patient herself. In the past, such objective interpretations have frequently led to medical paternalism, where the doctor decided what was best for a particular patient, based on the belief that doctors, because of their particular expertise in the medical and biological sciences, are best equipped to know what will serve the patient best. But, as we have seen in chapter 3, the decision whether a patient should or should not undergo treatment involves primarily an ethical not a medical judgement – and ethical judgements cannot be derived from medical or biological facts alone.

Owing to various factors – some already touched on in our discussion of changes in the self-perception of nurses – these traditional goals have been called into question and it is now generally assumed that health-care professionals have a primary obligation to act in their patients' best interests.[10] But what are 'interests'? How should we understand the term and the related notion of well-being?[11] Minimally, we should understand interests in the following way: any patient who is able to experience states of consciousness, that is, is able to experience pleasure and pain, has interests. Such patients have an interest in experiencing pleasant states of consciousness – well-being – and in not experiencing pain and suffering. This means that if a patient is in pain, health-care professionals have a prima facie obligation to relieve that pain and to restore well-being. If pain and discomfort are allowed to persist, the justification must be in terms of the overall or long-term interests of the patient.

There is no doubt that interests thus understood are morally significant and deserve consideration. But we need to broaden our understanding. While all conscious patients have the above simple interests, competent patients (patients who are able to make decisions for themselves) also have an interest in self-determination – in controlling and shaping their lives in accordance with their own values and plans for life. As far as health care is concerned, this means that patients should be able to make non-treatment decisions for themselves, based on their own understanding of health and well-being, of suffering and pain.

In one form or another, most contemporary ethical theories accept this broader notion of interests. While they will reach the conclusion by different routes, there is now near-universal agreement that competent and adequately informed patients should be able to accept and refuse life-sustaining treatment for themselves, and that it would be wrong, other things being equal, to override the patient's considered judgement. This conclusion is generally supported by an appeal to the value of autonomy or self-determination.[12] Some ethical theories will regard autonomy as an intrinsic value – a value that ought to be respected for its own sake – while others see it in instrumental terms. The latter view holds that we should respect autonomy because people generally value their autonomy very highly and are ordinarily the best judges of where their interests lie. On either one of these understandings of the value of autonomy, it might be argued that it was wrong to resuscitate Mac – not primarily because Mac was terminally ill and experiencing great pain and suffering, but rather because Mac had judged that this pain and suffering was too much *for him*, that he had decided that it was time to die.

The view outlined here entails that health-care decisions are personal decisions, that there are no objective standards of well-being that can or should be applied to everyone. And this is how it should be. As nurses have often pointed out, patients are unique individuals and it would be quite inappropriate to act on the basis of blunt rules or principles that prescribe certain treatments for particular groups of patients, without taking the particularities of these patients, including their values and beliefs, into account. Rather, nurses will often, and rightly, insist that our ethical responses must be finely tuned, and centre on what *this* particular patient – given her values and beliefs – judges to be best.

This recognition can be expressed in principled form, for example, 'Individuals have a right to make treatment decisions for themselves' or 'Health-care professionals have an obligation to respect the moral autonomy of their patients' and so on. Such principled responses are not only compatible with the care approach defended here, but seem to be presupposed by it. After all, we cannot sensitively respond to a patient unless we take account of the patient's own understanding of well-being, and respect her values, beliefs and plans for life.

Now, it is sometimes said that such autonomy-based approaches are excessively 'individualistic' and anathema to relational concerns. Such criticisms, however, are ill-conceived. In valuing autonomy and caring about a patient's interest in self-determination, we are not only showing respect for that person as an autonomous decision-maker, we are also showing care and concern for her as a relational being, that is, for her own particular understanding of relationships and of existing ties of love and affection.[13] One person may wish to undergo chemotherapy, for example, to increase her chances of seeing her first grandchild being born; another may wish to reject life-extending treatments, to spare herself and her loved ones a slow and drawn-out dying process. In other words, I am suggesting that one of the best ways of caring for people is to respect their autonomy and their rights.[14] To see how important respect for self-determination is, we need only look at the alternative where a dying person, like Mac, is denied the right to decide when enough is enough. Nel Noddings, ordinarily so critical of universal principles, including the principle of autonomy, seems to agree. As she puts it in her book *Women and Evil*: 'In so many of the stories with which we are familiar, the greatest suffering connected with dying lies in the . . . helpless exclusion [of the dying person] from autonomous action and community life.'[15]

It is true that patients will not always make the choices we think would be best. None the less, if their choice is an *autonomous* one, then the presumption must be that it ought to be respected. If we ignore or override a patient's choice in the name of a principle, such as vitalism or that the doctor knows best, we act, at best, paternalistically. If we deny a patient's choice in the name of an unprincipled feminine nursing ethics of care, we will, at best, act maternalistically. There are, however, no good reasons for thinking that maternalism has anything more to be said for it than does paternalism or, as Sarah Hoagland puts it, 'for preferring a society of mothers to a society of fathers'.[16]

To sum up, then, self-determination or autonomy is the interest every person has in making significant decisions affecting her life for herself, in accordance with her values, beliefs and plans for life. In health care, this entails that a person must, at the very least, be able to refuse treatment for herself.

Medical End-of-Life Decisions: The Traditional View

In many countries, including the US, there has been a welcome trend away from 'vitalism' and paternalism towards greater respect for patient autonomy, and patients like Mac are less likely to be resuscitated today than they were a decade or two ago. The contemporary moral and legal assumption is that competent patients must not be treated against their will – that they have a right to refuse medical treatment for themselves, and that the doctor (or the nurse, acting under the direction of a doctor) may, at least sometimes, collaborate with the patient in decisions that lead to the patient's foreseen death. Such decisions may not only involve the withholding or withdrawing of life-sustaining treatment, but also the administration of adequate pain and symptom relief that may foreseeably hasten death. What is much less accepted, both morally and legally, is that a doctor may at least sometimes deliberately end a terminally ill patient's life, through the prescription or administration of a lethal drug.[17]

Two initial questions present themselves: Is there a consistent way of distinguishing between these end-of-life decisions, and if there is, do these distinctions deserve our moral support? For the purposes of this discussion, we will accept the traditional assumption that the doctor–patient relationship is the appropriate locus for decision-making, and that the nurse's role is largely an instrumental one in implementing these decisions. We will question this assumption in the next and final chapter of this book.

Ordinary and extraordinary means of treatment

It is often assumed that so-called 'ordinary' treatments, but not 'extraordinary' or 'disproportionate' ones, must always be administered.[18] This distinction is, however, fraught with problems. First, it is not clear how the difference between ordinary and extraordinary means is to be understood. Some people understand it in terms of the distinction between usual and unusual treatments, between simple and sophisticated high-technology treatments, between non-invasive and invasive treatments, between burdensome and non-burdensome treatments and so on. As a first step, then, it would be necessary to specify how the term is to be used. Without a common understanding, there would be confusion.

This is not the main problem. If we are going to say that a patient must make use of ordinary treatments, but may forgo extraordinary ones, the distinction must be one in which we can find moral significance. Take the interpretation of the distinction in terms of simple versus high-technology treatments. On this view, a patient would presumably be entitled to refuse respiratory assistance but not antibiotics. The question is why? In some cases, the patient will – depending on her condition and prognosis – benefit from respiratory assistance. In others – when she is, for example, terminally ill and wishes to die – she will not derive any benefits from the treatment. And the same is true when it comes to 'ordinary' treatments, such as antibiotics. While antibiotics will often benefit a patient, there are clearly cases where a dying patient will not benefit from having a life-threatening infection treated, to linger for another day or two in a condition that she finds intolerable. This means that the distinction between ordinary and extraordinary treatments is redundant. Given that the aim of health care is to benefit patients, it will be clearer to focus directly on the benefits and burdens of particular treatments for particular patients, as judged by the patient herself.[19]

Causing death and allowing death to occur

Another way of attempting to draw a distinction between permissible and impermissible medical end-of-life decisions is to point at the distinction between deliberately ending life and merely allowing death to occur. Medical actions that deliberately end life or cause death are often described as 'killings' or 'euthanasia'; cases of withholding or withdrawing (extraordinary) treatment and of administering potentially life-shortening palliative care are generally described as instances of 'allowing to die'. Deliberately ending life is traditionally assumed to be impermissible; allowing death to occur is thought to be, at least sometimes, morally permissible or even legally mandatory. As it was put in the 1987 policy statement of the World Medical Association:

Euthanasia, that is the act of deliberately ending the life of a patient
. . . is unethical. This does not prevent the physician from respecting the desire of a patient to allow the natural process of death to
follow its course in the terminal phase of sickness.

But when does a doctor deliberately end life, and when does he
merely allow a patient to die? Consider the following four hypothetical examples:

Dr Adams' patient – Mr Angels – is dying from a progressively
debilitating disease. He is almost totally paralysed and needs a respirator to keep him alive. He is suffering considerable distress and
wants to die. He asks his doctor to disconnect the respirator. Dr
Adams complies, and Mr Angels dies three hours later, from respiratory failure.

Dr Bernard's patient – Mr Brown – is dying from the same disease as Mr Angels, needs a respirator to keep him alive and wants
to die. He asks Dr Bernard to give him a lethal injection and Dr
Bernard complies by administering potassium chloride. Mr Brown
dies a few minutes later.

Dr Clemens' patient – Mr Charles – is suffering from cancer
of the throat, which threatens to choke him. In great pain and
distress, he asks Dr Clemens to end his life. Dr Clemens explains
that this is not possible, but agrees to steadily increase the amount
of pain and symptom control. In a day or two, he says, the doses
will be such that Mr Charles will die, as a consequence of his (Dr
Clemens') attempts to make him comfortable. Dr Clemens starts
the infusion and 18 hours later Mr Charles dies.

Dr Daisy's patient – Mr David – is in virtually the same situation
as Mr Charles. When asked to end his life, Dr Daisy complies by
injecting a lethal dose of potassium chloride, and Mr David dies
within minutes.

Dr Adams, it might be said, 'allowed' his patient to die. His
patient died from an underlying disease, respiratory failure, and
not from the effects of a lethal injection, in the way Dr Bernard's
patient did. In this sense, it might be said that the two cases are
distinguishable – that Mr Angels' disease, not Dr Adams, caused

the patient's death, but that, in Mr Brown's case, Dr Bernard was the cause of death. It is, however, decidedly odd to say that Mr Angels' disease, not Dr Adams, caused the patient's death. Is not medicine ordinarily about *preventing* patients from dying from the diseases that afflict them, and was not the patient's death a direct consequence of the doctor's deliberate action – turning off a respirator, at the patient's request? And should we not, therefore, say that Dr Adams is, both causally and morally, as responsible for the consequences of his deliberate action – the patient's foreseen death – as is Dr Bernard?

Matters become even more complex when we turn to the next pair of cases. Dr Clemens clearly seems to have caused his patient's death in a way seemingly similar to the way Dr Bernard caused his patient's death. Both doctors administered drugs that they knew or expected would lead to their patients' earlier death. It is true, Dr Daisy used potassium chloride, whereas Dr Clemens administered drugs commonly used in pain and symptom control, but can this difference in the type of drug used allow us to distinguish, either causally or morally, between the two cases, and between the cases of Dr Adams and Dr Bernard? I think not.

This issue was raised in the 1996 US landmark decision *Compassion in Dying v. State of Washington*.[20] Compassion in Dying had argued that the State of Washington's prohibition of medically assisted suicide was untenable because the State already allowed patients and doctors to jointly make other, apparently similar, end-of-life decisions. In his carefully argued 8 to 3 majority opinion, Judge Reinhardt held that the current prohibition of medically assisted suicide must be based on the assumption that there is a relevant difference between medically assisted suicide and other 'conduct . . . the state has explicitly recognized'. But is there such a difference?

Reinhardt dismissed the distinction between actions and omissions as untenable. In many cases of forgoing treatment, he argued, health-care professionals unquestioningly perform actions that lead to the foreseen deaths of their patients. Nor would it help to bring in the notion of causation. A doctor who ceases treatment causes death, often with the same certainty as he would were he to administer a lethal injection. While some would say that it is the disease that causes death, Reinhardt continued that this is not a tenable position to take when the doctor administers life-shortening palliative care or withholds or withdraws fluid and nourishment. In those cases at least the doctor's action or omission, not the disease, is quite clearly the cause of death.

Given that these kinds of medical end-of-life decision are already permitted, and given that various other arguments for upholding the prohibition of medically assisted suicide were unconvincing, the Court ruled the prohibition of assisted suicide untenable. After all, there can be no doubt, Judge Reinhardt held, that in the case of already accepted practices 'the doctor intends that, as the result of his action, the patient will die.'

Reinhardt was surely right when he argued that the distinctions between actions and omissions and between causing and not causing death do not allow us to differentiate between permissible and impermissible end-of-life decisions. But, and this is important, proponents of the moral difference between killing and letting die have not generally understood the distinction between permissible and impermissible end-of-life decisions in this way. Rather, they have always held that some actions and omissions, such as the discontinuation of extraordinary means of treatment and the administration of potentially life-shortening pain and symptom control, are morally permissible. The presumption is not that it is wrong to 'do' certain things that cause death, but rather that it is wrong to *intend* death. As the Vatican's *Declaration on Euthanasia* puts it, an impermissible end-of-life decision ('mercy killing') is 'an act or an omission which of itself or by intention causes death'.[21]

This means that the crucial moral notion is that of intention, not that of doing or causing. It presupposes that we do not always intend all the foreseen consequences of our deliberate actions and omissions. In asserting that doctors who discontinue treatment and/or administer potentially life-shortening palliative care are intending the patient's death, Judge Reinhardt has thus challenged a whole body of traditional ethical thinking – and with it the so-called Principle of Double Effect. Should we accept Reinhardt's rejection of the Principle of Double Effect? There are, I believe, good reasons for doing so.

Rejecting the Traditional View for the Sake of Care

The Principle of Double Effect, long an important element in Catholic moral thinking, recognizes that one action can have more than one effect, and attempts to distinguish between the directly intended and the merely foreseen consequences of what we do. An otherwise impermissible effect – such as hastening a patient's death – may be permissible if the patient's death is only a foreseen rather than a directly intended consequence of what the agent does.[22] For example, if a doctor administers adequate pain and symptom control to a terminally ill and suffering patient, it is generally assumed that the doctor 'relieves pain' rather than 'hastens death', even if he expects that his action will, in fact, hasten or bring about the patient's death. In other words, while the patient will die as a consequence of what the doctor does, the patient's death is regarded as a merely foreseen and therefore permissible consequence of the doctor's action. Were the doctor to perform an outwardly similar action with the direct intention of shortening the patient's life, his action would be regarded as impermissible – and as a case of euthanasia.

Many palliative care specialists are willing to admit that some palliative treatments will hasten death.[23] But, in appealing to the intention/foresight distinction, many are also keen to distinguish their practice from voluntary euthanasia or the intentional termination of life. Take Dr Clemens' end-of-life decision in the example provided above. While Dr Clemens may agree that his action was causally related to Mr Charles' death, he might yet want to deny that he was *intending* his patient's death in the way in which, for example, Dr Bernard and Dr Daisy must have intended their patients' death. Since the Principle of Double Effect applies in the context of non-treatment decisions as well, Dr Adams would have been able to mount a similar argument about his intentions. While he had foreseen that his patient would die if he discontinued life-support, this was, he might say, merely a foreseen not an intended consequence of what he did.

The distinction between what we directly intend and what we merely foresee, however, is not a clear cut one. One anonymous Australian nurse gives the following example:

> If a patient is 'drowning' in his fluids and that patient is sitting up, it may be thought more humane to lay the patient flat thus quickening the process of dying. The patient may have lived a further four hours with much distress for himself . . . This is an example of simplified euthanasia but the same principle applies even when considering drug administration to hasten end.[24]

Sarah Shannon, a nurse now teaching at the University of Washington, makes a similar point:

> Any critical care nurse knows that if you turn a dying, hypotensive patient onto their right side you may drop their pressure and 'hasten' death. Knowing that, if I place the patient onto that side have I crossed that bright line between clearly right and clearly wrong? Usually at such a point, turning the patient to the right side isn't promoting comfort. The action can be anticipated to 'speed' dying. I may in fact *wish* the action to speed dying for the patient's and family's sake.

Anticipating the response that such actions are surely permissible, she pushes her point: 'If you answer that the turning in no way constitutes an unethical action, then tell me why it is wrong to provide a drug that would have the same effect.'[25]

Now, a defender of the view that it is always wrong to intend a patient's death might answer that Shannon has misunderstood what is at stake. *If* the agent *intends* that the patient die as a consequence of her turning the patient on the right side, then her action just *is* wrong, just as wrong as it would have been if she had provided a drug that had the same effect. In both cases the agent would have intended the patient's death and would hence have practised euthanasia or assisted suicide.

Whatever the theoretical merit of attempting to distinguish between the directly intended and merely foreseen consequences of medical end-of-life decisions, the above examples illustrate that such attempts will often not be helpful in practice. In many cases only the agent herself may be able to say what she intended to do when she did what she did. Another nurse's example, involving potassium chloride, the drug administered by Dr Bernard and Dr Daisy, will sharpen the point:

> In a situation where potassium is routinely added to IV solutions, if the nurse says to the doctor, 'This patient's potassium is already high enough to almost stop his heart,' and he answers, 'He's terminal, you know,' he means that a stopped heart is an easier death than being eaten away by cancer.[26]

Roger Hunt, a doctor who pioneered hospice and palliative care in South Australia, agrees that it is difficult to see how the Principle of Double Effect can help us to distinguish between 'euthanasia' and 'palliative care' in a consistent and practically useful way. Palliative care and euthanasia are not, he argues, distinct practices; rather they lie on a continuum of end-of-life decisions, where some forms of palliative care might be described as cases of 'slow active euthanasia'.[27] The same reasoning can, of course, also be applied to the forgoing of life-sustaining treatment at the end of life.

While there is thus no clear line separating permissible end-of-life decisions from impermissible ones, the continuing belief in the existence of such a line will, however, stand in the way of good patient care; it will foster and reinforce self-deception, secrecy and isolation, undercut professional responsibility, and may lead to the abandonment of a patient when the patient is most in need of care.[28]

Now, it is true that the principle that we may never intentionally end another person's life has a long history and is still widely accepted. But, as I suggested at the beginning of this chapter, we should not accept any principle *just because* it is widely accepted. Rather, if an accepted principle, rule or norm conflicts with good patient care, the presumption must be that it ought to be rejected. If we are to retain it, we must be provided with good reasons for doing so.

This leads to the following question: what is the relationship between the intention/foresight distinction and a health-care approach that takes dispositional care and the patient's best interests as its starting-point? If a terminally ill and suffering patient asks for help in dying, should it matter morally whether the doctor directly intends or merely foresees that the patient will die as a consequence of what he does? More important, what reasons would the dispositional carer have for thinking that 'merely foreseeing' or 'allowing' a patient to die is more expressive of care than 'intending' and 'helping' such a patient to die? To the extent that such actions or omissions are in the patient's best interests, as understood by the patient herself, should we not want to say that it is entirely appropriate for the carer to engage in actions or omissions that are not only *foreseen* to benefit the patient, but that are also *intended* to do so?[29]

Nel Noddings seems to make a similar point when discussing the question of euthanasia for terminally ill patients who want to die:

> We do not ask, guided by some symbolic body of thought, what this pain and suffering mean. Rather, we ask the far more direct and open question, What should I do in the face of this reality? In particular, the question before us now is, What should I do in the face of extreme suffering when there is a well-grounded judgement of hopelessness?

Noting that contemporary medicine can do much to help patients die with dignity, she goes on to say that patients might still be overwhelmed by 'psychic pain' and that in such cases 'active [voluntary] euthanasia might be a reasonable and compassionate choice', where the very possibility of making this choice 'may also reduce a patient's sense of helplessness'.[30] The central question from a relational care perspective is not, Nodding holds, 'whether and under what conditions *one man* may opt to end the life of another',[31] but rather how decision-making can grow out of an open and compassionate dialogue between the patient and all those involved in the decision.[32]

As we have already noted, Noddings holds that often 'the greatest suffering connected with dying lies in the dreadful separation from others that occurs even before death, in the helpless exclusion from autonomous action.' While the carers would certainly attempt to dissuade people from unreasonable attempts to end their lives, and even in the case of the hopelessly ill encourage the decision to continue to live, what is of the utmost importance is that 'The same spirit of genuine concern, open discussion, and loving sympathy should govern the decision to help live and the one to help die.'[33]

Noddings' central point, in line with her general critique of principles and rules, appears to be this: adherence to principles, such as the absolute prohibition of killing, the Principle of Double Effect, or any of the other principles or distinctions we discussed earlier, will not allow the carer to respond with sufficient sensitivity to the needs and wants of some patients at the end of life. In this she is surely correct. If we live our lives in accordance with blunt and inflexible principles, rules and norms, such as the principle: 'It is absolutely wrong to intentionally end a suffering patient's life,' then we will not always be able to respond to the needs and wants of particular patients. This does not entail, of course, that we should reject all principled ethical thinking. Rather, it may mean no more than rejecting the traditional distinction between permissible and impermissible medical end-of-life decisions, in favour of another more sensitive principle, such as respect for patient autonomy.

Some Objections

It is often said that there is no need for doctors to engage in the deliberate hastening of death. Patients are already permitted to refuse life-sustaining treatment, and palliative care can ensure that death is not the drawn-out and agonizing process it is often made out to be. Rather, most patients die in relative comfort and with dignity.

It is certainly true that the public recognition of a patient's right to refuse medical treatment, coupled with the provision of good palliative care, can ensure a dignified death for many patients. It cannot, however, help all patients. Patients will not always die swiftly, and in ways acceptable to them, when treatment is withheld or withdrawn. Rather, they may linger on for hours, days and sometimes weeks. In some 5 per cent of cases, even the best palliative care cannot satisfactorily relieve all pain.[34] The case of Lillian Boyes, briefly described in chapter 1 by Roisin Hart, may have been a case in point. Let us take a closer look at her case.

Lillian Boyes

In August 1991, 70-year-old Lillian Boyes was dying in the Royal Hampshire County Hospital, in Winchester, England. She had been suffering from a very painful form of rheumatoid arthritis for some 20 years, and Nigel Cox had been her consultant rheumatologist for 13 of those 20 years. Lillian Boyes had deformed hands and feet, swollen joints and gangrene from steroid treatment. She had also developed ulcers and abscesses on her arms and legs; she had fractured vertebrae, experienced internal bleeding, and it caused her great pain to be touched.

When Lillian Boyes asked Nigel Cox to end her life, he initially refused. This led her to refuse further treatment. Her pain got worse: her body could no longer metabolize the opioid painkillers, including heroin, that Nigel Cox was giving her. According to one nurse, she 'howled and screamed like a dog' whenever she was touched, and the hospital chaplain said he had never seen anyone 'so much eaten by pain'. When it appeared that Lillian Boyes had hours, rather than days, to live, she again asked Nigel Cox to help her die. Her two sons supported her request. This time her doctor responded. He injected a lethal dose of potassium chloride. Lillian Boyes relaxed, and for the first time in a long time, her son could clasp her hand. Then she died.

As we already know, Nigel Cox recorded details of the injection he had given in the medical records, without discussing it with Roisin Hart or any of the other nurses. Roisin Hart reported the case to hospital management. By the time the police had been called, Lillian Boyes' body had been cremated, and it was not possible to prove that the potassium chloride had caused her death. Nigel Cox was charged with attempted murder and was subsequently found guilty. The judge held that he had 'betrayed his unequivocal duty as a physician', and imposed a 12-month suspended prison sentence.

The case was also reviewed by the General Medical Council. The Council found that it was appropriate for a doctor to ease pain and suffering, but that it was 'wholly outside that duty to shorten life in order to relieve suffering'.[35]

There is little doubt that Nigel Cox acted contrary to the law, and contrary to accepted medical principles. But do we also want to say that he 'betrayed his unequivocal duty as a physician'? Or should we say that Lillian Boyes' plight and her doctor's response raised questions about the validity of an accepted professional and legal principle – the principle that a doctor must never intentionally and openly end a patient's life?

Doctors and nurses are well aware that palliative care and withdrawal of treatment cannot help all patients, and many regard voluntary euthanasia and/or medically assisted suicide as not only compatible with their role as carers, but as required by it.[36] Surveys of doctors and nurses in countries such as the US, Britain and Australia, have consistently shown that a large number of health-care professionals already practise voluntary euthanasia, and want the law changed so that they can openly and lawfully provide direct help in dying to those who need and want it.[37]

Even patients receiving excellent hospice or palliative care will frequently ask for direct help in dying.[38] The most frequent reason is not pain, but rather what these patients regard as an intolerable and, from their point of view, undignified dying process.[39] Some patients – a significant minority – can be helped only by medically assisted suicide or voluntary euthanasia. This means that there is a strong presumption in favour of permitting the practice. It is, however, only a presumption. As we have seen, an exclusive focus on our responsibility to particular others is inadequate from the moral point of view. We must consider wider questions of justice as well. Expressed in terms of the Minimum Conception of Ethics: voluntary euthanasia should be allowed – unless the practice is incompatible with the equal consideration of the interests of all those affected by our actions.[40]

This brings us to the question of public policy, an area where the primary focus is not on the interests of particular others, but rather on the just promotion and protection of the interests of all.

Public Policy, Impartiality and Justice

Protecting the interest in self-determination

There is no consensus on the morality of voluntary euthanasia. While there is, in many countries, majority support for allowing the practice, many members of society – including many nurses and doctors – regard direct help in dying as intrinsically wrong and contrary to their professional role. As one Australian nurse put it when asked to describe her attitudes to voluntary euthanasia:

> I have already been involved in . . . termination of pregnancies and have found that the guilt will stay with me for the rest of my life.

> Yes, I do pity the terminally ill patient who requests euthanasia
> . . . However, if euthanasia were made legal in Australia, then I
> would have to be sure that I never ever worked with patients who
> are likely to request such a 'procedure'. I believe life is precious. It
> is good to be alive (in pain even). It is not up to us to decide when
> we should stop living . . . Life is given to us. It is wrong to termin-
> ate it.[41]

Another nurse, however, reached a different conclusion, arguing
as follows:

> If I was in the position where the illness was terminal and incur-
> able, I would wish that I had the opportunity of active euthanasia.
> Therefore patients in the same situation should be able to make that
> decision.[42]

This raises the following question: What is the proper relation
between the moral views held by individual members of society,
including patients, doctors and nurses, and the moral principles
we should adopt to govern the provision of health care in liberal
and pluralist societies, such as, for example, Australia, Britain and
the United States?

Our earlier discussion of the nature of ethics has obvious implications for what counts as an acceptable answer. Anyone who
accepts the Minimum View of Ethics would have to reject the
view that ethics is one thing, public policy quite another. To the
extent that we subscribe to the view that morality requires us to
give equal consideration to the interests of all those affected by
what we do, we must also accept that public policy considerations
will, of necessity, fall within the realm of the ethical. After all, the
public policies we adopt will typically have a direct bearing on the
interests and well-being of members of society – they can make
the lives of individuals go better or worse, and treat them fairly
or unfairly.

Then there is the issue of ethical plurality, and of respect for
the religious and moral views of individuals and groups. Modern societies are typically made up of people who have different
visions of the 'good life' and who will sometimes arrive at different answers to morally sensitive questions, such as 'the right to
die'. Because these different answers have their source in particular

value systems, they cannot be shown to be true or false in the ordinary sense of those terms.[43] This means that it would be quite inappropriate to enforce a particular moral point of view. Rather, as self-determining moral beings, people should be free to live their lives in accordance with their values and beliefs – as long as their doing so is compatible with the rights or interests of others.

This general idea was memorably expressed by John Stuart Mill in his essay *On Liberty*:

> the only purpose for which power can be rightfully exercised over any member of a civilised community, against his will, is to prevent harm to others . . . over himself, over his own body and mind, the individual is sovereign.[44]

The implication of this liberal point of view is that terminally ill patients should be free to make end-of-life decisions for themselves, and that willing doctors should be able to comply with the patient's request. There are, of course, grey areas in the application of this principle, where people make decisions without reflection or where there are doubts about their competency. But when an adult person of sound mind makes a carefully considered medical end-of-life decision, the state should not interfere with that decision and seek to prevent doctors from assisting the person in the implementation of her decision. We have already accepted this principle with regard to non-treatment and palliative care decisions, and there is a strong presumption that it should be extended to cover medically assisted suicide and voluntary euthanasia as well.

Voluntary euthanasia, as we have already noted, will be unacceptable to some members of society. Their ideas are, however, implicitly respected in the very idea of *voluntary* euthanasia – it is an *option* (like palliative care and the withholding of treatment) available to those who want it, and is not a mode of dying that must be taken up by everyone. Palliative care and non-treatment will remain the preferred option for many people; but the fact that palliative care can give many people the kind of dignified death they want does not mean that this mode of dying is appropriate for everyone. As one writer in the field puts it, a dignified or 'good death' is not so much a pain-free or a 'happy' death, but rather an autonomous death:

a good death is one over which a person has some degree of control so that it is, to the greatest degree feasible in the circumstances, an expression of that person's life values and of their conception of the good life. A good death is then an autonomous death – a death I choose and determine for myself – and from this point of view it is something that a liberal society should favour and foster.[45]

No patient should, without good reason, be made to die in ways that, while meeting the moral or religious precepts of some, are anathema to their own. As the legal philosopher Ronald Dworkin puts it: 'Making someone die in a way that others approve, but he regards as a horrifying contradiction of his life, is a devastating, odious form of tyranny.'[46]

Discrimination

If the patient's interest in self-determination and respect for her own understanding of well-being is one reason for a liberal approach towards medical end-of-life decisions, there is another justice-related reason as well. The traditional view unfairly discriminates against particular individuals and groups. This issue was raised in a second 1996 US landmark case, that of *Timothy E. Quill* et al. v. *State of New York*, heard before the Second Appeals Court of New York.[47] Building on the legal permissibility of doctors withdrawing treatment, Dr Timothy Quill, a well-known supporter of medically assisted suicide, argued:

> The removal of a life support system that . . . results in the patient's death requires the direct involvement by the doctor . . . When such patients are mentally competent, they are consciously choosing death as preferable to life under the circumstances that they are forced to live . . . [U]nfortunately, some dying patients who are in agony that can no longer be relieved, yet are not dependent on life-sustaining treatment, have no such options under current legal restrictions. It seems unfair, discriminatory and arbitrary, and inhumane to deprive some dying patients of such vital choices because of arbitrary elements of their condition which determine whether they are on life-sustaining treatment that can be stopped.

The Appeals Court concurred and struck down the prohibition on medically assisted suicide, on the grounds that it discriminates unfairly against patients not so 'fortunate' as to require life-support which they can then refuse. This argument must be taken seriously.[48] We ought not to support public policies that unjustly discriminate against particular individuals and groups.

Some More Objections

It is frequently conceded that existing policies do not serve all patients equally well. But, it is said, in an imperfect world that is the best we can do. If we depart from our traditional assumption that doctors must never intentionally terminate life, then it will be to the detriment of society as a whole.

Many of the claims about the bad consequences of the legalization of voluntary euthanasia, however, rest on the erroneous assumption that there is a clear distinction between voluntary euthanasia and other already accepted medical end-of-life decisions, that is, that voluntary euthanasia raises new issues – issues that are not already raised by practices long since regarded as good medical practice. But this assumption, as we have already seen, is largely wrong. Voluntary euthanasia is very much like other accepted medical end-of-life decisions.

It is thus sometimes claimed that dying patients cannot rationally or autonomously choose euthanasia, because they might be depressed or their minds clouded by medication. But if opponents of voluntary euthanasia really believed this, then they would also have to hold that no patient can ever autonomously refuse life-sustaining treatment or choose life-shortening palliative care. In either case the patient makes a decision that will foreseeably lead to her death. To hold that a patient can, for example, competently refuse treatment, but not competently request direct help in dying, is inconsistent. The question is whether a patient can rationally choose an earlier death over a later one, and that choice is made in either case. Hence, if a patient can rationally opt for an earlier death by refusing treatment or by accepting life-shortening palliative care, then she must also be able rationally to opt for an earlier death by euthanasia. The views of health-care professionals lend support to this. According to a 1993 study, an overwhelming majority of nurses (95 per cent) think that a patient's request for a hastening of death can be rational.[49]

A similar response is called for when it is alleged that voluntary euthanasia is contrary to the proper goals of health-care. Shortly after the 1996 landmark rulings of the Ninth and Second Circuit Courts of Appeals on medically assisted suicide, *American Medical News*, a publication of the American Medical Association, ran an editorial under the headline 'Court-Assisted Ethicide'. The editorial argued that these rulings have dealt medical ethics a series of damaging blows:

> We can't recall a time when medical ethics has suffered such a damaging series of blows in rapid succession. However well-intentioned, these courtroom decisions undermine medicine's most fundamental ethical tenet: First do no harm.[50]

But are doctors who are helping terminally ill patients end their lives really harming patients, thereby acting contrary to the goals of medicine? Are they not, rather, *benefiting* patients in the same way that they are now benefiting patients by withholding or withdrawing treatment, and providing potentially life-shortening palliative care? It seems that the answer must be 'yes'. This means that the time has come seriously to question some widely accepted principles, values and beliefs. As Sarah Shannon puts it:

> Bioethics has held up the active versus passive, withdrawal/withholding of life support versus assisted suicide as a shield for far too long. Let's put it down, listen to clinicians . . . and challenge ourselves to a bit of 'moral growth' by re-visiting this debate. Perhaps the increasing use of technology has blurred the distinction? Perhaps the original reasoning was flawed?[51]

Would the doctor–patient relationship be threatened if doctors were permitted to practise voluntary euthanasia? I cannot see why. On the contrary, many patients would derive considerable peace of mind from the knowledge that their doctors would not only be willing to allow them to die, but would be willing to give death a helping hand if this should ever become necessary, which it may not. One might thus liken voluntary euthanasia to fire insurance. Having our house insured will give us peace of mind, even if our house will never burn down.[52]

Nor does it make good sense to suggest that the legalization of voluntary euthanasia would brutalize doctors and nurses and lead to moral decline in the health services. Voluntary euthanasia is best seen as a form of particularized caring. Rather than brutalizing health-care professionals, it will allow them to respond more sensitively to the needs of *all* terminally ill patients – including those who request direct help in dying.

Of course, the vulnerable must be protected from harm, from being pressured into asking for 'voluntary' euthanasia. These dangers must be taken seriously, particularly in countries where universal health-care insurance is not available. But again, these dangers are not specific to voluntary euthanasia. Pressure cannot only be applied to patients in the context of euthanasia, but also in the context of other medical end-of-life decisions, such as non-treatment decisions. Patients can be pressured into 'voluntarily' refusing treatment or, more insidiously, such treatment may simply not be offered to them in the first place. This means that patients must be protected from coercion and undue persuasion at the end of life, not that they must be prevented from making medical end-of-life decisions for themselves.

The legalization of voluntary euthanasia does not mean that doctors and nurses who disagree with the practice on moral or religious grounds should be compelled to provide it. Rather, the very same principle – respect for self-determination or autonomy – that leads us to give patients the right to make medical end-of-life decisions for themselves will also lead us to the conclusion that the moral values and beliefs of doctors and nurses must be taken seriously and deserve respect. No health-care professional should be compelled to participate in the provision of services she finds morally repugnant.[53]

The slippery slope objection

More recently, another claim has been put forward by people opposed to the legalization of voluntary euthanasia. They argue that voluntary euthanasia should not be permitted because the experience from the Netherlands (where doctors have been able openly to practise voluntary euthanasia for a number of years) shows that it will lead to abuse.[54] The argument is usually based on the findings of a 1992 Dutch study of medical end-of-life decisions – the so-called Remmelink Report.[55] The argument is that the study shows that the introduction of voluntary euthanasia has led to abuse, that is, to the termination of life without consent. Doctors, the study showed, did not always have their patients' consent when they withdrew or withheld treatment, administered life-shortening palliative care or administered euthanasia – typically, but not always, because the patient was suffering much, was close to death and was unable to give consent.

But how can a single study – so far the only one of its kind anywhere in the world – possibly show that the practice of voluntary euthanasia *has led to* abuse? To demonstrate that, one would need at least two studies – one conducted before the practice of voluntary euthanasia was introduced and one conducted some time after it. Only then would one be able to compare the incidence of various practices and say that there is more or less abuse. What is more, we do not know whether there is more or less abuse in the Netherlands than in countries such as, for example, Australia, Britain and the United States, where voluntary euthanasia is practised frequently, even though it is unlawful.[56] It may be less or more. We simply do not know.

Surely, the best way of preventing abuse is to make medical end-of-life decisions transparent, through the implementation of procedures that allow public scrutiny. In the case of competent patients, this could be achieved by shifting the focus from the doctor's intention to the patient's consent.

The Malleability and Constructability of End-of-Life Decisions

As we have seen, the traditional assumption is that doctors are not presumed to intend all the foreseen consequences of their medical end-of-life decisions. This makes for the extreme malleability and 'constructability'[57] of end-of-life decisions. Doctors who do not, for whatever reasons, want to practise 'euthanasia' have other means of achieving the same result.[58] Dr Adams and Dr Clemens, in our above hypothetical examples, might well have intended their patients' death when they did what they did (and would hence have practised voluntary euthanasia); and Dr Bernard and Dr Daisy could, had they so chosen, have used accepted drugs rather than potassium chloride to bring about the same result – and their actions would, on the face of it, have been transformed from criminal homicide into 'good medical practice'. In real life, Dr Cox could most likely have done the same.

The slippery nature of the notion of intention was highlighted in one of the 1996 trials of Dr Jack Kevorkian, who was accused of having assisted two terminally ill persons end their lives by inhaling deadly carbon monoxide gas. According to Michigan law, 'a person is not guilty of criminal assistance of suicide if that person was administering medication and procedures with the intent to relieve pain and discomfort and not to cause death,' even if the treatment 'may hasten or increase the risk of death'. Kevorkian claimed he had no such intent. Rather, he maintained, he had never wanted either patient to die: their deaths were an 'unfortunate, repugnant, unavoidable' consequence of relieving their suffering. The jury found him not guilty.[59]

Jack Kevorkian's claim that he did not intend the deaths may be unconvincing. But it takes the traditional view that a doctor can knowingly and deliberately bring about a morally significant event – such as a patient's death – without having intended what may well be its logical conclusion. It sits at the opposite end of the approach underpinning the reasoning of Judge Reinhardt: that doctors should be presumed to have intended death not only when they administer non-therapeutic lethal injections, but also when they engage in other already accepted medical end-of-life decisions. It seems to me that we ought to side with Reinhardt. The reason is simple: if we continue to base our laws, at least to some significant extent, on the slippery notion of intention, this entails that these laws will often be unclear, difficult to enforce, that they will encourage and entrench hypocrisy, undermine trust in the doctor–patient relationship, do not treat patients fairly (in that a patient's treatment may depend on the doctor's willingness and ability to manipulate the law) and do not ensure sound ethical decision-making. Bringing in such notions as 'direct' causation – or the distinction between standard and non-standard drugs – may occasionally bring a Dr Cox (who uses potassium chloride) before the courts, when most of his colleagues would have used some other 'indirect' method to end life, but this is not very helpful in ensuring good medical practice.[60]

The solution lies in changing our focus. When it comes to end-of-life decisions for competent patients, we should abolish the intention/foresight distinction and focus on the patient's consent. As a consequence, the central questions would no longer be, 'What did the doctor intend when he did what he did?' and 'How, or by what method, did the patient's foreseen death come about?' but rather: 'Is this the kind of death the patient wants? Does it comply with the patient's understanding of a dignified death?' and 'Has the patient given her consent?' While it may be possible to draw increasingly fine scholastic distinctions between actions or omissions that cause or merely allow death and between intending and foreseeing and so on, these distinctions are not very helpful in framing public policies and laws. This is not to deny that such conceptual distinctions may well play a role in some people's private lives (and deserve respect); it is rather to suggest that, for the purposes of public policy formation, the focus must be on principles that can be shared by all, such as the principle defended here that competent patients and their doctors should be free to make medical end-of-life decisions that best meet the patient's needs. A sufficiently rich notion of consent – and the requirement that *all* medical end-of-life decisions require the competent patient's consent – would capture this principle in a workable procedural standard.

This approach would obviate the need to distinguish in what are often practically useless ways between permissible and impermissible end-of-life decisions. Rather, with the patient's consent doctors would now be at liberty to aid each patient's dying in a way that best meets the needs of that particular patient. For one patient this would involve refusal of treatment; for another the acceptance of life-shortening palliative care; and for a third it would mean medically assisted suicide or voluntary euthanasia.

This approach has various advantages over the existing situation: first, it meets the requirements of dispositional care, for it will allow health-care professionals sensitively to respond to the needs of *all* their patients; second, it eliminates unjust discrimination against particular individuals and groups; and third, by focusing

on consent, it replaces the malleable and opaque distinction between deaths that are directly intended and those that are merely
foreseen with a transparent and workable procedural approach.

Conclusion

If one of the reasons for the above discussion was to argue for the
substantive conclusions, another no less important reason was to
demonstrate the importance of moral argument. Moral reasoning
starting with – but not ending with – the insights derived from
dispositional care can challenge some long-accepted principles, rules
and laws, principles and laws that are unjust and stand in the way
of good patient care.

Injustices, however, can only be challenged by way of principled argument. This means that it is important to distinguish
the rejection of particular ethical principles from the rejection of
principled ethical reasoning. Without principled reasoning we cannot, as we noted before, establish even our most basic values and
claims, and would be opting out of ethical discourse altogether. If
we want to remain participants in ethical discourse, we must engage
in principled ethical thinking, and with the help of *our* principles
challenge existing principles incompatible with the goals of care.
Take vitalism and paternalism. Is there any way of challenging
these principles, other than by appeal to other principles, such as
'the right to self-determination', 'respect for persons' and the like?
I think not. If this is correct, it might be best to regard principles,
rules, rights and laws as 'tools' – tools that can be employed to
protect the helpless and ensure justice for all.[61]

In addition to that, it is important to recognize that the ability
to appeal to commonly shared principles, rules and rights is critically important in public endeavours, such as health care, where
we need to ensure that some basic moral rights or expectations –
such as a competent patient's right to make end-of-life decisions
for herself – are met. Some feminists and others have been critical of moral analyses based on rights and, as we have seen, various
writers, Nel Noddings foremost among them, have suggested
that we should reject rights, principles and rules in favour of care.

I can see no reason why we should regard moral rights as inconsistent or competitive with the ends of dispositional care. Rather,
whereas we might see dispositional care as an ideal, we might see
respect for rights as a 'moral floor' – in the words of Mary Ann
Warren, as 'a minimum protection for individuals which remains
morally binding even where appropriate caring relationships are
absent or have broken down'.[62] The doctor treating Mac, for
example, may not have been sensitive to the plight of Mac, but
– as Barbara Huttmann realized – recognition of such rights as
'the right to die' can at least protect terminally ill patients from
the zealous efforts of others to keep them alive against their will.

In this chapter I have mapped an approach to medical end-of-
life decisions that is, I believe, not only demanded by the insights
derived from dispositional care, but by those of impartialist principled ethical thinking as well. While the traditional approach does
not allow health-care professionals to respond sensitively to the
needs of all their patients, and unfairly discriminates between similarly situated patients who are seeking direct help in dying, the
approach sketched here meets the demands of both justice and
care – and the gap between the justice and care perspective, at
least in this particular area of patient care, would have been bridged.

I have not given an answer to the wider question raised at the
beginning of this chapter of how the justice and care perspectives might be bridged. Nor would I be foolish enough to attempt
to do so, at the end of a long book, and in an area where many
others have failed. While I have, I believe, been successful in showing that, in our area of concern at least, the insights derived from
care for particular others coincide with the demands of justice, I
am quite certain that this will not always be the case. Rather, in
areas such as the allocation of scarce medical resources, conflict
would be inevitable. While it might clearly benefit a particular
patient to receive an expensive treatment, there may be justice-
based reasons for denying her the treatment. In a case such as
this, it may be impossible to bridge the demands of justice and
of care.

I tend to think that the attempt to transcend or bridge the dichotomy between justice and care in a global sense is wrong-headed.
We may be able to bridge the dichotomy in some domains, but
not in others. Rather, as I suggested in chapter 6, in some areas

the conflict between partialist and impartialist concerns will be irresolvable and our choice often a tragic one. Setting these larger questions aside, we will, in the next and final chapter, deal with questions relating to the role of nurses in end-of-life decisions, and discuss the vexed issue of how much-needed changes might best be implemented.

9

Nursing: The Slumbering Giant

Three critical care nurses . . . worked together efficiently as they resuscitated an irreversibly dying man. All the while, tears ran down their cheeks. This man had suffered for weeks. He had begged them to let him die. But there were orders and policies, and . . .

Leah Curtin, 'A Nurse's Conscience' (1983)

A common and natural result of an undue respect for law is that you see a file of soldiers, colonel, captain, corporal, private, powder-monkeys and all, marching in admirable order over the hill and dale to the wars, against their wills, aye, against their common sense and conscience . . . They have no doubt that it is a damnable business in which they are concerned.

Henry David Thoreau, *Civil Disobedience* (1849)

A profession that does not govern itself will nevertheless be governed – from without.

Margaret Styles, 'Coming of Age: Issues before the Nursing Profession' (1986)

Nurses as Patient Advocates

We began this book with the stories of two nurses – Roisin Hart and Barbara Huttmann. Both stories involved medical end-of-life decisions. In the first case the treating doctor, Nigel Cox, helped his patient, Lillian Boyes, to die; in the second case, the unnamed doctor kept his patient, Mac, alive. What was significant from the nurses' point of view was not only the substantive question of whether the doctors' actions were right or wrong, but also the implicit assumption that it is appropriate for doctors to make morally significant end-of-life decisions and for nurses to carry them out (or at least to consent to them) regardless of their own moral or professional point of view. These cases signal that nurses are not regarded as autonomous health-care professionals and moral agents, but as dependent functionaries whose role it is to do the moral bidding of others.

In 1983 Roland Yarling and Beverly McElmurry wrote that the nurse

> *is often not free to be moral*, that is, a nurse is often not free to honor the commitment to the patient, whether the commitment takes the form of responding to the patient's request for no further treatment, of keeping the patient free from unnecessary suffering, or of performing whatever functions may be required by professional standards of nursing and by excellence in nursing practice.[1]

For many nurses these observations are as true today as they were then, and there is an urgent need for change. The reason is not, or not only, that many nurses experience disillusionment, moral outrage and burn-out as a consequence of their inability to honour their commitments to patients;[2] it is rather that the moral voice of nurses must be heard *for the patients' sake*. This does not mean, of course, that nurses should *make* morally relevant decisions for patients. As we have seen, that is the role of neither the doctor nor the nurse, but of the patient herself. The moral voice of nurses must be heard so that members of the health-care team can respond sensitively and adequately to the needs and wants of those for whom they care. Why should this be so?

The reason lies in the link between what I called 'dispositional care' and the adequacy of our moral response. Moral action presupposes not only sound ethical principles, but also the willingness and ability to give lucid attention to the particularities of situations and individuals. If the willingness or ability to pay attention to particularity and to respond sensitively to it is lacking in the providers of clinical care, there is a danger that patients are treated as either malfunctioning biological organisms or as the mere bearers of broad interests or rights.

Dispositional care presupposes a degree of 'closeness' between the carer and the cared-for. If this closeness is lacking, we are unable to treat the cared-for as a *particular* other – although we are still able to treat her as the bearer of broad interests or rights. Nurses are often, in a physical and relational sense of the term, closer to individual patients than doctors. They care for patients for extended periods of time and may, as a consequence, not only develop the relevant caring dispositions traditionally associated with women, but also the requisite insights into *this* patient's needs, wants and values. As one nurse puts it:

> The unique position of the nurse in the health care system . . . enhances the nurse's ability to develop an interactive/interpersonal therapeutic relationship that permits her/him to gain knowledge of the whole person and the ways in which each person defines their experience of illness.[3]

Doctors are typically more distant from their patients – a point forcefully made by an intensive-care nurse:

> [doctors] basically sit back there and make the decisions. They have basically no contact with the patient as an individual . . . Early in the morning they draw their bloods, they listen to their lungs, they listen to their bellies, maybe chitchat a bit, and the only other times they're back in there is usually to start an IV or to draw blood.[4]

Another nurse makes a similar observation: 'It is far too easy for a doctor to impose his will when he sees the patient for only 10 minutes a day. When a patient says he's ready to die but the doctor insists that he live, the *doctor* should take care of that patient for 8 hours a day.'[5] While some doctors – and Dr Cox may have been an example of this – will have had the opportunity to develop long-term caring relationships with particular patients, it would none the less be true, as a general rule, that nurses are better placed than doctors to function as dispositional carers. This means that they would also, other things being equal, be better placed than doctors to develop the relevant insights into their patients' health-related needs and wants.

The recognition that nurses occupy a special position in the health-care team has led to claims, already briefly touched on in chapter 3, that nurses have a professional and moral obligation to defend the health-related interests of those for whom they care. This idea – enthusiastically embraced by many nurses at the time – found expression in the metaphor of the nurse as patient advocate. No longer were nurses to be seen as the subservient servants of doctors, but rather as the courageous advocates of patients.

Over the years, various criticisms have been voiced with regard to the advocacy role. For example, some critics have claimed that it would give rise to an overly narrow understanding of the nurse's role, where nurses would function as the mere guardians of their patients' legal rights, such as the right to self-determination; others claimed that adoption of the advocacy role would require too much of nurses; and a third group of critics have suggested that the advocacy role would encourage adversarial relationships between different members of the health-care team.[6]

Some of these criticisms may well be justified – but only in so far as they apply to particular *interpretations* of the advocacy role. They do not touch the core idea of advocacy itself. The core idea is that nurses must, *in some sense of the term*, always conceive of themselves as patient advocates. This is so because nurses are health-care professionals, and all health-care professionals must, by virtue of their professional role, also speak and act on behalf of those for whom they care. One may thus disagree with particular interpretations of the advocacy role, but one cannot consistently reject the central idea that nurses, just like doctors and other health-care professionals, have a prima facie obligation to act in ways that will protect and enhance the interests and rights of their patients. Indeed, this is what contemporary nursing codes suggest. The American Nurses' Association Code, for example, states that nurses should act in ways that 'support and enhance the client's responsibility and self-determination to the greatest extent possible';[7] the Australian Nursing Council Code admonishes nurses to 'respect the rights of persons to make informed choices in relation to their care';[8] and, to give one other example, the United Kingdom Central Council for Nursing, Midwifery and Health Visiting exhorts nurses always to act 'in such a way as to promote and safeguard the well being and interests of patients/clients.'[9] What the debate over advocacy is or ought to be about, is thus not whether nurses should be patient advocates, but rather how this professional ideal is to be understood and best translated into practice.

One central problem in articulating a substantive view of what advocacy entails lies in the disparate character of the various roles performed by nurses in different health-care settings. Another problem is that the obligation to act in a particular patient's best interests is not absolute; rather, it is a prima facie obligation – an obligation that must, at the critical level of ethical thinking, be tested against the impartialist consideration of the interests of all those affected by the action. This means that it is not possible to give clear directives as to how individual nurses should act if they find themselves in situations where an individual patient's interests are not being met. Different circumstances and different health-care settings may require different context-dependent responses and, in the end, each actor has to make a moral judgement appropriate to the problem at hand.

Another problem – and the one we shall be focusing on here – lies in the individualistic nature of the metaphor of the nurse as patient advocate. Like all traditional nursing ethics, the metaphor fixes our gaze firmly on individual patients and nurses. It focuses on situations where 'the nurse' finds herself in circumstances that call for an activation of the advocacy role; it does not encourage us to ask critical questions about the context that forms the backdrop to these kinds of situation and may thus conceal important social and structural issues from view.[10] In other words, the metaphor does not encourage us to ask why it is that nurses so often find themselves in situations where they are not, in the words of Yarling and McElmurry, 'free to honor the commitment to the patient'.[11] This question, however, must be asked, for the sake of good patient care.

Nursing: The Slumbering Giant

As we have seen, during the 1970s and early 1980s the idea of patient advocacy became a symbol of courage and of power. Many nurses saw themselves as brave warriors who were willing to defend the rights and interests of those for whom they cared. If the contemporary nursing literature is taken as primary evidence, this enthusiasm has waned somewhat. The outward-looking activist metaphor of the nurse as patient advocate has been eclipsed by the inward-looking metaphor of the nurse as feminine carer. No longer is the primary focus on protecting the patient from the harmful actions or omissions of others, but rather on the development of inner qualities and virtues, such as compassion, empathy and care. Why should this be so?

The answer may well be that the idea of advocacy is fine in theory, but difficult to apply in practice. After all, individual nurses are not acting in a social vacuum, but in the context of institutional and social frameworks and constraints that strongly discourage assertiveness and independent action. To begin with, there is an important difference between the 'social fit' of the old metaphors of subservience and the new metaphor of advocacy. As we saw in chapter 2, when the old metaphors were born they reflected fairly accurately social expectations about the role of women in society, about the relationship between the sexes and about the relationship between doctors and nurses. Things are different when it comes to the advocacy role. Some doctors find it difficult to see nurses as professional colleagues rather than as subordinate functionaries, and medical organizations are clinging to traditional notions of exclusive medical responsibility for treatment decisions.[12] As one Australian nurse notes, the historical 'master and handmaiden' relationship is still affecting nursing as a profession: '[N]ursing is still regarded as a female calling and hence occupies an inferior role in male dominated society.'[13] Another nurse laments:

> If the changing role of women in society has become widely accepted . . . in general, I may be working in a hospital which is atypical – a pocket of resistance. Senior nurses constantly battle with attitudes which are chauvinistic and paternalistic . . . it makes it very wearing.[14]

Even today, many nurses still feel intimidated by doctors. A 1988 government inquiry in New Zealand showed that hundreds of women suffering from carcinoma *in situ* had been involved, without their consent, in an 'unfortunate experiment' at the National Women's Hospital in Auckland.[15] Some of these women had not been receiving adequate treatment for their condition. The National inquiry also revealed that anaesthetized women at the hospital had, over a 20-year period, been subjected without their consent to vaginal examinations by groups of medical students. While doctors sought to defend the latter practice by arguing that in a teaching hospital the rights of patients had to be balanced against the need to teach, this kind of defence sits very uncomfortably with the nurse's advocacy role and the now widely shared belief that 'penetration without consent', even if performed by doctors and medical students, is morally wrong.[16] This defence raised obvious questions about the role of nurses involved. Should nurses not at the very least have *raised* the issue, and made it the subject of professional and public debate? In commenting on the *Report of the Cervical Cancer Inquiry*, Joy Bickley, the professional officer of the New Zealand Nurses' Association observed: 'Nurses who most appropriately should be the advocates for the patient, feel sufficiently intimidated by the medical staff . . . that even today they fail to confront openly the issue arising from the 1988 trial.'[17]

It would be a mistake, however, to see the problem exclusively in terms of either sexism or the non-assertiveness of nurses. There are also unresponsive institutional structures and frequently lack of support from nursing management and the nurses' own professional organizations.[18] As a 1988 Australian report on professional issues in nursing concludes, many nurses who wanted to give 'any effect to their ethical viewpoint' experienced a strong 'sense of powerlessness'. Their attempts to have an input into ethical decisions were 'usually met with resistance by those with the formal decision-making function'.[19]

All these factors conspire to make the adoption of the advocacy role a very hazardous and often futile activity for nurses. While individual nurses have been able to implement some reforms and achieve some victories on behalf of those for whom they care, others have paid the high price of dismissal and have found themselves charged with unprofessional or unlawful conduct.[20]

The fact that many nurses have suffered as a consequence of their attempts to act as patient advocates may explain why the contemporary nursing literature seems inclined to reject the advocacy role in favour of that of relational carer. For the relational carer the primary focus is not so much on right action or on 'fighting the system' for the patient's sake, but rather on the development of relational dispositions and virtues in the nurse–patient encounter. But, as we have already seen, the fact that the care approach does not challenge existing structures and relationships, even if these be unjust and unfair, is one reason why this approach is morally inadequate and ought to be rejected by proponents of both feminist and traditional approaches to ethics. Rather than see the care approach as a *moral* approach, it is perhaps best regarded as a set of coping strategies for the powerless and dispossessed.[21]

While adoption of the advocacy role has often been costly for individual nurses and may frequently have failed to achieve the goal of better patient care, it would none the less be a mistake, I believe, for nurses to reject the metaphor of the nurse as patient advocate. The central value of the metaphor lies in its power to shape actions. It focuses attention firmly on the proper primary 'object' of nursing care – the individual patient or client – and highlights such positive qualities as courage and assertiveness.[22] These qualities – traditionally strongly discouraged in nurses and women – are sorely needed if nurses are to fulfil their professional and moral responsibilities to patients. At the same time it must be realized, however, that the attempts by individual nurses to bring about change are not likely to be successful. To the extent that the main reasons for nurses feeling compelled to act as patient advocates are systemic, that is, have their source in social arrangements and institutional structures, such reforms require collective rather than individual action. To achieve success, nurses must act collectively. Individually, nurses are like dwarfs; collectively, they are a powerful giant. Nursing is the largest health-care profession and potentially has great strength. So far it has only rarely exercised its strength and hence might best be regarded as a powerful but slumbering giant.[23] This means that it would be best if nurses were to see themselves not only as patient advocates, but also as part of a potentially powerful professional group – a group that needs to mobilize itself for the sake of good patient care.

To be effective such change must, I believe, proceed on at least two levels. First, it must ensure that guidelines, policies and laws are sound; and second, it must pay attention to the soundness of the division of labour between nurses and doctors in different areas of health care.

End-of-Life Decisions

Because of the complexity of the health-care context and the various roles performed by doctors and nurses, there cannot be a uniform approach to reforms. Rather, any such reforms must proceed issue by issue, and must be justified primarily by the good of patients. Our focus will once again be on end-of-life decisions for competent patients. Professional nursing organizations have not been at the forefront of social and political debates directed at the implementation of structures and laws that would protect the patient's right to be self-determining at the end of life. This is true not only when it comes to voluntary euthanasia, but – at least in Australia – also as far as not-for-resuscitation orders, enduring powers of attorney and so-called living wills are concerned. Organized nursing is not generally a major player in public debates, and the silence of nursing organizations stands in stark contrast to the assertive and aggressive stance generally taken by professional medical associations on a wide range of social and ethical issues.

The Australian Medical Association (AMA), for example, has condemned point-blank as 'unethical' the introduction of legislation permitting voluntary euthanasia and medically assisted suicide in the Northern Territory of Australia.[24] The Australian Nursing Federation (ANF), on the other hand, has been silent on the matter, neither condemning nor supporting the legislation. One may attempt to justify the ANF's approach as the adoption of a neutral position, necessitated by the lack of unanimity among members of the Federation. But such attempts are clearly missing the point. There can be no neutral position on the issue of voluntary euthanasia. A so-called 'neutral' stance will implicitly support the status quo, and the status quo cannot be regarded as an acceptable option for nurses and for nursing. The point is not only that there are, as my arguments in chapter 8 have suggested, good reasons for thinking that existing laws prohibiting voluntary euthanasia and assisted suicide are discriminatory and unjust, there is also the professional commitment of nurses to the goal of patient self-determination. In other words, to the extent that nurses ought to *care* about the self-determination of patients, and about such principles as equality and justice at the end of life, they cannot, I believe, consistently maintain a position of 'neutrality' on the issue of voluntary euthanasia. To the extent that the status quo unjustifiably limits patient self-determination, and is unjust and unfair, it ought not, explicitly or implicitly, to be supported by professional nursing organizations.

If there are strong patient-centred reasons for seeking legal change, there are closely related nurse-centred reasons as well. As we have seen, the ANF exhorts nurses to 'respect the rights of persons to make informed choices in relation to their care.'[25] But how can nurses reasonably be expected to fulfil this obligation when their own Federation implicitly supports social arrangements that will prevent them from respecting the rights of their patients? Similarly, as we have seen, the American Nurses' Association (ANA) code states that nurses should act in ways that 'support and enhance the client's responsibility and self-determination to the greatest extent possible',[26] and yet the ANA adopted, in 1994, the position that nurses should not participate in assisted suicide or active euthanasia.[27] This means that the ANA is, on the face of it, exhorting nurses to act in accordance with two incompatible principles: that they should and should not act in ways that support and enhance their patients' responsibility and self-determination. It also means that individual nurses will frequently find themselves in situations where moral conflict is unavoidable, because they cannot fulfil both obligations at once. In other words, whatever nurses do in such situations, they may feel that they have failed morally – that they have either failed the patient by not respecting her right to be self-determining or that they have failed their profession by acting contrary to the law or the values articulated by their professional leaders.

If existing laws governing medical end-of-life decisions and the support by professional nursing organizations of the status quo stand in the way of good patient care, so does the division of professional and moral responsibility between doctors and nurses. Doctors are expected to devise treatment plans for patients, and nurses are expected to carry them out – even though nurses will often be better placed than doctors to develop the relevant insights into the patient's health-related needs and wants at the end of life. While there are thus once again good patient-centred reasons for challenging this division of labour, I am not aware that professional nursing organizations have acted decisively and assertively to bring about change. And yet, as long as the present division of labour between doctors and nurses persists, practising nurses will frequently and unavoidably find themselves in situations where they must choose between failing the patient or acting contrary to some other perceived professional or moral obligation.

Two recent empirical surveys demonstrate these difficulties well. According to a 1991 survey of 943 Australian nurses, conducted by myself and my colleague, Peter Singer, 55 per cent of respondents engaged in the care of terminally or incurably ill patients had been asked by a patient to hasten death – either by withholding or withdrawing treatment or by directly ending the patient's life through active euthanasia.[28] One in 10 of those asked to withhold treatment indicated that he or she had acted on a patient's request at least once – *without having been asked by the doctor to do so*; and among those who had been asked for active euthanasia the rate was one in 20 – where the action was again performed without medical authorization. When asked by a doctor to take part in an action that would directly and actively end a patient's life, 85 per cent of the nurses asked had done so.[29]

In response to an open-ended question as to why they withheld or withdrew treatment, without having been asked by a doctor to do so, almost two out of three nurses referred to the patient's wishes, sometimes stressing the rationality of the request and at others the intensity of the patient's wish to die. The same is true when it came to active voluntary euthanasia. Most answers indicated that respondents gave decisive weight to a reiterated request from the patient. Several mentioned discussions over some period of time, involving the family as well. One nurse explained her response by referring to 'the patient's desire to die knowing they were loved by someone because they were *listened* to'. Some worked under the implicit direction of doctors to increase narcotic infusions 'as necessary', but others had overridden a medical decision:

> I have temporarily sped up a morphine infusion to a greater rate than ordered on a terminally ill patient who had signed a form to reject treatment and be allowed to die. I had requested a medical order to increase the rate because the patient was in pain (unconscious but

moaning), but it had been refused. I gave the patient several bolus (unordered) doses during the shift because medical staff were wrong.

Another respondent wrote: 'The woman's request was pleading, and I felt it was honest. I did not wish to impose my will or the will of the doctor on this woman.' Other nurses explained their actions in the following way:

It was his wish. I had placed him on a pan and the last thing he said to me was 'Go away and let me die.' Standing outside the curtain I could hear him saying: 'Die you bastard, die!' When I went back in, he had arrested. I did not commence CPR although there was no Not for Resuscitation Order.

I felt it was immoral to go against the patient's expressed wishes.

[I acted] out of respect for the patient's wishes, as often nurses are the only people the patient has who can/will respect their feelings.

These nurses had acted without the authorization of the treating doctor – certainly in some and perhaps in most cases – because they believed that the doctor would not listen to their representation of the patient's point of view, and they had in most – if not in all – cases broken the law.

A 1996 US study, conducted by David Asch, a physician and member of the University of Pennsylvania's Center for Bioethics in Philadelphia, paints a somewhat similar picture.[30] Of 852 critical care nurses, 141 had received requests from patients or family members to perform euthanasia or to assist in suicide. 129 nurses stated that they had provided such assistance, sometimes without the advance knowledge or request of the doctor, and an additional 35 had withheld life-sustaining treatment that had been ordered by a doctor.

These American nurses gave very similar reasons to the ones advanced by their Australian colleagues for their actions – a profound responsibility for the patient's welfare and the fact that doctors are frequently unresponsive to the patient's point of view and unwilling to listen to nurses who may attempt to speak on the patient's behalf. As one nurse put it:

I have experienced tremendous frustration and anger with physicians who either stress the possibility of a good prognosis, giving false hope – or place their belief system above that of their patients. The physician spends 5 to 10 minutes each day with the patient and then leaves me to carry out his orders and deal with the patient and his/her family for 8 to 12 hours. I'm left with the dilemma of carrying out orders that I believe – and sometimes know – are not in the patient's best interests or what the patient or family has expressed as their desires.[31]

A study which shows that large numbers of nurses are willing to act contrary to institutional policies and the law, in attempts to meet the goals of good patient care, should, I would have expected, at the very least give some pause for thought. After all, might these findings not suggest that institutional policies, professional structures and laws are such that individual nurses – well aware of their impotence to change 'the system' – feel compelled to step outside the bounds of policy and law, for the sake of those for whom they care?

This was seemingly not a question the American Nurses' Association and the American Association of Critical Care Nurses put to themselves. Rather, in a joint public statement, coinciding with the publication date of the survey, the two organizations categorically declared: 'Nurses do not kill the patients entrusted to their care,' adding that the study was 'erroneous and not to be relied on'.[32] In other words, two professional nursing organizations chose to implicate the messenger, rather than give careful consideration to the message which, surely, would not have come as a total surprise to American nursing leaders. After all, the authoritative 1995 SUPPORT study had already referred to reports by nurses that the preferences of terminally ill patients frequently did change neither the behaviour of doctors nor the outcome of treatments.[33]

The important point here is that denial of the findings will not only implicitly support the status quo, but will also legitimize inaction on the part of nursing leaders. If it is denied point-blank that nurses ever 'kill' patients and that a study which purports to show that they do is flawed, then there is no need to look at ways in which a clearly unsatisfactory situation might be changed. But, in avoiding facing the issue squarely, nursing leaders are failing in their responsibilities to patients and to nurses. This suggests that, although it may still be appropriate to think of nurses as a group as a slumbering giant, a more appropriate metaphor for organized nursing might be that of a wakeful but timid giant – a giant who lacks the assertiveness and courage to do what, clearly, it ought to be doing.[34]

In an editorial accompanying the survey, Colleen Scanlon, a nurse and lawyer who directs the American Nurses' Association's Center for Ethics and Human Rights, accepts that some nurses may, in fact, practise euthanasia. But, she holds, the study does not allow us to draw any conclusions about the prevalence of such actions. The reason is that the questions put to nurses were ambiguous and that even those who might have acted entirely within prescribed guidelines may have been counted as performing euthanasia. Referring to the reported finding that many nurses had given a lethal amount of opiates to patients, Scanlon suggests that the administration of these drugs does not necessarily constitute euthanasia, but may have been an instance of good terminal care.[35]

But is this argument sound? Nurses participating in the study were not asked whether they had ever practised 'euthanasia' – a term that can be understood in a number of different ways – but rather whether they had ever performed 'an act with the specific intent of causing or hastening a patient's death . . . [by, for example,] providing an intentional overdose of narcotics or potassium chloride.'[36] Unless Scanlon assumes that some respondents did not read the instructions carefully, it is difficult to see how she could arrive at the conclusion that nurses who administered lethal doses of an opiate 'with the specific intent of causing or hastening a patient's death' were performing anything other than euthanasia in its 'classical' sense, that is, were intentionally ending the patient's life, for the patient's sake.[37]

Moreover, even if we were to accept that we cannot be entirely confident about the prevalence of 'euthanasia'-type actions by nurses, this would not significantly alter the importance of the study. The reason is that it is a mistake to think that the central issue is how often these nurses practised 'euthanasia' or engaged in some other end-of-life decision. As we have seen, there is, for a number of reasons (including the extreme 'constructability' of these kinds of decision) no bright line separating 'euthanasia' from other widely accepted practices known or intended to bring about the patient's death. What is centrally significant is that the study shows that many nurses implemented end-of-life decisions on their own, that is, without having been asked by a doctor to do so. This suggests that the problem is not only one of voluntary euthanasia not being lawful (this problem is, in principle, the same for nurses and for doctors), but also one of the role responsibilities of nurses when it comes to decision-making at the end of life. In other words, the central question for nurses is how they can adequately respond to patients' needs and wants at the end of life, when they lack the formal authority to take responsibility for end-of-life decisions.

David Asch, the author of the study, seems to have reached a similar conclusion when he holds that his survey has shown 'that these nurses struggle to uphold important personal values under extremely challenging circumstances – often with little support from physicians.'[38] This leaves us with the question of what should be done. Asch believes that, to the extent that national opinion surveys reveal that the majority of the public supports policies that would allow euthanasia under certain circumstances, '[t]he result of this study should prompt nurses, physicians, and other health care professionals to examine their practices more openly and collaboratively, with the aim of understanding and reducing disagreements over goals and plans.'[39]

On this point, Asch is surely right. Such examinations should focus not only on the question of whether there are any good reasons for health-care professionals continuing to adhere to the traditional distinctions between various consented-to end-of-life decisions, but also the important practical question of what role nurses and doctors should play in the decision-making process at the end of life. To illustrate the importance of the second point, let us assume that voluntary euthanasia has been legalized, as I have no doubt will soon be the case in many parts of the world. This would mean that the permissibility of medical end-of-life decisions would now no longer depend on such dubious distinctions as that between the directly intended and the merely foreseen death-producing (or death-allowing) consequences of various actions or omissions, but rather on the terminally ill patient's consent. This approach would overcome some of the obstacles that currently hamper good patient care: all terminally ill patients would now, in principle, be treated equally, and not be discriminated against on the basis of whether or not they needed life support, which they could then refuse, or whether a doctor was willing to stretch the notion of intent. There would no longer be any need for self-deception, for secrecy and for the abandonment of patients when they are most in need of care.

This is the theoretical view. In practice, the situation would most likely be very different. Good medical practice presupposes not only sound laws, but also sound decision-making structures. In many countries, competent patients have long had a well-recognized moral and legal right to refuse medical treatment for themselves, and there is also a general consensus that adequate pain and symptom control may be administered, even if this is expected to hasten death. None the less, in practice patients are not always free to refuse treatment for themselves, and frequently will not receive adequate pain and symptom control.[40] These findings should not be interpreted as demonstrating that doctors are villains and nurses are exemplars of moral and professional virtue; rather, if doctors are less sensitive to the patient's needs and wants, this is more likely than not due to the fact that doctors lack the kind of particularized insights into the patient's wishes at the end of life that is more readily available to nurses.

If this is correct, it means that ways must be found to ensure not only that we have the correct substantive principles and laws in place, but also that decision-making structures are such that they will allow those best situated in relation to the patient to have final responsibility for decision-making at the end of life – and in many cases, this will be the nurse, rather than the doctor.

The Need for Collective Action

Such fundamental changes in laws and in formal decision-making structures are difficult for individuals to bring about. For individuals engaged in direct patient care, it will often seem easier to circumvent established policies and laws, for the sake of good patient care. The widespread silent practice of voluntary euthanasia by doctors and nurses may be an example of this.[41] But the covert breaching of policies and laws is not an acceptable solution.

The reasons are fairly obvious. Not only are such actions in the long term likely to undermine trust and cooperation between different members of the health-care team (Nigel Cox's unlawful action and the difficult position Roisin Hart found herself in as a consequence can serve as an example), they may also undermine respect for the law, put individual health-care professionals at risk and – most important – do not allow for public scrutiny and fail to ensure that all patients will be receiving the kind of care they ought to be receiving. In other words, covert individual action will, at best, deal with some of the symptoms of systemic failure, but does not address itself to the source of the problem.

A doctor has presented the following vision to highlight the need for structural change when it comes to the *saving* of lives. The same kind of analogy might also be applied, at least in some settings, when it comes to saving individual patients from the fate of *not* being allowed or helped to die:

> You know, sometimes I feel like this. There I am standing by the shore of a swiftly flowing river and I hear the cry of a drowning man. So I jump into a river, put my arms towards him, pull him to the shore and apply artificial respiration. Just when he begins to breathe, there is another cry for help. So I jump into the river, reach him, pull him to shore, apply artificial respiration, and then just as he begins to breathe, there is another cry for help. So back into the river again, reaching, pulling, applying, breathing and then another yell. Again and again, without end, goes the sequence. You know, I am so busy jumping in, pulling them to shore, applying artificial respiration, that I have *no* time to see who the hell is upstream pushing them all in.[42]

The only way in which individual patients who are nearing the end of their lives can be prevented from needing 'rescuing' is through the implementation of 'upstream' structural changes. Leah Curtin presents the case of a nurse who has just been fortunate enough to be 'let off' with a severe reprimand for not having resuscitated a terminally ill young child, Christy:

> I feel no guilt about my care for Christy . . . However, there are other children like Christy; doctors still won't write no code orders

(no matter what they may say) and the hospital policy remains the same. If I fail to resuscitate some other dying child, I don't know what will happen. What will (or should) I do when faced with similar situations in the future?[43]

What I am suggesting, then, is that health-care professionals show a healthy disrespect for existing policies and laws determining end-of-life care – not by quietly breaching existing policies and laws, but by questioning them publicly and working towards systemic change. Covert action can, at best, help a few patients. *Systemic* change will minimize the need for rescue.

While both nurses and doctors have an obligation to seek systemic change, it would, I believe, be too optimistic to think that a majority of doctors and their professional organizations will in the near future willingly share formal responsibility for end-of-life decisions with nurses. Doctors might, in principle, recognize the need for clearly documented not-for-resuscitation orders, they may even support legislation allowing voluntary euthanasia, but this is not the same as saying that they would also be willing to relinquish their position of 'captain of the team'. If this is correct, the burden of attempting to bring about structural change in the doctor–nurse relationship will fall squarely on the shoulders of nurses and their professional organizations.

How any such changes are best to be achieved will very much depend on the relevant political, social and professional context in which individual nurses and their organizations find themselves. In some contexts, it might be most appropriate for the nursing profession to concentrate its energies on producing sound and high-profile research that demonstrates that current arrangements do not serve patients well and that existing laws regulating end-of-life decisions for competent terminally ill patients are unfair and unjust, and do not allow for public scrutiny. In others, it might be more appropriate for it to direct its energies towards attacking the powerlessness and corruption that have enveloped and crippled the aspirations of nurses for a very long time.[44] And in some contexts, there might be merit in focusing on statutory protection of patients' rights, and in creating protective frameworks for nurses who 'blow the whistle' on doctors who fail to respect the patients' right to be self-determining at the end of life. While strike action always requires strong moral justification, it may be justifiable in some circumstances. In almost all cases, there would have to be some emphasis on nursing education, and on ensuring that individual nurses are not only good carers, but also good and assertive moral reasoners who are willing to defend publicly the rights and interests of those for whom they care. To the extent, however, that organized nursing has not, until now, chosen to exercise its very great strength, it could well be that the most important contribution individual nurses can make at this point in time is to devise avenues for collective action, and to cajole their professional organizations into fulfilling their political and social responsibilities through the adoption of an assertive and courageous stance in outlining and defending an appropriate patient-centred response to decision-making at the end of life. Such an approach would not only, I believe, have to include the endorsement of voluntary euthanasia and assisted suicide, but would also seek to ensure that nurses, at the very least, share formal responsibility in the making of end-of-life decisions with doctors.

My own view would be that ultimately, at least in the area of terminal care, final decision-making authority should be vested in nurses. While this would not exclude shared decision-making, that is, the consultation of doctors by nurses, the final responsibility would be the nurse's. This means that the relevant nurse (a primary care nurse, perhaps) would not only be able to write not-for-resuscitation orders for patients, take responsibility for the administration of adequate pain and symptom control, the employment or non-employment of life-sustaining treatment, but also for the provision of voluntary euthanasia and assisted suicide. While doctors would function as technical advisers and would, if so requested, provide technical services, they would hold no formal decision-making authority.[45]

It is true that this is a somewhat utopian model and may be more difficult to implement than a model that aims at shared decision-making only, while leaving the formal decision-making powers in the hands of doctors. The reason why I am advocating that authority be placed in the hands of nurses is that I am somewhat dubious about the general success of shared decision-making in a climate where the doctor's traditional position as decision-maker is securely buttressed by law and tradition. As one weary nurse put it: 'You can put forward your opinion as many times as you like but the doctors have the ultimate decision on treatment, it is entirely up to them.'[46]

Would nurses want this role, and would they be prepared to provide direct help in dying to terminally ill patients who request it? There are no good reasons for thinking that they would not. According to the above Australian study, some 78 per cent of nurses surveyed wanted the law changed to allow voluntary euthanasia to be performed by doctors, and among 1210 US oncology nurses, 47 per cent of respondents indicated that they would vote to legalize physician-assisted death, with 16 per cent indicating that they would, if instructed by a doctor to do so, administer a lethal injection to a competent, terminally ill patient who requests such assistance.[47] These surveys suggest that there is considerable support for voluntary euthanasia among nurses and, as we know, many nurses are already, often without having been asked by the doctor to do so, implementing end-of-life decisions on behalf of those for whom they care.[48] Moreover, even if some nurses today feel somewhat reluctant to accept this responsibility, what does this show? It may show no more than that these nurses have been socialized, corrupted if you like,[49] into accepting a subservient role – a role that is, of course, incompatible with professionalism.

Conclusion

Social institutions are not natural phenomena. Rather, they operate in particular social and historical contexts and more often than not are the outcome of accidental or arbitrary social arrangements; they are also frequently· bastions of the unequal distribution of power and privilege. Medicine and nursing, and the traditional relationship between doctors and nurses, are examples of this, and of the sexism that has, for a very long time, shaped the relations between women and men. The traditional assumption, supported by laws and various institutional structures, that nursing is subservient to medicine must be seen in this historical context. Given that there are good reasons for rejecting it, individual nurses and their professional organizations have a moral obligation to seek to bring about change. Rational moral argument and debate must play a central role in this. If nurses fail to free themselves from the historical constraints that have led to the assumption that it is appropriate for doctors to make end-of-life decisions, and for nurses to carry them out, then they have not only failed their patients but also themselves.

Notes

Chapter 1   Two Nurses

1 On the centrality of this question for nursing, see also M. Benjamin and J. Curtis, 'Ethical autonomy in nursing', in Donald Van De Veer and Tom Regan (eds), *An Introduction to Health Care Ethics* (1987), p. 395.

2 See Nina Fletcher et al., *Ethics, Law and Nursing* (1995), pp. 209–10; also Peter Singer, *Rethinking Life and Death* (1994), pp. 139–140.

3 Janet Snell, 'Dr Cox: the nurse's story', *Nursing Times* (7 Oct. 1992), p. 19.

4 Barbara Huttmann, 'One nurse's story: what I had to do for my patient Mac', *Nursing Life* (Jan./Feb. 1984), p. 21.

5 See, for example, James L. Muyskens, *Moral Problems in Nursing: A philosophical investigation* (1982); Robert M. Veatch and Sara T. Fry, *Case Studies in Nursing Ethics* (1987); Martin Benjamin and Joy Curtis, *Ethics in Nursing*, 3rd edn (1992); Megan-Jane Johnstone, *Bioethics: A nursing perspective*, 2nd edn (1995).

6 The Nightingale Pledge is one of the earliest nursing codes of ethics. It was devised in 1893 in the United States by Lystra Grecter, principal of the Farrand Training School for Nurses at the Harper Hospital in Detroit. See Ian E. Thompson, Kath M. Melia and Kenneth M. Boyd, *Nursing Ethics*, 2nd edn (1988), p. 55.

7 See John O. Godden, 'No longer silent', *Humane Medicine* (May 1988), p. 1.

8 Margaret Steinfels, 'Ethics, education, and nursing practice', *Hastings Center Report* (August 1977), pp. 20–1.

9 Jean Watson citing N. Noddings in 'Introduction: an ethics of caring/curing/nursing *qua* nursing', in Jean Watson and Marilyn

A. Ray (eds), *The Ethics of Care and the Ethics of Cure: Synthesis and chronicity* (1988), p. 2.

10 Margaret Adams, 'The compassion trap', in Vivian Gornick and Barbara K. Moran (eds), *Women in Sexist Society: Studies in power and powerlessness* (1971), pp. 401–16.

11 H. Morrow, 'Nurses, nursing and women', *World Health Organisation Chronicle* (1986), pp. 216–21.

12 American Nurses Association, *Facts About Nursing, 1986–1987* (1987).

13 Florence Nightingale, *Cassandra* (1979), p. 49.

Chapter 2 A History of Subservience

1 *Webster's Third New International Dictionary of the English Language* (1971), vol. II, p. 1551.

2 Lavinia L. Dock and Isabel Maitland Stewart, *A Short History of Nursing*, 3rd edn (1934; first edition 1920), p. 4.

3 Lisa H. Newton, 'In defence of the traditional nurse', *Nursing Outlook* (June 1981), pp. 348–54.

4 See R. H. Shyrock, *The History of Nursing* (1959).

5 Barbara Melosh, *'The Physician's Hand' – Work Culture and Conflict in American Nursing* (1982), p. 3.

6 V. L. Bullough and B. Bullough, *The Care of the Sick: The emergence of modern nursing* (1979); Margaret Connor Versluysen, 'Old wives' tales? Women healers in English history', in Celia Davies (ed.), *Rewriting Nursing History* (1980), pp. 175–99.

7 M. Benjamin and C. Curtis, 'Ethical autonomy in nursing', in Donald Van De Veer and Tom Regan (eds) *An Introduction to Health Care Ethics* (1987), p. 395.

8 Karl Marx, 'Eighteenth Brumaire', in Karl Marx and Friedrich Engels, *Selected Works* (1975), p. 96.

9 Karl Marx, 'The German ideology', in L. D. Easton and K. H. Gudat (eds), *Writings of the Young Marx on Philosophy and Society* (1967), p. 421.

10 See, for example, Max Black (ed.), *Models and Metaphors* (1962); Andrew Ortony (ed.), *Metaphor and Thought* (1979); George Lakoff and Mark Johnson, 'Conceptual metaphor in everyday language', *Journal of Philosophy*, 78 (Aug. 1980), pp. 435–86. George Lakoff and Mark Johnson, *Metaphors we Live by* (1980); Janet Martin Soskice, *Metaphor and Religious Language* (1985); James F. Childress, 'Metaphor and analogy', in W. T. Reich (ed.), *Encyclopedia of Bioethics* (1995), pp. 1765–73.

11 As cited by Andrew Jameton: *Nursing Practice: The ethical issues*

(1984), p. 21. Florence Nightingale herself did not appear to believe that being a 'good woman/mother' was sufficient for being a good nurse. While Florence Nightingale would have regarded being a 'good woman' (a woman of good character) as a necessary condition for being a good nurse, it was not a sufficient one. As she put in *The Art of Nursing*: 'It has been said and written scores of times that every woman makes a good nurse. I believe, to the contrary, that the very elements of nursing are all but unknown' (1946, p. 7). Elsewhere she wrote: 'It seems a commonly received idea among men, and even among women themselves, that it requires nothing but a loving heart, the want of an object, and a general disgust or incapacity for other things to turn a woman into a good nurse. This reminds me of the parish where a stupid old man was set to be schoolmaster because he was "past keeping the pigs".' (*Notes on Nursing* (1952, p. 143); first published in 1859).

12   See, for example, Max Black, 'Metaphor', in Max Black (ed.), *Models and Metaphors*, pp. 25–47.

13   Gerald R. Winslow, 'From loyalty to advocacy: a new metaphor for nursing', *Hastings Center Report* (June 1984), p. 32. In this and the next chapter I draw extensively on Winslow's excellent analysis.

14   See, for example, Gerald R. Winslow, 'From loyalty to advocacy'; Michael Bayles, 'Betwixt and between: juggling ethical responsibilities in today's nursing scene', *Canadian Nurse*, 78 (1982), pp. 36–9; J. Ashley, *Hospitals, Paternalism and the Role of the Nurse* (1977); M. Josephine Flaherty, *Nursing Ethics: Theories and pragmatics* (1982), pp. 67–78.

15   Sarah Dock, 'The relation of the nurse to the doctor and the doctor to the nurse', *American Journal of Nursing*, 17 (1917), p. 394. Cited in Martin Benjamin and Joy Curtis, 'Ethical autonomy in nursing'. (Sarah Dock was an influential leader in the nursing profession at the time.)

16   This characterization of nurses appeared in a 1903 issue of the *Journal of the American Medical Association* and is cited by Barbara Ehrenreich, 'The purview of political action', in National League of Nursing, *The Emergence of Nursing as a Political Force* (1979), p. 13.

17   Brian Abel-Smith, *A History of the Nursing Profession* (1960), p. 52. The discussion in this chapter owes much to this excellent account of the recent history of nursing.

18   A. J. Davis and M. A. Aroskar, *Professional Ethics and Institutional Constraints in Nursing Practice* (1978), p. 32.

19   Abel-Smith, *A History of the Nursing Profession*, p. 9. See also Cecil Woodham-Smith, *Florence Nightingale* (1951), p. 51, and Gerald Bowman, *The Lamp and the Book* (1967), p. 21.

20   Florence Nightingale, 'Suggestions on the subject of providing training and organising nurses for the sick poor in workhouse infirmaries': *Letter to Sir Thomas Watson, Bart.*, member of the committee appointed by the President of the Poor Law Board, p. 1: London, 19th January 1867: British Library of Political and Economic Science Pamphlet Collection (Coll./c/x3), as cited by Abel-Smith, *A History of the Nursing Profession*, p. 5.

21   One of Florence Nightingale's pupils, Miss Pringle, wrote after 12 years' practical experience of hospital nursing: 'Some of the nurses were the best type of women – clever, dutiful, cheerful, and kind, endowed above all with that motherliness which is the most precious attribute of a nurse.' Cited by Abel-Smith, *A History of the Nursing Profession*, p. 5.

22   Charles Dickens, *Martin Chuzzlewit* (1968). In the preface to the 1849 cheap edition, Dickens made it clear that his tale was intended to reveal the evils of contemporary hospitals and the short-comings of persons then working as nurses. Nineteen years later, in the preface to the 'Charles Dickens Edition', Dickens wrote that Sarah Gamp and Betsy Prig had been 'fair specimens' of nurses in the early 1840s, but that since then 'that class of persons' had 'greatly improved through the agency of good women'. (The prefaces are reprinted in the 1968 Penguin edition, pp. 39–42.)

23   Ibid., p. 378.

24   Ibid., pp. 378–9.

25   Bowman, *The Lamp and the Book*, p. 20.

26   Abel-Smith, *A History of Nursing*, pp. 2–3.

27   As cited in C. Woodham-Smith, *Florence Nightingale*, p. 352.

28   'Hospital nurses' in *Fraser's Magazine*, May 1848, cited by Katherine Williams, 'From Sarah Gamp to Florence Nightingale: a critical study of hospital nursing systems 1840–1897', in Celia Davies (ed.), *Rewriting Nursing History* (1980), p. 54.

29   See Abel-Smith, *A History of the Nursing Profession*, pp. 10–11, and Bowman, *The Lamp and the Book*, p. 22.

30   Mary Wollstonecraft, *A Vindication of the Rights of Woman (1792)* (1967).

31   'On liberty' was published in 1859 and 'On the subjection of women' in 1869. 'On liberty' is reprinted in E. A. Burtt (ed.), *The English Philosophers from Bacon to Mill* (1939), pp. 949–1041. 'On the subjection of women' is reprinted in A. S. Rossi (ed.), *Essays on Sex and Equality* (1970), pp. 125–242.

32   *Australian Women's Magazine and Domestic Journal* (June 1884), p. 826; *Women's World* (June 1886), p. 86. I owe these (and many later) references to Monica Mackay, *Handmaidens of Medicine: Hospital nursing*

in Victoria 1880–1905 (unpublished Master of Economics thesis, Monash University, 1983), p. 73, and its excellent research on original sources.

33 Abel-Smith, *A History of the Nursing Profession*, p. 17. See also J. Perkins, *Women and Marriage in Nineteenth Century England* (1987) and K. Williams: 'Ideologies of nursing: their meanings and implications', in R. Dingwall and J. McIntosh (eds), *Readings in the Sociology of Nursing* (1978), pp. 36–44.

34 Myra Stark, 'Introduction' in Florence Nightingale, *Cassandra* (1979), p. 4.

35 See L. M. Hektor, 'Florence Nightingale and the women's movement: friend or foe?', *Nursing Inquiry*, 1 (1994), p. 41.

36 R. Strachey, *The Cause: A short history of the women's movement in Great Britain* (1928), p. 95, as quoted by L. M. Hektor, 'Florence Nightingale . . .', p. 41.

37 Cited by Myra Stark, 'Introduction', to *Cassandra*, p. 6.

38 Florence Nightingale, *Cassandra* (1852), with an introduction by Myra Stark, (1979).

39 Myra Stark, 'Foreword' to Florence Nightingale. *Cassandra*, p. 10.

40 C. Woodham-Smith, *Florence Nightingale*, p. 72.

41 *Encyclopaedia Britannica*, 16 (1961), p. 641.

42 See also L. M. Hektor, 'Florence Nightingale . . .'

43 See Brian Abel-Smith: *A History of the Nursing Profession*, p. 21.

44 It is true, Florence Nightingale did not want blind obedience; she wanted *intelligent* obedience. As she put it in her *Notes on Nursing:* 'Let no woman suppose that obedience to the doctor is not absolutely necessary. Only neither doctor nor nurse lay sufficient stress upon *intelligent* obedience, upon the fact that obedience *alone* is a very poor thing.' *Notes on Nursing* (first published 1859), (1952), p. 5.

45 See Susan Sontag, *Illness as Metaphor* (1959), pp. 273–84; also James F. Childress, 'Metaphor and Analogy'.

46 Gerald Winslow, 'From loyalty to advocacy', p. 33.

47 St John's House, King's College Hospital, 'Hints for Nurses', p. 1, cited by Katherine Williams, 'From Sarah Gamp to Florence Nightingale', p. 69.

48 Grace Jennings Carmichael, *Hospital Children: Sketches of life and character at the Children's Hospital Melbourne* (1891).

49 Carmichael, *Hospital Children*, p. 66.

50 The reforms envisaged by Florence Nightingale did, after all, have as one of their central planks the idea that the control of the nursing staff as to discipline and teaching be taken out of the hands of men, to be firmly lodged in the hands of a woman. As Nightingale put

it in a letter to Mary Jones: 'The whole reform in nursing both at home and abroad has consisted in this; to take all power over Nursing out of the hands of men, and put it in the hands of *one female trained* head and make her responsible for everything (regarding internal management and discipline) being carried out. Usually it is the Medical staff who have injudiciously interfered as "Masters". How much worse it is when it is the Chaplain . . . Don't let the Doctor make himself Head Nurse.' Cited in Abel-Smith, *A History of the Nursing Profession*, p. 25.

51 Charlotte M. Perry, 'Nursing ethics and etiquette', *American Journal of Nursing* (April 1906), pp. 450–1, cited by Gerald Winslow, 'From loyalty to advocacy', p. 33.

52 Isabel Hampton Robb, *Nursing Ethics: For hospital and private use*, first published in 1900; 2nd edn (1928), p. 173.

53 As cited by Richard Trembath and Donna Hellier, *All Care and Responsibility: A history of nursing in Victoria 1850–1934* (1987), p. 28.

54 R. H. McNeill, 'The ideal nurse', *Australasian Nurses Journal*, 8 (June 1910), p. 194.

55 Sarah Dock, 'The relation of the nurse to the doctor and the doctor to the nurse', p. 394.

56 Isabelle Rathie is cited by Richard Trembath and Donna Hellier in *All Care and Responsibility*, p. 19.

57 As cited by Megan-Jane Johnstone, *Nursing and the Injustices of the Law* (1994), p. 133.

58 As cited by Martin Benjamin and Joy Curtis, 'Ethical autonomy in nursing' (1987), p. 394.

59 'Nurses' schools and illegal practice of medicine', *Journal of the American Medical Association*, 47 (1906), p. 1835. (I owe this reference to Megan-Jane Johnstone, *Nursing and the Injustices of the Law* (1994), p. 16.)

60 Janet Wilson James, 'Isabel Hampton Robb and the professionalisation of nursing in the 1890's', in M. J. Vogel and C. E. Rosenberg (eds), *The Therapeutic Revolution: Essays in the social history of medicine* (1979), p. 2, as cited by Monica Mackay, *Handmaidens of Medicine*, p. 146.

61 G. Burbridge, *Lectures for Nurses*, 4th edn (1950), pp. 26–7, as cited by Ann Woodruff, 'Divided loyalties – the nurse's dilemma', in Royal Australian Nursing Federation, *Ethics: Nursing perspectives* (1987), vol. 1, pp. 26–7.

62 Florence Nightingale, *Notes on Nursing*, p. 131.

63 Isabel M. Stewart, as cited by Andrew Jameton, 'Physicians and Nurses', p. 68.

64   Florence Nightingale, 'Nursing the sick', from *Dictionary of Medicine*, ed. Richard Quain (1882), p. 1048, as cited by Brian Abel-Smith: *A History of the Nursing Profession*, p. 22.

65   As cited by Brian Abel-Smith: *A History of the Nursing Profession*, p. 22.

66   Charlotte Haddon, 'Nursing as a profession for ladies', *St Paul's Monthly Magazine* (Aug. 1871), pp. 458 and 461, as cited by Brian Abel-Smith, *A History of the Nursing Profession*, pp. 186 and 283.

67   See Richard Trembath and Donna Hellier, *All Care and Responsibility*, p. 8; also Monica Mackay, *Handmaidens of Medicine*, pp. 74ff. and 131.

68   See n. 11 above.

69   Florence Nightingale, *Notes on Nursing* (1859), p. 143.

70   This is what Florence Nightingale says on p. 52 of *The Art of Nursing* (1946):

> I would earnestly ask my sisters to keep clear of both the jargons now current everywhere . . . of the jargon namely about the 'rights' of women, which urges women to do all that men do, including the medical and other professions, merely because men do it, and without regard to whether this *is* the best that women can do; and of the jargon which urges women to do nothing that men do, merely because they are women, and should be 'recalled to a sense of their duty as women' and because 'this is women's work' and 'that is men's' and 'these are things which women *should* not do', which is all assertions and nothing more. Surely woman should bring the best she has, *whatever* that is. . . . without attending to either of these cries.

See also Florence Nightingale, *Cassandra* (1979), and Andrea Dworkin's discussion of Florence Nightingale in 'The politics of intelligence', in Elizabeth Frazer, Jennifer Hornsby and Sabina Lovibond (eds), *Ethics: A feminist reader* (1992), pp. 100–31.

71   As cited by Richard Trembath and Donna Hellier, *All Care and Responsibility*, p. 16.

72   As cited by M. Mackay, *Handmaidens of Medicine*, p. 145.

73   Andrew Jameton, 'Physicians and nurses: A historical perspective', in B. A. Brody and H. T. Engelhardt, Jr (eds), *Bioethics: Readings and cases* (1987), pp. 68–9. See also J. A. Ashley, *Hospitals, Paternalism and the Role of the Nurse* (1976).

74   As cited in Margaret Connor Versluysen, 'Old wives tales?', in Celia Davies (ed.), *Rewriting Nursing History*, p. 182.

75   Florence Nightingale, *Cassandra*, p. 52.

76   See Monica E. Baly, 'Florence Nightingale and "her" schools of nursing', p. 51; 1890 Royal Commission Into Charitable Institu-

tions (Victoria), Minutes, p. 492; see also Beatrix Tracey, 'The ministering angel', *Lone Hand* (1 July 1908), p. 236. (I owe the last two references to Monica Mackay, *Handmaidens of Medicine*, pp. 55 and 57 respectively.)

77 Josephine L. De Pledge, 'Nursing as a profession', *Nursing Record* (6 July 1893), p. 336.

78 *Una Journal of Nursing*, 1 (1903), p. 33, as cited by Monica Mackay, *Handmaidens of Medicine*, p. 161.

79 *Fraser's Magazine*, May 1848, as cited by Katherine Williams, 'From Sarah Gamp to Florence Nightingale: A critical study of hospital nursing systems from 1840 to 1987', in Celia Davies (ed.), *Rewriting Nursing History*, p. 54.

80 *Medical Times and Gazette*, no. 80 (10 Jan. 1852), as cited by Katherine Williams: 'From Sarah Gamp to Florence Nightingale', p. 54.

81 *Australian Medical Journal* (15 June 1880), p. 274.

82 James Barrett, *Argus* (30 June 1885), p. 4, as cited by Monica Mackay, *Handmaidens of Medicine*, p. 46.

83 Letter to the Editor, *Argus* (8 June, 1885), as cited by Monica Mackay, *Handmaidens of Medicine*, p. 63.

84 Genesis 2:18: 'I will make a help meet for him.'

85 Haddon, 'Nursing as a profession for ladies', *St Paul's Monthly Magazine* (Aug. 1871), p. 458, as cited by Brian Abel-Smith, *A History of the Nursing Profession*, p. 19.

86 See, for example, Florence Nightingale's early feminist essay: *Cassandra*, and the introduction to it by Myra Stark. Lavinia Dock (who, together with Isabel Maitland Stewart, wrote the influential book *A Short History of Nursing*) was active in the American suffrage movement, and went to jail three times for her involvement in that cause. See K. L. Brand and L. K. Glass, 'Perils and parallels of women and nursing', *Nursing Forum*, 14 (1975), p. 169.

87 Andrew Jameton, 'Physicians and nurses', p. 68.

Chapter 3 Advocacy or Subservience for the Sake of Patients?

1 Personal communication. A good 60 years have passed since the incident occurred, but the nurse still does not want her identity revealed.

2 The story of the Tuskegee study is brilliantly retold by James H. Jones in *Bad Blood: The Tuskegee syphilis experiment* (1981). (To mark the 20th anniversary of the end of the Tuskegee study, and to

discuss its legacy, a number of articles by leading bioethicists have been published in the Nov./Dec. issue of the *Hastings Center Report*, 22 (1992), pp. 29–40.)

3   Ibid., p. 161.

4   Ibid., p. 163.

5   Ibid., p. 110.

6   See, for example, 'Where does loyalty to the physician end?' (editorial), *American Journal of Nursing*, 10 (Jan. 1910), pp. 230–1; 'Where does loyalty to the physician end?' (letters), *American Journal of Nursing*, 10 (Jan. 1910), pp. 274, 276. (I owe these reference to Gerald R. Winslow, 'From loyalty to advocacy: a new metaphor for nursing', *Hastings Center Report*, 14 (June 1984), p. 34.)

7   Parts of this chapter have greatly benefited from Gerald R. Winslow, 'From loyalty to advocacy'.

8   While the Tuskegee syphilis study is one of the most infamous and highly publicized episodes in the history of human subjects research, there are others as well. In a large-scale New Zealand experiment, for example, female patients were denied potentially effective treatment to determine the invasive potential of carcinoma *in situ* of the cervix. See *Report of the Cervical Cancer Inquiry*, prepared by the Committee of Inquiry into Allegations Concerning the Treatment of Cervical Cancer at National Women's Hospital and into Other Related Matters (1988). The story is recounted in S. Coney's book, *The Unfortunate Experiment* (1988).

9   See, for example, Erica Bates and Helen Lapsley, *The Health Machine: The impact of medical technology* (1985).

10   Stephen Rice, *Some Doctors make you Sick* (1988), p. 9.

11   Health Call, *Health Complaints Advisory Link Annual Report: 1 May 1986–30 April 1987* (1987).

12   *The Age* (Melbourne, 3 June 1995), p. 3.

13   Paul Starr, *The Social Transformation of American Medicine* (1982), pp. 379, 389; as cited by Gerald R. Winslow, 'From loyalty to advocacy', p. 36.

14   See Gerald R. Winslow, 'From loyalty to advocacy', p. 36.

15   An abridged version of the judgement, 'In the matter of Karen Quinlan, an alleged incompetent', is reprinted in B. Steinbock (ed.), *Killing and Letting Die* (1980), pp. 23–44.

16   *Report of the Study of Professional Issues in Nursing* (Melbourne: Health Department of Victoria, 1988), p. 163.

17   A. M. Sadler, Jr, B. L. Sadler, and A. A. Bliss, *The Physician's Assistant: Today and tomorrow* (1972), p. 63. (In 1972 neither England nor Australia had introduced nursing education in universities. Both countries have since moved towards higher education for nurses.)

18 The term 'physician extender' is used by Susan Costello, H. Tristram
    Engelhardt, Jr and Mary Ann Gardell, 'Licensing, certification, and
    the restraint of trade: the creation of differences among the health
    care professions', in Baruch A. Brody and H. Tristram Engelhardt,
    Jr (eds), *Bioethics: Readings and cases* (1987), pp. 89–95.

19 As cited by Michael Gawenda, 'The hospitals are sick. The symp-
    toms start here', *Age* (Melbourne): *Saturday Extra* (19 October 1985),
    p. 2. See also *Report of the Study of Professional Issues in Nursing*. For
    a discussion of the strike, see Megan-Jane Johnstone, *Bioethics: A
    nursing perspective*, pp. 342–8; and Carol Fox, *Enough is Enough: The
    1986 Victorian nurses' strike* (1991).

20 *Report of the Study of Professional Issues in Nursing*, p. 191.

21 This point is also noted by Gerald W. Winslow, 'From loyalty to
    advocacy', p. 37.

22 See, for example, Sandra Henry Kosik, 'Patient advocacy or fighting
    the system', *American Journal of Nursing*, 72 (Apr. 1972), pp. 694–
    8; Christine Spahn-Smith, 'Outrageous or outraged: a nurse advo-
    cate story', *Nursing Outlook* (Oct. 1980), pp. 624–5; Leah Curtin,
    'Case Study X: cardiopulmonary resuscitation and the nurse', in
    Leah Curtin and Josephine Flaherty (eds), *Nursing Ethics: Theories
    and pragmatics* (1982), pp. 293–4.

23 See, for example, Sara Paretsky, *Guardian Angel* (1987).

24 Sandra Henry Kosik, 'Patient advocacy or fighting the system',
    p. 694.

25 Patricia Murphy, 'Helping Joanne die with dignity – a nursing pro-
    file in courage', *Nursing* (Sept. 1990), pp. 45–9.

26 See, for example, Natalie Abrams, 'A contrary view of the nurse as
    patient advocate', *Nursing Forum*, XVII (1978), pp. 258–67; Leah
    L. Curtin: 'The nurse as advocate: a cantankerous critique', *Nursing
    Management* (May 1983), pp. 9–10.

27 Jeane C. Quint, 'Institutionalized practices of information control',
    Psychiatry, 28 (1965), pp. 119–32; as cited by Shelley van Kempen,
    'The nurse as client advocate', in Carolyn Chambers Clark and Carole
    A. Shea (eds), *Management in Nursing: A vital link in the health care
    system* (1979), p. 189.

28 M. P. Donahue, 'The nurse – a patient advocate?', *Nursing Forum*,
    17 (1978); as cited by Jean Jenny, 'Patient advocacy – another role
    for nursing?', *International Nursing Review*, 26 (1979), p. 176.

29 S. H. Kosik, 'Patient advocacy or fighting the system', p. 698.
    Nurses received considerable encouragement from proponents of
    the patient rights movement. See, for example, George J. Annas,
    'The patient rights advocate; can nurses effectively fill the role?',
    Supervisor Nurse, 5 (July 1974), pp. 21–5, and G. J. Annas and J. M.

Healey, 'The patient rights advocate: redefining the doctor-patient relationship in the hospital context', *Vanderbilt Law Review*, no. 243 (1974), pp. 266–8.

30   Patricia Fay, 'In support of patient advocacy as a nursing role', *Nursing Outlook*, 26 (Apr. 1978), pp. 252–3.

31   Jo Ann Ashley, *Hospitals, Paternalism, and the Role of the Nurse* (1976), p. 5.

32   See, for example, the 1973 International Council of Nurses *Code for Nurses*, which holds that '[t]he nurse's primary responsibility is to those people who require nursing care.' See also the 1980 report on revisions to the Principles of Medical Ethics endorsed by the American Medical Association, which states that '[t]he profession does not exist for itself; it exists for a purpose and increasingly that purpose will be defined by society.' (As quoted by Robert M. Veatch, 'Medical ethics: an introduction', in R. M. Veatch (ed.), *Medical Ethics* (1989), p. 22.)

33   See, for example, Carolla A. Quinn and Michael D. Smith, *The Professional Commitment: Issues and ethics in nursing* (1987), ch. 1.

34   Robert Barker, 'Care of the sick and cure of the disease: comment on "The Fractured Image"', in Stuart F. Spicker and Sally Gadow (eds), *Nursing: Images and ideals – Opening dialogue with the humanities* (1980), pp. 42–3. See also James L. Muyskens, *Moral Problems in Nursing: A philosophical investigation* (1982), pp. 31ff.

35   On this point, see also H. Tristram Engelhardt, Jr, 'Physicians, patients, health care institutions – and the people in between: nurses', in Anne Bishop and John R. Scudder, Jr, *Caring, Curing, Coping* (1985), p. 63.

36   Ibid., p. 62.

37   American Psychiatric Association, *Diagnostic and Statistical Manual of Mental Disorders*, 3rd edn (1980), as cited by Engelhardt, ibid., p. 71.

38   See Martin Benjamin and Joy Curtis, *Ethics in Nursing*, 3rd edn (1992), pp. 91–5.

39   Ibid., p. 92.

40   H. Tristram Engelhardt, Jr, 'Physicians, patients, health care institutions – and the people in between: nurses', pp. 62–79.

41   See, for example, Jean Watson, 'Introduction: an ethic of caring/curing/nursing *qua* nursing', in *The Ethics of Care and the Ethics of Cure: Synthesis in Chronicity*, ed. Jean Watson and Marilyn A. Ray (1988), pp. 1–3.

42   *Report of the Study of Professional Issues in Nursing* (Melbourne: Health Department of Victoria, 1988), pp. 25–6.

43 James L. Muyskens, *Moral Problems in Nursing*, p. 36.

44 Robert Zussman, *Intensive Care: Medical ethics and the medical profession* (1992), ch. 5, at p. 80.

45 Lisa Newton, 'In defense of the traditional nurse', *Nursing Outlook*, 29 (June 1981), pp. 348–54. See also Lisa H. Newton, 'A vindication of the gentle sister: comment on "The Fractured Image"', in Stuart F. Spicker and Sally Gadow (eds), *Nursing: Images and ideals*, pp. 34–40.

46 Lisa H. Newton, 'In defense of the traditional nurse', p. 350.

47 Of course, it also leaves open the question of whether bureaucratic, hierarchical structures are the ones we should adopt in the first place. While I believe that there might well be other and more satisfactory arrangements, I will set this question aside and not discuss it any further.

48 As H. Tristram Engelhardt, Jr, notes ('Physicians, patients, health care institutions' p. 68), the now famous phrase by which doctors were construed as 'captain of the ship', was used in the case of *McConnel* v. *Williams*, 361 Pa.355, 65 A. 2nd 243 (1959).

49 Lisa H. Newton, 'In defense of the traditional nurse', p. 351.

50 Ibid.

51 John Ladd, 'Some reflections on authority and the nurse', in Stuart F. Spicker and Sally Gadow (eds), *Nursing: Images and ideals* (1980), p. 171.

52 This point is made by Andrew Jameton, *Nursing Practice: The ethical issues*, p. 46. There might, however, be some advantage in having doctors – on account of their expertise – in charge of the treatment plans of emergency-prone patients *if* the agreed goal is to save life. This would ensure that the person most qualified to conduct the relevant procedure would not have to defer to the authority in charge of the overall treatment plan before implementing a procedure.

53 C. K. Hofling et al., 'An experimental study in nurse–physician relationships', *Journal of Nervous and Mental Disease*, 143 (1966), pp. 171–80, as cited by Martin Benjamin and Joy Curtis, *Ethics in Nursing*, p. 23.

54 Martin Benjamin and Joy Curtis, *Ethics in Nursing*, pp. 99–100.

55 Sarah Dock, 'The relation of the nurse to the doctor and the doctor to the nurse', *American Journal of Nursing*, 17 (1917), p. 394.

56 See Robert Baker, 'Care of the sick and cure of disease', p. 43.

57 Ibid., p. 45.

58 Ibid.

59 See also Andrew Jameton, *Nursing Practice*, p. 46.

60 Lisa H. Newton, 'In defense of the traditional nurse', p. 351.

61 Ibid., p. 352.
62 Ibid.
63 Ibid.
64 Susan Sherwin, *No Longer Patient: Feminist ethics and health care* (1992), p. 229.
65 Megan-Jane Johnstone, *Nursing and the Injustices of the Law* (1994), p. 1.
66 M. Thornton, 'A fair day's pay for work of equal value', *Lamp*, 41 (1984), p. 11, as quoted by Megan-Jane Johnstone: *Nursing and the Injustices of the Law*, p. 1.
67 See, for example, J. Ashley, *Hospitals, Paternalism and the Role of the Nurse* (1976), ch. 5; Andrew Jameton, *Nursing Practice*, ch. 3; Virginia S. Cleland, 'Sex discrimination: nursing's most pervasive problem', *American Journal of Nursing*, 81 (1981), pp. 1542–7; and Megan-Jane Johnstone, *Nursing and the Injustices of the Law*.
68 Andrew Jameton, *Nursing Practice*, pp. 47–8. On this point, see also Alasdair MacIntyre, 'To whom is the nurse responsible', in C. P. Murphy and H. Hunter (eds), *Ethical Problems in the Nurse – Patient Relationship* (1983), p. 82.

Chapter 4 Ethics

1 This chapter contains material from a number of earlier articles of mine, including: 'An ethical approach to IVF and ET: what ethics is all about', in W. Walters and P. Singer (eds), *Test-tube Babies* (1982), pp. 22–35; Helga Kuhse and Peter Singer, 'The nature of ethical argument', in P. Singer, H. Kuhse et al. (eds), *Embryo Experimentation* (1990), pp. 37–42, and draws especially on Peter Singer, *Practical Ethics* (1993), ch. 1 and James Rachels, *The Elements of Moral Philosophy*, 2nd edn (1993).
2 For an excellent survey of the field of ethics see Peter Singer (ed.), *A Companion to Ethics* (1991). See also R. B. Brandt, *Ethical Theory* (1959).
3 Here I follow James Rachels, *The Elements of Moral Philosophy*.
4 F. Dostoyevsky, *The Brothers Karamazov* (1964), vol. 1, pp. 77 and 274.
5 E. J. Carnell, *An Introduction to Christian Apologetics* (1950), as cited by R. B. Brandt, *Ethical Theory*, p. 67.
6 St Thomas Aquinas, *Summa Theologica*, II–II Q. XI, art. iii–iv, in *The Basic Writings of Saint Thomas Aquinas*, ed. Anton C. Pegis, vol. 1 (1946). (I owe this reference to H. Tristram Engelhardt, *The Foundations of Bioethics* (1986), p. 16 and subsequent communication.)

7 Williston Walker, *A History of the Christian Church* (1957), p. 367.
8 Joan C. Callahan, 'Basics and background', in Joan C. Callahan (ed.), *Ethical Issues in Professional Life* (1988), p. 12.
9 For a good collection of articles on the Divine Command Theory, see Paul Helm (ed.), *Divine Commands and Morality*, 1981.
10 Plato, 'Euthyphro', in *The Dialogues of Plato*, trans. Benjamin Jowett, ed. R. M. Hare and D. A. Russell (1970), vol. 1, pp. 35–56. For a discussion of this point, see also Peter Singer, *Practical Ethics*, 2nd edn (1993), pp. 3–4, and James Rachels, *The Elements of Moral Philosophy*, 2nd edn (1993), pp. 47–50.
11 It is sometimes thought that the problem raised by Plato can be avoided by postulating the goodness of God. If God is good, so the argument goes, then God would not approve of cannibalism and torture. But if we accept the view that good and bad are defined by reference to what God commands, then the notion that God is good is deprived of all meaning. For if 'good' means 'commanded by God', then 'God is good' would mean only 'God is commanded by God' – an empty self-referential truism.
12 Antony Flew, *God and Philosophy* (1966), p. 109. (I owe this reference to James Rachels, *The Elements of Moral Philosophy*, p. 47.)
13 But see my discussion below on *social practice*, where I touch on the vexed problem of moral relativism.
14 Plato, 'Euthyphro', p. 46.
15 See R. B. Brandt, *Ethical Theory*, pp. 56ff.
16 See, for example, G. E. Moore, *Principia Ethica* (1978); R. M. Hare, *Moral Thinking* (1981), ch. 4.
17 For a further discussion of this and some related points, see Martin Benjamin and Joy Curtis, *Ethics in Nursing*, 2nd edn (1986), pp. 5–11.
18 For an excellent brief discussion of natural law theory see Stephen Buckle, 'Natural law', in Peter Singer (ed.), *A Companion to Ethics*, pp. 161–74.
19 See also James Rachels, *The Elements of Moral Philosophy*, pp. 50–5.
20 H. Tristram Engelhardt, Jr, *The Foundations of Bioethics*, p. 30.
21 James Cook, *Captain Cook's Journal 1768–71*, ed. Capt. W. S. L. Wharton (1893), pp. 91–5, as quoted by H. Tristram Engelhardt, Jr, *The Foundations of Bioethics*, p. 30.
22 St Thomas Aquinas, *Summa Theologica*, II–II, pp. 153–4, as quoted by H. Tristram Engelhardt, Jr, *The Foundations of Bioethics*, p. 197.
23 J. Finnis, *Natural Law and Natural Rights* (1980).
24 Stephen Buckle, 'Natural law', in Peter Singer (ed.), *A Companion to Ethics*, p. 171.
25 See for example, Bernard Williams, *Ethics and the Limits of Philosophy*

(1985) and David B. Wong, *Moral Relativity* (1984). For a shorter statement of David Wong's views, see his 'Relativism', in Peter Singer (ed.), *Companion to Ethics* (1991), pp. 442–50. Rosemarie Tong, *Feminist Thought: A comprehensive introduction* (1989); and Carol Gilligan, *In a Different Voice: Psychological theory and women's development* (1982).

26   W. G. Sumner, *Folkways* (1934), pp. 418 and 28, as cited by R. B. Brandt, *Ethical Theory* (1959), p. 59.

27   Karl Marx, 'The German ideology', in *Writings of the Young Marx on Philosophy and Society*, ed. and trans. L. D. Easton and K. H. Gudat (1967), p. 463.

28   See James Rachels, 'Can ethics provide answers?', *Hastings Center Report*, 10 (June 1980), pp. 32–40.

29   David Hume puts this view in *A Treatise of Human Nature*, Book III, and in *An Inquiry Concerning the Principles of Morals*. The above paragraph covers a number of different views under the general term 'subjectivism'. For a more extensive discussion, see James Rachels, *The Elements of Moral Philosophy*, ch. 3. Rachels himself defends a form of subjectivism.

30   James Rachels, *The Elements of Moral Philosophy*, pp. 38–9.

31   See Justin Oakley, *Morality and the Emotions* (1992), ch. 4.

32   Asen Balikci, *The Netsilik Eskimo* (1970), pp. 148–9.

33   H. Tristram Engelhardt, Jr, *The Foundations of Bioethics*, p. 7.

34   David Hume, 'Essay on suicide', in S. Gorovitz et al. (eds), *Moral Problems in Medicine* (1976), p. 384.

35   See, for example, Helga Kuhse and Peter Singer, 'Individuals, humans and persons: the issue of moral status', in Peter Singer, Helga Kuhse et al., *Embryo Experimentation*, pp. 65–75.

36   David Hume, *An Enquiry Concerning the Principles of Morals*, Section IX, Part I.

37   Luke 6: 31; see also Matthew 7: 12.

38   Tobit 4: 15.

39   Matthew 22: 40.

40   *Encyclopaedia Britannica* (1975), vol. 4, p. 608.

41   *Analects* 15: 23 and 6: 28.

42   For this formulation of the categorical imperative see Immanuel Kant, *Groundwork of the Metaphysics of Morals*, trans. H. J. Paton (1976).

43   This position is attributed to Jeremy Bentham by John Stuart Mill, 'Utilitarianism' (1960; first published 1863), p. 58.

44   See R. M. Hare, *The Language of Morals* (1952); R. M. Hare, *Freedom and Reason* (1963); R. M. Hare, *Moral Thinking* (1981).

45 See Peter Singer, *Practical Ethics.*

46 John Rawls, *A Theory of Justice* (1973).

47 R. M. Dworkin, *Taking Rights Seriously* (1977), pp. 180 and 272.

48 For a discussion of the 'Ideal Observer Theory', see R. B. Brandt, *Ethical Theory*, pp. 173–6. The image of an 'archangelic viewpoint' is used by R. M. Hare, *Moral Thinking: Its levels, method and point* (1981), p. 44.

49 For a good account of the arguments for and against consequentialism, see Samuel Scheffler (ed.), *Consequentialism and its Critics* (1988).

50 See, for example, the excellent collection *Consequentialism and its Critics*, ed. Samuel Scheffler (1988).

51 Jeremy Bentham, *Principles of Morals and Legislation* (1948); John Stuart Mill, 'Utilitarianism', in various collections.

52 R. M. Hare states his basic position in *The Language of Morals* (1952); *Freedom and Reason* (1963); *Moral Thinking* (1981). For a brief outline of these views, see R. M. Hare, 'Universal prescriptivism', in P. Singer (ed.), *A Companion to Ethics*, pp. 451–63.

53 For a useful discussion of deontological approaches to ethics, see Tom L. Beauchamp and James F. Childress, *Principles of Biomedical Ethics*, 3rd edn (1989), ch. 2. See also Nancy (Ann) Davies, 'Contemporary deontology', in Peter Singer (ed.), *A Companion to Ethics*, pp. 205 18.

54 For a good discussion of absolutism, see the collection *Absolutism and Its Consequentialist Critics*, ed. J. G. Haber (1994).

55 Immanuel Kant, *The Moral Law.*

56 Kant, 'On a supposed right to lie from altruistic motives', in *Critique of Practical Reason and Other Writings in Moral Philosophy*, trans. Lewis White Beck (1949).

57 See Justin Oakley, 'Virtue ethics', *Ratio*, 9 (Sept. 1996), pp. 128–52.

58 John Rawls, *A Theory of Justice*, p. 190.

59 John Stuart Mill, 'Utilitarianism', in *Utilitarianism, On Liberty, and Essay on Bentham*, ed. Mary Warnock (1974).

60 R. M. Hare, *Moral Thinking*, p. 39; see also Robert M. Adams, 'Motive utilitarianism', *Journal of Philosophy*, 73 (1976); and Peter Railton, 'Alienation, consequentialism, and the demands of morality', in Samuel Scheffler (ed.), *Consequentialism and its Critics* (1988), pp. 93–133.

61 See, for example, Brad Hooker, 'Rule consequentialism', *Mind*, 99 (1990), pp. 67–77.

62 See, for example, Tom L. Beauchamp, 'What's so special about the virtues?', in Earl E. Shelp (ed.), *Virtue and Medicine* (1984),

pp. 307–27; Justin Oakley, 'Virtue ethics', forthcoming in *Ratio*, 9, no. 2 (Sept. 1996).

63 See, for example, Helga Kuhse, *The Sanctity-of-Life Doctrine in Medicine: A critique* (1987); Helga Kuhse and Peter Singer, *Should the Baby Live: The problem of handicapped infants* (1985).

64 James Rachels, *The Elements of Moral Philosophy*, p. 13; see also Peter Singer, *Practical Ethics*, pp. 12–14.

65 Peter Singer, *Practical Ethics*, pp. 12–13.

66 James Rachels, *The Elements of Moral Philosophy*, p. 13; see also Peter Singer, *Practical Ethics*, pp. 12–14.

67 Ibid., pp. 13–14.

68 James Rachels, *The Elements of Moral Philosophy*, p. 14.

69 See, for example, the Report of the Warnock Committee on *in vitro* fertilization, where committee members found that they agreed or could agree on solutions, even though they started from quite different value premises: *Report of the Committee of Inquiry into Human Fertilization and Embryology* (HMSO, London, cmnd 9314, 1984). The report, with two new chapters by Mary Warnock, was subsequently published as a book: Mary Warnock, *A Question of Life: The Warnock Report on human fertilisation and embryology* (1985).

70 For a brief discussion of some of the issues raised in this context, see R. M. Hare, 'Public policy in a pluralist society', in P. Singer, H. Kuhse et al., *Embryo Experimentation* (1990), pp. 183–94; for another approach, see H. Tristram Engelhardt, Jr, *The Foundations of Bioethics* (1986), esp. chs. 1 and 2.

Chapter 5 Women and Ethics

1 Aristotle, 'Politics', Book I, ch. 13.

2 See, e.g., *Philosophy of Woman*, ed. Mary Briody Mahowald (1978); *Philosophy and Women*, ed. Sharon Bishop and Majorie Weinzweig (1989); see also Genevieve Lloyd, *The Man of Reason: 'Male' and 'female' in Western philosophy* (1984).

3 Of all the influential political theorists, Rousseau devoted most attention to women and their role in society. How he should be understood, from a feminist point of view, is by no means uncontentious. For a sensitive discussion of the complexity of his views, and the various interpretations given to them, see Karen Green, *The Woman of Reason: Feminism, humanism and political thought* (1995), chs. 4 and 5.

4 Jean-Jacques Rousseau, *Emile*, trans. Barbara Foxley (1966).

5 Ibid., p. 321.
6 As quoted in Jane Roland Martin, *Reclaiming a Conversation: The ideal of the educated woman*, (1985), p. 41.
7 Rousseau, as quoted in ibid., p. 52.
8 Rousseau, *Emile*, p. 359.
9 Alfred Lord Tennyson, 'The Princess'. The poem can be found in various anthologies.
10 See Rosemarie Tong, *Feminine and Feminist Ethics*, (1993), pp. 28–30.
11 See, for example, Genevieve Lloyd, *The Man of Reason: 'Male' and 'female' in Western philosophy* (1984).
12 John Milton, *Paradise Lost*, Book 4, at l. 300; in *The Poetical Works of John Milton*, ed. H. C. Beeching (1916), p. 254.
13 Immanuel Kant, 'On the distinction of the beautiful and sublime in the interrelations of the two sexes', reprinted in Mary Briody Mahowald (ed.), *Philosophy of Woman* (1978), pp. 193–203. The quotations are from pp. 194 and 195.
14 Jean-Jacques Rousseau, *Emile*, pp. 340, 349, 350.
15 Sigmund Freud, 'Some psychical consequences of the anatomical distinction between the sexes', in *The Standard Edition of the Complete Psychological Works of Sigmund Freud*, trans. and ed. James Strachey (1961), vol. XIX, pp. 257–8, as quoted by Carol Gilligan, *In A Different Voice* (1982), p. 7.
16 Arthur Schopenhauer, 'On women', in Mary Mahowald (ed.), *Philosophy of Woman* (1983), p. 231 (emphasis in original).
17 Alison M. Jaggar, 'Feminist ethics: projects, problems, prospects', in Claudia Card (ed.), *Feminist Ethics* (1991), p. 79.
18 Theresa Harris, *Woman: The Angel of the Home and the Saviour of the World* (1890), p. 1, as cited by Monica Mackay, *Handmaidens of Medicine: Hospital nursing in Victoria 1880–1905* (unpublished Master of Economics thesis, Monash University, 1983), p. 134.
19 Donna Dickinson (ed.), *Woman in the Nineteenth Century and Other Writings by Margaret Fuller* (1994).
20 The above passage is quoted in Jean Grimshaw, 'The idea of a female ethic', in Jean Grimshaw, *Feminist Philosophers: Women's perspectives on philosophical traditions* (1986), p. 200.
21 See, for example, Nel Noddings, *Caring: A feminine approach to ethics and moral education* (1984).
22 Helen Bequaert Holmes, 'A call to heal medicine', in *Hypatia* (special issue on feminist ethics and medicine), 4, no. 2 (1989), pp. 2 and 3.
23 Martha Lear, *Heartsounds* (1980), pp. 38–9.
24 There is considerable debate as to whether Rousseau believed that

his account reflected his views on 'the true nature' of women and men, or whether it was based on mere expediency. S. Moller Okin (*Women in Western Political Thought* (1980), pp. 130ff.) puts forward a convincing argument, according to which Rousseau was not so much concerned with 'the nature' of women and men as with familial and social stability that would serve everyone (and most of all men) well.

25 Mary Wollstonecraft, *A Vindication of the Rights of Woman* (1967), pp. 68 and 69.

26 Ibid., p. 50

27 Ibid., p. 42.

28 The term 'familiar ghetto' is Margaret Urban Walker's, in 'Moral understandings: Alternative "epistemology" for a feminist ethics', *Hypatia*, 4 (1989), p. 16.

29 Beverley Wildung Harrison, *Our Right to Choose: Toward a new ethics of abortion* (1983), pp. 39–40, as cited by Janice G. Raymond, 'Reproductive gifts and gift giving: the altruistic woman', *Hastings Center Report* (Nov./Dec. 1990), p. 8.

30 Ibid., p. 62.

31 For an early 'essentialist' view see, for example, Mary Daly, *Gyn/Ecology: The metaethics of radical feminism* (1978). For a critique of essentialism see, Elizabeth Spelman, *Inessential Woman* (1988); for a defence, see Diana Fuss, *Essentially Speaking: Feminism, nature and difference* (1989); and Martha C. Nussbaum, 'Human functioning and social justice: in defense of Aristotelian essentialism', *Political Theory*, 20 (May 1992), pp. 202–46.

32 Carol Gilligan, *In A Different Voice: Psychological theory and women's development* (1982); Carol Gilligan, 'Moral orientation and moral development', in Eva Feder Kittay and Diana T. Meyers, *Women and Moral Theory* (1987), pp. 19–33.

33 See, for example, Eva Feder Kittay and Diana T. Meyers (eds), *Women and Moral Theory*. (This book is devoted to a discussion of various implications of Gilligan's work.)

34 For an excellent concise account of the history of feminist ethics, see Alison M. Jaggar, 'Feminist ethics: projects, problems, prospects', in Claudia Card (ed.), *Feminist Ethics* (1991), pp. 78–104.

35 Nancy Chodorow, 'Family structure and feminine personality', in M. Z. Rosaldo and L. Lamphere (eds), *Woman, Culture and Society* (1974); Nancy Chodorow, *The Reproduction of Mothering* (1978). See also Chodorow's more recent collection of essays, *Feminism and Psychoanalytic Theory* (1989). For a comprehensive recent discussion of Gilligan and feminist ethical theory, see Susan J. Hekman, *Moral*

Voices – Moral Selves (1995). Hekman provides a brief but useful discussion of Chodorow's views, and some of the debates surrounding them, on pp. 67ff.

36 Carol Gilligan, *In a Different Voice*, pp. 7–8.
37 Ibid., p. 2.
38 Ibid., pp. 173–4.
39 See also Carol Gilligan, 'Moral orientation and moral development', pp. 19–33.
40 Carol Gilligan, *In a Different Voice*, p. 18.
41 Lawrence Kohlberg, *The Philosophy of Moral Development* (1981); Lawrence Kohlberg, *Essays in Moral Development* (1981), vol. 1, pp. 409–12.
42 Carol Gilligan, *In a Different Voice*, p. 73.
43 Ibid., pp. 25–6. The original Heinz Dilemma is found in Lawrence Kohlberg, 'Stage and sequence: the cognitive development approach to socialization', in D. A. Goslin (ed.), *Handbook of Socialization Theory and Research* (1969), p. 379.
44 Ibid., p. 25.
45 Carol Gilligan, *In a Different Voice*, pp. 26–7.
46 Ibid., p. 28.
47 Ibid.
48 Ibid.
49 Ibid., pp. 28 and 29.
50 Ibid., p. 30.
51 Ibid., pp. 70ff.
52 Carol Gilligan bases her view that women and men (and boys and girls) typically approach ethics differently on those of the psychologist Nancy Chodorow (*In a Different Voice*, pp. 7–9). According to Chodorow, general and near universal differences in the male and female personality and roles are the result not of men's and women's anatomy, but rather of women's involvement in early child care – and of girls' identifying themselves as female, and of experiencing themselves as like their mothers. Nancy Chodorow, 'Family structure and feminine personality', in M. Z. Rosaldo and L. Lamphere (eds), *Woman, Culture and Society* (1974); Nancy Chodorow, *The Reproduction of Mothering* (1978).
53 Carol Gilligan, 'Moral orientation and moral development', pp. 19–33; and Carol Gilligan, *In a Different Voice*, p. 174.
54 At least one philosopher holds that Amy – in her discussion of the above-mentioned Heinz dilemma – does not adopt a care approach, but that her way of dealing with the dilemma shows her to be reasoning according to Kantian principles of justice. (Jonathan Dancy,

'Caring about justice', *Philosophy*, 67 (Oct. 1992), pp. 447–66, at 462).

55 This would, on my reading, be the likely response of someone who adopted the approach put forward by Nel Noddings in *Care: A feminine approach to ethics* (1984). See also the discussion of her views in chs. 6 and 7 below.

56 John M. Broughton, 'Women's rationality and men's virtues: a critique of gender dualism in Gilligan's theory of moral development', *Social Research*, 50 (Aug. 1983), pp. 597–642; J. C. Tronto, 'Beyond gender difference to a theory of care', *Signs*, 12 (1987), pp. 644–63.

57 See, for example, Catherine C. Greeno and Eleanor E. Maccoby, 'How different is the "different voice"?', in Mary Jeanne Larrabee, *An Ethic of Care* (1993), pp. 193–8. Sandra Harding, 'The curious coincidence of feminine and African moralities – challenges for feminist theory', in Eva Feder Kittay and Diana T. Meyers (eds), *Women and Moral Theory* (1987), pp. 226–315.

58 For a representative list of studies, see Marilyn Friedman, *What are Friends For? Feminist Perspectives on Personal Relationships and Moral Theory* (1993), pp. 119 and 120.

59 Lawrence J. Walker, 'Sex differences in the development of moral reasoning: a critical review', in Mary Jeanne Larrabee (ed.), *An Ethic of Care: Feminist and interdisciplinary perspectives* (1993), pp. 157–76, at 176. The article was initially published in *Child Development*, 55 (1984), pp. 677–91. Walker's findings are not without their critics. See, for example, Diana Baumrind, 'Sex differences in moral reasoning: response to Walker's (1984) conclusion that there are none', in Mary Jeanne Larrabee (ed.), *An Ethics of Care*, pp. 177–92. Baumrind's article was initially published in *Child Development*, 57 (1986), pp. 511–21. See also M. Rickard, H. Kuhse and P. Singer, 'Caring and justice: a study of two approaches to health-care ethics', *Nursing Ethics*, 3 (1996), pp. 212–23.

60 Joan C. Tronto, *Moral Boundaries: A political argument for an ethic of care* (1993), p. 84.

61 Susan Faludi, *Backlash* (1991), p. 365.

62 Catherine G. Greeno and Eleanor E. Macoby, 'How different is the "different voice"?', *Signs*, 11 (1986), pp. 314–15.

63 See, for example, G. T. Kaplan and L. J. Rogers, 'The definition of male and female: biological reductionism and the sanctions of normality', in S. Gunew (ed.), *Feminist Knowledge, Critique and Construct* (1990), pp. 205–28.

64 Carol Gilligan and Grant Wiggins, 'The origin of morality in

early childhood relationships', in J. Kagan and S. Lamb (eds), *The Emergence of Morality in Young Children* (1978), p. 278. I owe this reference and the following argument to Michele M. Moody-Adams, 'Gender and the complexity of moral voices', in Claudia Card (ed.), *Feminist Ethics* (1990), pp. 198–9.

65 Carol Gilligan, *In a Different Voice*, p. 2.

66 Shortly after having drawn the distinction between the two 'moral voices' in terms of theme rather than gender on p. 2 of her book, Gilligan already draws generalizations in terms of gender on p. 3, where she states that one of the intentions of her research is to provide psychologists with the appropriate tools to give a 'clearer representation of women's development'. Similar generalizations appear throughout the book. On this point, see also, Michele M. Moody-Adams, 'Gender and the complexity of moral voices', p. 197.

67 Moody-Adams puts the following argument on pp. 197–8.

68 Carol Gilligan and Grant Wiggins, 'The origins of morality in early childhood relationships', in Jerome Kagan and Sharon Lamb (eds), *The Emergence of Morality in Young Children* (1987), p. 279.

69 On this point, see also Rosemarie Tong, *Feminine and Feminist Ethics* (1993), p. 94.

70 Ibid.

71 A similar point is made by Moody-Adams.

72 Michael Levin, *Feminism and Freedom* (1987), p. 38; Nicholas Davidson: *Failure of Feminism* (1988), p. 230, both cited by Susan Faludi, *Backlash*, p. 365.

73 Carol Gilligan, 'Reply by Gilligan', *Signs*, 11 (1986), p. 333, as cited by Susan Faludi, p. 365.

74 Susan Faludi, *Backlash*, pp. 365–6.

75 The debate revolving around essentialism has become very complex, and it is not possible, in a few paragraphs, to map this debate. For a useful brief discussion of essentialism and difference, see E. Grosz, 'A note on essentialism and difference', in S. Gunew (ed.), *Feminist Knowledge* (1990). See also, Alice Echols, 'The new feminism of yin and yang' in Ann Snitow, Christine Stansell and Sharon Thomson (eds), *Powers of Desire: The politics of sexuality* (1983), p. 441; D. Fuss, *Feminism, Nature and Difference* (1989). For a good introductory discussion of cultural feminism, see Linda Alcoff, 'Cultural feminism versus post-structuralism: the identity crisis in feminist theory', in Nancy Tuana and Rosemarie Tong (eds), *Feminism and Philosophy: Essential readings in theory, reinterpretation, and application* (1995), pp. 434–56.

76   For a trenchant critique of essentialism, see Elizabeth Spelman, *Inessential Woman* (1988).
77   See also Allison M. Jaggar, 'Feminist ethics: projects, problems, prospects', in Claudia Card (ed.), *Feminist Ethics* (1991), p. 94.
78   See also Alison M. Jaggar, 'Human biology in feminist theory: sexual equality reconsidered', in Carl C. Gould (ed.), *Beyond Domination: New perspectives on women and philosophy* (1984), pp. 21–42. In this paper Jaggar defends the view that 'biologism' is ultimately incoherent.
79   Carol Gilligan, *In A Different Voice*, pp. 7ff.
80   See, for example, Mary Jean Larrabee, 'Gender and moral development: a challenge for feminist theory', in Mary Jeanne Larrabee (ed.), *An Ethics of Care: Feminist and interdisciplinary perspectives* (1993), pp. 3–16.
81   See Susan J. Hekman, *Moral Voices, Moral Selves* (1995), pp. 73ff. Joan C. Tronto, *Moral Boundaries: A political argument for an ethic of care* (1993), p. 85.
82   Nel Noddings, *Caring* (1984); Sara Ruddick, *Maternal Thinking: Toward a politics of peace* (1989). There are important differences between these books. Sara Ruddick, for example, holds that mothering is open to men; Nel Noddings, on the other hand, seems to suggest that 'caring' has, at least in part, a biological basis.
83   For an excellent account of such 'standpoint' theories – theories that rely on the idea of caring labour – see Sandra Harding, *The Science Question in Feminism* (1986); see also Carol Whitbeck, 'A different reality: feminist ontology', in Ann Garry and Marilyn Pearsall (eds), *Women, Knowledge, and Reality: Explorations in feminist philosophy* (1989), p. 59; Sarah Ruddick, 'Maternal thinking', *Feminist Studies*, 6 (Summer 1980), pp. 342–67; Virginia Held, *Rights and Goods: Justifying social action* (1984); and Virginia Held: *Feminist Morality: Transforming culture, society and politics* (1993).
84   The distinction between the public and the private sphere, and the moralities to which activities in these spheres might give rise, may not be as sharp as I have drawn it here. Principles of justice are also required in the private sphere, and the care approach may sometimes be the appropriate one in the public sphere. See, for example, Marilyn Friedman, *What Are Friends For?* (1993), pp. 131ff.; and Virginia Held, 'The meshing of care and justice', *Hypatia* (Special Issue Feminist Ethics and Social Policy, Part II), 10 (1995), pp. 128–32.
85   See also Jean Grimshaw, 'The idea of a female ethic', in P. Singer (ed.), *A Companion to Ethics* (1991), p. 493.
86   Alison M. Jaggar, 'Feminist ethics', p. 85.

87   It must be borne in mind that there is no clear separation between the 'public' and the 'private' sphere. Rather, the 'public' and 'private' lives of women and men have always overlapped in important ways. In addition to that, there are variations in male and female role assignment between cultures. None the less, when all is said and done, it is largely correct to say that women's lives were more predominantly played out in the 'private sphere', whereas men's lives have generally had a more public focus.

88   See Alison M. Jaggar, 'Human biology in feminist theory'.

89   Marilyn Friedman, *What Are Friends For?*, pp. 118ff.

Chapter 6   Care versus Justice

1   Carol Gilligan, *In a Different Voice: Psychological theory and women's development* (1982).

2   See also Leslie Cannold, Peter Singer, Helga Kuhse and Lori Gruen, 'What is the justice/care debate *really* about?' *Midwestern Studies in Philosophy*, 20 (1996), pp. 357–77. For some other recent characterizations of the differences between so-called ethics of care and ethics of justice, see Lawrence Blum, 'Gilligan and Kohlberg: Implications for moral theory', *Ethics*, 98 (Apr. 1988), pp. 472–91, and Jonathan Dancy, 'Caring about justice', *Philosophy*, 67 (Oct. 1992), pp. 447–66.

3   C. Gilligan, *In a Different Voice*; Carol Gilligan, 'Moral orientation and moral development', in Eva Feder Kittay and Diana T. Meyers (eds), *Women and Moral Theory* (1987); C. Gilligan and J. Attanucci, 'Two moral orientations', in C. Gilligan, J. V. Ward and J. B. Bardige (eds), *Mapping the Moral Domain: A contribution to women's thinking to psychological theory and education* (1988).

4   Nel Noddings, *Caring*.

5   See Anne Colby and Lawrence Kohlberg, *The Measurement of Moral Judgment* (1987), vol. 1, p. 24. (There are grounds for being somewhat wary of describing all aspects of Kohlberg's 'justice approach' as Kantian: the fact that Kohlberg sees his account as deriving from Immanuel Kant does not mean that his understanding of Kant is necessarily correct. Nor does it mean that all those who refer to the 'justice approach' to ethics are necessarily understanding it in a strictly Kohlbergian sense. This is why I am speaking rather broadly of a Kantian or deontological approach.)

6   See, for example, Michael Stocker, 'The schizophrenia of modern ethical theories', *Journal of Philosophy*, 73 (1976), pp. 453–66; Michael Stocker, 'Values and purposes: the limits of teleology and the ends of friendship', *Journal of Philosophy*, 78 (1981), pp. 747–65; Peter

Railton, 'Alienation, consequentialism and morality', *Philosophy and Public Affairs*, 13 (1984), pp. 134–71; G. Fletcher, *An Essay on the Morality of Relationships* (1993).

7   M. Nussbaum, in S. J. Hekman, *Moral Voices, Moral Selves* (1995), p. 37.

8   R. Manning, *Speaking from the Heart* (1992), pp. xii–xiv.

9   Jean Watson, 'Introduction: An ethic of caring/curing/nursing *qua* nursing', in Jean Watson and Marilyn A. Ray (eds), *The Ethics of Care and the Ethics of Cure: Synthesis and chronicity* (1988), p. 1.

10   Carol Gilligan, 'Moral orientation and moral development', in E. F. Kittay and D. T. Meyers (eds), *Women and Moral Theory*, p. 23.

11   Ibid.

12   Nel Noddings' *Caring* provides one of the strongest care critiques of impartialist ethics. See also her 'A response', *Hypatia*, 5 (Spring 1990), pp. 120–6, where she appears to have somewhat softened her views.

13   T. L. Beauchamp and J. F. Childress, *Principles of Biomedical Ethics*, 4th edn (1995), p. 88. The quotation is from T. Quill and P. Townsend, 'Bad news: delivery, dialogue and dilemmas', *Archives of Internal Medicine*, 151 (Mar. 1991), pp. 463–4.

14   Ibid.

15   Nel Noddings, *Caring*.

16   Ibid., pp. 36–7.

17   Sara Ruddick, as quoted in Jean Grimshaw, *Philosophy and Feminist Thinking* (1986), p. 204.

18   See I. Kant, 'On a supposed right to tell lies from benevolent motives', trans. T. K. Abbott (1909), pp. 361–5.

19   On this point, see also George Sher, 'Other voices, other rooms? Women's psychology and moral theory', in E. F. Kittay and D. T. Meyers (eds), *Women and Moral Theory*, p. 180.

20   Ibid.

21   Claudia Card, 'Caring and Evil', *Hypatia*, 5 (Spring 1990), p. 105. (In an endnote, Claudia Card adds (p. 107) that 'Nel Noddings agreed with this point during discussion at the April 1988 presentation of this essay.')

22   Laura Purdy, 'Feminist healing ethics', *Hypatia* (Special issue on feminist ethics and medicine), 4 (1988), p. 11.

23   Carol Gilligan, *In a Different Voice*, p. 100.

24   Nel Noddings, *Caring*, p. 2.

25   Henry Sidgwick, *The Methods of Ethics*, 7th edn (1907), pp. 353–4.

26   Nel Noddings, *Caring*, p. 5.

27   Marilyn Friedman, 'Beyond caring', in Marilyn Pearsall (ed.), *Women and Values* (1986), p. 105.

28 Seyla Benhabib, 'The generalized and the concrete other', in Marilyn Pearsall (ed.), *Women and Values* (1986), p. 164.
29 See R. M. Hare, *Moral Thinking: Its levels, method and point* (1981), p. 140.
30 See, for example, Margaret Urban Walker, 'Moral understanding: alternative "epistemology" for a feminist ethics', *Hypatia*, 4 (1988), p. 22.
31 Robin S. Dillon, 'Respect and care: toward moral integration', *Canadian Journal of Philosophy*, 22 (1992), p. 117.
32 See R. M. Hare, *Moral Thinking*, p. 41.
33 Nel Noddings, *Caring*, p. 1.
34 Ibid., p. 96.
35 Carol Gilligan, *In a Different Voice*, p. 28. See also Annette Baier, 'What do women want in a moral theory?', in M. L. Larrabee (ed.), *An Ethic of Care* (1993), p. 55, on 'mathematical systematizing' in traditional ethics.
36 Nel Noddings, *Caring*, p. 53.
37 Ibid., p. 5.
38 See Rita C. Manning, *Speaking from the Heart: A feminist perspective on ethics* (1992).
39 R. M. Hare, *Moral Thinking*.
40 See, for example, T. L. Beauchamp and J. F. Childress, *Principles of Biomedical Ethics*, 4th edn (1994), pp. 14ff.
41 Anne Colby and Lawrence Kohlberg, *The Measurement of Moral Judgment*, p. 21.
42 Marilyn Friedman, 'Care and context in moral reasoning', in D. T. Meyers and E. F. Kittay (eds), *Women and Moral Theory*, p. 203.
43 Lawrence Kohlberg, Charles Levine and Alexandra Hewer, *Moral Stages: A current reformulation and response to critics* (1983), pp. 145–8. (I owe this reference to Marilyn Friedman, 'Care and context in moral reasoning', p. 350.)
44 See also Marilyn Friedman, 'Care and context in moral reasoning', pp. 203–4.
45 R. M. Hare, *Moral Thinking* (1981), pp. 32–3.
46 Ibid., p. 34.
47 Ibid.
48 This does not mean that single-principle approaches, including utilitarianism, are without problems of their own. For a critical discussion of some of these problems, see Samuel Scheffler (ed.), *Consequentialism and its Critics* (1988).
49 Susan Sherwin, 'Feminist and medical ethics: two different approaches to contextual ethics', *Hypatia*, 4 (Summer 1989), p. 61.

50   Lawrence Blum, 'Iris Murdoch and the domain of the moral', *Philosophical Studies*, 1 (1986), p. 344.

51   William Godwin, *An Enquiry Concerning Political Justice and its Influence on General Virtue and Happiness* [1793], ed. Raymond Preston (1926), p. 42. (In the third edition Godwin changed 'chambermaid' to 'valet' and 'mother' to 'father', apparently to avoid giving the impression that he regarded women as of less worth than men.) For a discussion of Godwin's views on partiality and impartiality, see Peter Singer, Leslie Cannold and Helga Kuhse, 'William Godwin and the defence of impartialism', *Utilitas*, 7 (May 1995), pp. 67–86. See also Marilyn Friedman, 'The social self and the partiality debate', in Claudia Card (ed.), *Feminist Ethics* (1991), pp. 174ff.

52   For a range of these kinds of criticism see, e.g., Bernard Williams, 'Critique of utilitarianism', in *Utilitarianism: For and Against*, ed. B. Williams and J. J. C. Smart (1973); Michael Stocker, 'The schizophrenia of modern ethical theories', *Journal of Philosophy*, 73 (1976), pp. 453–66; Bernard Williams, *Moral Luck* (1980); Bernard Williams, *Ethics and the Limits of Philosophy* (1985); G. E. M. Anscombe, 'Modern moral philosophy', *Philosophy*, 33 (1958), pp. 1–19; Lawrence A. Blum, *Friendship, Altruism and Morality* (1980); Susan Wolf, 'Moral saints', *Journal of Philosophy*, 79 (1982), pp. 419–39; Margaret Urban Walker, 'Partial consideration', *Ethics*, 101 (1991), pp. 758–74; Dean Cocking and Justin Oakley, 'Indirect consequentialism, friendship and the problem of alienation', *Ethics*, 106 (Oct. 1995), pp. 86–111; see also the 'Symposium on impartiality and ethical theory', *Ethics*, 101 (July 1991). For a powerful defence of impartialist ethics see Shelly Kegan, *The Limits of Morality* (1989).

53   Bernard Williams, 'Persons, character and morality', in *Moral Luck* (1981).

54   Rita C. Manning, *Speaking from the Heart: A feminist perspective on ethics* (1992), p. 24.

55   Anne Colby and Lawrence Kohlberg, *The Measurement of Moral Judgment*, p. 21.

56   Nel Noddings, *Caring*, p. 34.

57   Ibid., p. 3.

58   Ibid., p. 34.

59   Michael Stocker, 'The schizophrenia of modern ethical theories', *Journal of Philosophy*, 73 (1976), pp. 453–66.

60   See Henry Sidgwick, *The Methods of Ethics*, 7th edn (1907), Book III, ch. XIII; J. J. C. Smart, 'An outline of a system of utilitarian ethics', in J. J. C. Smart and B. Williams, *Utilitarianism – For and Against* (1973).

61   On this point, see, for example, Bernard Williams, 'A critique of

utilitarianism', in J. J. C. Smart and Bernard Williams, *Utilitarianism – For and Against* (1973), pp. 97ff.

62 Noddings, *Caring*, p. 5.

63 William Godwin, *Memoirs of the Author of a Vindication of the Rights of Woman*, ch. vi, p. 90, second edition, quoted in William Godwin, *Thoughts Occasioned by the Perusal of Dr Parr's Spital Sermon* (1801); reprinted in J. Marken and B. Pollin (eds), *Uncollected Writings (1785–1822) by William Godwin* (1968), pp. 314–15. For a further discussion of Godwin's views on impartiality and partiality, see Peter Singer, Leslie Cannold and Helga Kuhse, 'William Godwin and the defence of impartialism'. *Utilitas*, 7 (1995), pp. 67–86.

64 Charles Dickens, *Bleak House*, first published in 1853. I owe this reference to Christina Hoff Sommers, 'Filial morality', in E. F. Kittay and D. T. Meyers (eds), *Women and Moral Theory* (1987), p. 72.

65 R. M. Hare, *Moral Thinking*.

66 See also J. E. Adler, 'Particularity, Gilligan and the two-level view', *Ethics*, 100 (Oct. 1989), pp. 149–56.

67 See also Peter Singer, Leslie Cannold and Helga Kuhse, 'William Godwin and the defence of impartialist ethics'.

68 On this point, see Marilyn Friedman, 'The practice of partiality', *Ethics*, 101 (July 1990), pp. 818–35.

69 In her book *Caring*, Nel Noddings speaks of concern for those distant from us – for example, those starving in Africa – as a form of 'romantic rationalism' (p. 3). She now seems to agree that this response is inadequate. (Nel Noddings, 'A response', *Hypatia*, 5 (Spring 1990), pp. 120–6.)

70 See, for example, the authors listed in notes 6 and 52 above.

71 See, for example, Peter Singer, Leslie Cannold, and Helga Kuhse, 'William Godwin and the defence of impartialist ethics'.

72 See note 64 above.

73 Charlotte Perkins Gilman, 'The unnatural mother', in *The Charlotte Perkins Gilman Reader*, ed. Ann J. Lane (1980), pp. 57, 58 and 65; first published in *The Forerunner* (Nov. 1916), pp. 281–5. See also P. Singer, L. Cannold and H. Kuhse, 'William Godwin and the defence of impartialist ethics'.

74 R. M. Hare, *Moral Thinking*; Peter Railton, 'Alienation, consequentialism and the demands of morality', *Philosophy and Public Affairs*, XIII (1984), pp. 134–71.

75 See also P. Singer, L. Cannold and H. Kuhse, 'William Godwin and the defence of impartialism', pp. 81–2.

76 Alison M. Jaggar, 'Feminist ethics: projects, problems, prospects', p. 90.

77 See, for example, Catherine MacKinnon, *Feminism Unmodified:*

Discourses on Life and Law (1987); Susan Moller Okin, *Justice, Gender, and the Family* (1989).

78   Ibid.

79   Annette Baier, 'What do women want in a moral theory?', in *Nous*, 19 (1985), p. 56.

80   Marilyn Friedman, 'The social self and the partiality debate', in Claudia Card (ed.), *Feminist Ethics* (1991), p. 170.

Chapter 7   'Yes' to Caring – But 'No' to a Nursing Ethics of Care

1   This chapter draws on the following papers, Helga Kuhse, 'Caring is not enough: reflections on a nursing ethics of care', *Australian Journal of Advanced Nursing*, 11, no. 1 (Sept.–Nov. 1993), pp. 32–42; Helga Kuhse, 'Clinical ethics and nursing: "Yes" to caring, but "No" to a female ethics of care', *Bioethics*, 9 (1995), pp. 207–19.

2   For a variety of interpretations of a care approach, see, for example, A. P. Griffin, 'A philosophical analysis of caring in nursing', *Journal of Advanced Nursing*, 8 (1983), pp. 289–95; Dena S. Davis, 'Nursing: an ethics of caring', *Humane Medicine*, 2 (1985), pp. 19–25; Jean Watson and Marilyn A. Ray (eds), *The Ethics of Care and the Ethics of Cure: Synthesis and chronicity* (1988); Mary Carolyn Cooper, 'Gilligan's different voice: a perspective for nursing', *Journal of Professional Nursing*, 5 (1989), pp. 10–16; Sarah T. Fry, 'The role of caring in a theory of nursing ethics', *Hypatia*, 4, no. 2 (Summer 1989), pp. 89–103; B. Kelly, 'Respect and caring: ethics and essence of nursing', in M. M. Leininger, *Ethical and Moral Dimensions of Care* (1990), pp. 67–79; P. R. Schultz, 'Noddings's caring and public policy: a linkage and its nursing implications', in ibid., pp. 81–7; Randy Spreen Parker, 'Nurses' stories: the search for a relational ethics of care', *Advances in Nursing Science*, 13 (1990), pp. 31–40; Alisa L. Carse, 'The "voice of care": implications for bioethical education', *Journal of Medicine and Philosophy*, 16 (1991), pp. 5–28; Jean Harbison, 'Gilligan: a voice for nursing?', *Journal of Medical Ethics*, 18 (1992), pp. 202–5; Ann Bradshaw, 'Yes! There is an ethics of care: an answer for Peter Allmark', *Journal of Medical Ethics*, 22 (Feb. 1996), pp. 8–12.

3   Madeleine Leininger, 'Caring: the essence and central focus of nursing', in *The Phenomenon of Caring: Part V* (1977), pp. 2–14. Jean Watson, *Nursing: Human Science and Human Care* (1985).

4   Jean Watson: *Nursing*.

5   Jean Watson, 'Introduction: an ethics of caring/curing/nursing *qua*

nursing', in Jean Watson and Marilyn A. Ray (eds), *The Ethics of Care and the Ethics of Cure* (1988), p. 2.

6   Verena Tschudin, *Ethics in Nursing: The caring relationship* (1986), p. 19.

7   Sarah T. Fry, 'The role of caring in a theory of nursing ethics', p. 89.

8   Alison M. Jaggar, 'Feminist ethics: projects, problems, prospects', in Claudia Card (ed.), *Feminist Ethics* (1991), p. 82. (Card makes this point in the context of her discussion of a feminist ethics.)

9   Quoted in Richard T. Hull, 'Defining nursing ethics apart from medical ethics', in J. E. Thompson and H. O. Thompson (eds), *Professional Ethics in Nursing* (1990), p. 49. See also Jean Watson, 'Introduction: an ethics of caring/curing/nursing *qua* nursing', p. 2: 'nursing ethics of human care cannot be reduced to medical ethics. That is, nursing ethics should be distinguished by its philosophical and moral ideals that affirm the personal unique contextual experiences associated with human caring, inherent in nursing *qua* nursing.'

10 See, for example, the following widely used nursing ethics texts: M. Benjamin and J. Curtis, *Ethics in Nursing* (1981); James L. Muyskens, *Moral Problems in Nursing: A philosophical investigation* (1982); Leah Curtin and M. Josephine Flaherty, *Nursing Ethics: Theories and Pragmatics* (1982); Mary F. Kohnke, *Advocacy: Risk and Reality* (1982); Catherine P. Murphy and Howard Hunter, *Ethical Problems in the Nurse–Patient Relationship* (1983); A. J. Davis and M. A. Aroskar, *Ethical Dilemmas and Nursing Practice* (1983); Ian E. Thomson, Kath M. Melia and Kenneth M. Boyd, *Nursing Ethics* (1983); A. Jameton, *Nursing Practice: The ethical issues* (1984); E. E. Bandman and B. Bandman, *Nursing Ethics in the Life Span* (1985).

11 Carol Gilligan, *In a Different Voice: Psychological theory and women's development* (1982).

12 Some nurses had already, prior to 1982, engaged in philosophical and trans-cultural explorations of the notion of care, without, however, seeing themselves engaged in the project of fashioning a feminist nursing ethics of care. See, for example, Madeleine Leininger, 'Caring: the essence and central focus of nursing', in *The Phenomenon of Caring*; Leah Curtin, 'Ethical issues in nursing practice and education', in *Ethical Issues in Nursing and Nursing Education* (1980), pp. 25–6; and Madeleine Leininger (ed.), *Caring: An Essential Human Need: Proceedings of Three National Caring Conferences* (1981); see also Ann Bradshaw, 'Yes! There is an ethics of care', on the traditional religious basis of the caring approach.

13 Nel Noddings, *Caring* (1984).

14 Ann Bradshaw, 'Yes! There is an ethics of care', p. 9. (Bradshaw refers here specifically to Patricia Benner, 'The role of experience, narrative, and community in skilled ethical comportment', *Advances in Nursing Science*, 14 (1991), pp. 1–21.)

15 Sara T. Fry, 'The role of caring in a theory of nursing ethics'; see also Sara T. Fry, 'Toward a theory of nursing ethics', *Advances in Nursing Science*, 11, no. 4 (1989), pp. 9–21; and Sara T. Fry, 'The philosophical foundation of caring', in M. M. Leininger (ed.), *Ethical and Moral Dimensions of Care* (1990), pp. 13–24.

16 Sara T. Fry, 'Toward a theory of nursing ethics', p. 16.

17 Warren Thomas Reich, 'History of the notion of care', *Encyclopedia of Bioethics* (1995), pp. 319–31.

18 On the richness of the notion of 'caring', see Nel Noddings, *Caring*, pp. 9–16.

19 In addition to the authors already cited, see for example: E. O. Bevis: 'Caring: a life force', in Madeleine Leininger (ed.), *Caring: An Essential Human Need* (1981); Barbara Carper, 'The ethics of caring', *Advances in Nursing Science*, 1 (1979), pp. 11–19; Sally Gadow, 'Nurse and patient: the caring relationship', in A. Bishop and J. Scudder, *Caring, Curing, Coping: Nurse, physician, patient relationships* (1982); Diana Gendron, *The Expressive Form of Caring* (1988); P. Benner and J. Wrubel, *The Primacy of Caring: Stress and coping in health and illness* (1989); Mary Carolyn Copper, 'Reconceptualizing nursing ethics', *Scholarly Inquiry for Nursing Practice*, 4 (1990), pp. 209–21; Jane K. Brody, 'Virtue ethics, caring, and nursing', *Scholarly Inquiry for Nursing Practice*, 2 (1988), pp. 87–96.

20 Madeleine Leininger, 'Caring is nursing: understanding the meaning, importance, and issues', in M. M. Leininger (ed.), *Care: The essence of nursing and health* (1988), p. 92. For two recent philosophical reflections on ethics and caring, see Jeffrey Blumstein, *Care and Commitment: Taking the personal point of view* (1981) and Stan van Hooft, *Caring: An essay in the philosophy of ethics* (1995).

21 Megan-Jane Johnstone, *Bioethics: A nursing perspective*, 2nd edn (1995), p. 132.

22 E. O. Bevis, 'Caring: a life force', in M. Leininger (ed.), *Caring: An essential human need* (1981), p. 50.

23 Jean Watson, *Nursing: Human science and human care* (1985), p. 66.

24 P. Benner and J. Wrubel, *The Primacy of Caring: Stress and coping in health and illness* (1989).

25 B. Blattner, *Holistic Nursing* (1981), p. 70.

26 M. Leininger, 'Caring: a central focus of nursing and health care

services', *Nursing and Health Care* (Oct. 1980), p. 143, as cited by Hilde L. Nelson, 'Against caring', *Journal of Clinical Ethics*, 3 (Spring 1992), p. 9.

27 M. Leininger, 'The phenomenon of caring: importance, research questions and theoretical considerations', in M. Leininger (ed.), *Caring: An essential human need* (1981), p. 9.

28 See A. P. Griffin, 'A philosophical analysis of caring in nursing', *Journal of Advanced Nursing*, 8 (1983), pp. 289–95. (Griffin distinguishes between 'caring' in an affective sense from 'caring' in 'seeing to the needs of X'.) On this point, see also Stan van Hooft, 'Caring and professional commitment', *Australian Journal of Advanced Nursing*, 4 (1987), pp. 30–1.

29 See also Peter Allmark, 'Can there be an ethics of care?', *Journal of Medical Ethics*, 21 (1995), p. 21.

30 There is considerable debate about the different and sometimes conflicting ways in which individual authors, as well as different authors, seem to understand the term. For a trenchant critique of Sarah Fry's concept of care, see Howard J. Curzer, 'Fry's concept of care in nursing ethics', *Hypatia*, 8 (Summer 1993), pp. 174–83.

31 Jean Watson, 'Introduction: an ethics of caring/curing/nursing *qua* nursing', p. 2.

32 Verena Tschudin, *Nursing Ethics*.

33 Nel Noddings, 'In defense of caring', *Journal of Clinical Ethics*, 3 (Spring 1992), p. 16.

34 Milton Mayeroff, *On Caring* (1971).

35 Martin Buber, *I and Thou*, 3rd edn, trans. W. Kaufmann (1970).

36 Stan van Hooft, 'Caring and professional commitment'.

37 M. Mayeroff, *On Caring*, p. 48, as cited by Stan van Hooft, 'Caring and professional commitment', p. 30.

38 Stan van Hooft, 'Caring and professional commitment'.

39 Nel Noddings, *Caring*, pp. 73–4.

40 Ibid., pp. 179–80.

41 Jean Watson, *Nursing*, p. 63. (My emphasis.)

42 Ibid., p. 66.

43 For some other criticisms of the requirement that nurses should not only care for but also about their patients, see H. J. Curzer, 'Is care a virtue for health care professionals?', *Journal of Medicine and Philosophy*, 18 (1993), pp. 51–69.

44 N. I. Komorita, K. M. Doehring and P. W. Hirchert, 'Perception of caring by nurse educators', *Journal of Nursing Education*, 30 (Jan. 1991), p. 23.

45 Rita C. Manning, *Speaking from the Heart: A feminist perspective on ethics* (1992), p. 61.

46 Lawrence Blum, 'Gilligan and Kohlberg: implications for moral theory', *Ethics*, 98 (Apr. 1988), p. 485. See also Lawrence Blum, 'Moral perception and particularity', *Ethics*, 101 (July 1991), pp. 701–25.

47 See also Lawrence A. Blum, *Moral Perception and Particularity* (1994). (A contemporary philosophical question is whether 'particularism' must lead to the rejection of impartialism and to moral scepticism and relativism. We will not be able to examine this complex question here. My assumption is that there is no necessary link between particularism and the rejection of universality, and that a moral approach, such as utilitarianism, can be both particular and universal. For a good recent discussion of some of these questions, see Torbjörn Tännsjö, 'In defence of theory in ethics', *Canadian Journal of Philosophy*, 25 (Dec. ·1995), pp. 571–94.)

48 Mina Mills, Huw T. O. Davies and William A. Macrae, 'Care of dying patients in hospital', *British Medical Journal*, 309 (3 Sept. 1994), pp. 583–6.

49 Rita C. Manning, *Speaking from the Heart*, p. 61.

50 Of course, these nurses' behaviour may not have been due to lack of caring, but to a mere lack of observation – a 'nursing fault' already commented on by Florence Nightingale in a chapter in her *Notes on Nursing* (1969, pp. 105–26). For a useful attempt to draw a distinction between 'observational vigilance' and 'affect' (or care), see Margaret Olivia Little, 'Seeing and caring: the role of affect in feminist moral epistemology', *Hypatia*, 10 (1995), pp. 117–37. Little discusses Nightingale's approach on p. 122.

51 There are important differences between these interpretations, which need not concern us for the purposes of our present discussion. See, for example, Howard J. Curzer, 'Fry's concept of care', *Hypatia*, 8 (1993), pp. 174–83, and Peter Allmark, 'Can there be an ethics of care?', *Journal of Medical Ethics*, 21 (1995), pp. 19–24.

52 Nel Noddings, *Caring*. But see also her more recent 'A response' (*Hypatia*, 5 (Spring 1990), pp. 120–6, where Noddings allows for the possibility that 'care' alone may not be enough).

53 Nel Noddings, *Caring*, p. 3.

54 Ibid., p. 5.

55 Ibid., p. 3.

56 Ibid.

57 Ibid., p. 53.

58 Ibid., pp. 82–3.

59 Peter Allmark, 'Can there be an ethics of care?', p. 20.
60 See D. Putnam, 'Relational ethics and virtue theory', *Metaphilosophy*, 22 (1991), pp. 231–8. (I owe this reference to Peter Allmark, ibid., p. 20.)
61 Peter Allmark, 'Can there be an ethics of care?'
62 Sarah Luca Hoagland, 'Some thoughts on "Caring"', in Claudia Card (ed.), *Feminist Ethics* (1991), pp. 246–63.
63 Jean Watson, 'Introduction: an ethic of caring/curing/nursing *qua* nursing', pp. 1–2.
64 Nel Noddings, *Caring*, p. 3.
65 Peter Allmark, 'Can there be an ethics of care?', p. 20.
66 Nel Noddings, *Caring*, pp. 56–7.
67 Ibid., p. 105.
68 Ibid., p. 106.
69 Noddings cannot avoid this example by relying on the traditional distinction between actions or omissions, or killing and allowing to die. It is not part of her moral scheme. (See Nel Noddings, *Women and Evil* (1989), pp. 130–55.)
70 Nel Noddings, *Caring*, pp. 109–10.
71 Ibid., p. 25.
72 *Warthen v. Toms River Community Memorial Hospital*, 488 A.2d 229, NJ Super AD 1985. (Following her refusal to continue to dialyse a terminally ill and distressed patient, Corinne Warthen was dismissed by the hospital. She took her case first to the Lower and then the Superior Court. Both courts ruled in favour of the hospital.)
73 Nel Noddings, *Caring*, p. 3.
74 On this point, see also Ann Bradshaw, 'Yes! There is an ethics of care'.
75 Jean Watson, 'Introduction: an ethics of caring/curing/nursing *qua* nursing', p. 2.
76 Randy Spreen Parker, 'Nurses' Stories', *Advances in Nursing Science*, 13 (1990), pp. 31–4.
77 Ibid., pp. 33–4.
78 The phrase is Mildred Dickemann's as quoted by Dianne Romain in 'Care and Confusion', in Eve Browning Cole and Susan Coultrap-McQuin (eds), *Explorations in Feminist Ethics: Theory and Practice* (1992), p. 35.
79 Jean Grimshaw, *Philosophy and Feminist Thinking* (1986), pp. 216–17.
80 Ibid., p. 217.
81 Ibid.
82 Megan-Jane Johnstone, *Bioethics: A nursing perspective*, p. 469.

83   *Una Journal of Nursing*, 1, no. 2 (1903), p. 33.
84   See, for example, Susan Moller Okin, 'Reason and feeling in thinking about justice', *Ethics*, 99 (Jan. 1989), pp. 229–49.
85   Janice Raymond, 'Reproductive gifts and gift giving: the altruistic woman', *Hastings Center Report* (Nov./Dec. 1990), p. 9.
86   Marilyn Friedman, *What Are Friends For?*, pp. 118ff.
87   Catharine A. MacKinnon, *Feminism Unmodified: Discourses on life and law* (1987), p. 39. See also Megan-Jane Johnstone, *Nursing and the Injustices of the Law* (1994); Steve H. Miles and Alison August, 'Courts, gender and "the right to die"', *Law, Medicine and Health Care*, 18 (Spring/summer 1995), pp. 85–95.
88   Janice Raymond, 'Reproductive Gifts', pp. 216ff.
89   Alison M. Jaggar, 'Feminist ethics', in Claudia Card (ed.), *Feminist Ethics* (1991), p. 92.
90   Jean-Jacques Rousseau, *Emile*, trans. Barbara Foxley (1988), pp. 340, 349, 350.
91   John O. Goden, 'Editorials – no longer silent', *Humane Medicine*, 4 (May 1988), p. 1.

Chapter 8   Just Caring at the End of Life

1   See, for example, the contributions to the 'Symposium on Care and Justice', in *Hypatia*, 10 (1995), pp. 113–52; also Joy Kroeger-Mappes, 'The ethic of care *vis-à-vis* the ethic of right: a problem for contemporary moral theory', *Hypatia*, 9 (Summer 1994), pp. 108–31.
2   See, for example, Anne J. Davis, 'Are there limits to caring? Conflict between autonomy and beneficence', in M. M. Leininger (ed.), *Ethical and Moral Dimensions of Care* (1990), pp. 25–32; Brighid Kelly, 'Respect and caring: ethics and essence of nursing', in M. M. Leininger (ed.), *Ethical and Moral Dimension of Care*, pp. 67–79; Phyllis R. Schultz, 'Noddings's *Caring* and public policy: a linkage and its nursing implications', in M. M. Leininger (ed.), *Ethical and Moral Dimension of Care*, pp. 80–8; G. Dalley, *Ideologies of Caring* (1988); J. Salvage, *The Politics of Nursing* (1985); Peter Allmark, 'Can there be an ethics of care', *Journal of Medical Ethics*, 21 (1995), pp. 19–24; Linda Hanford, 'Nursing and the concept of care: an appraisal of Noddings' theory', in G. Hunt (ed.), *Ethical Issues in Nursing* (1994), pp. 181–97.
3   A. Bradshaw, 'Yes! There is an ethics of care: an answer to Peter Allmark', *Journal of Medical Ethics*, 22 (1996), p. 8.
4   Ibid., pp. 11–12.

5   In his 'Reply to Ann Bradshaw' (*Journal of Medical Ethics*, 22 (1996), pp. 13–15) Peter Allmark makes a similar point.

6   See, for example, Susan Sherwin, *No Longer Patient: Feminist ethics and health care* (1992).

7   Laura Purdy, 'Feminist healing ethics', *Hypatia*, 4 (Summer 1988), p. 11.

8   See ch. 1.

9   See for example, Catherine P. Murphy, 'The changing role of nurses in making ethical decisions', *Law Medicine and Health Care* (Sept. 1984), p. 175; J. M. Wilkinson, 'Moral distress in nursing practice: experience and effect', *Nursing Forum*, 88 (1987), p. 16; Editors of *Nursing Life*, 'The right to die: what 3504 nurses had to say about one of the most important – yet one of the "grayest" – issues in health care today', *Nursing Life*, 4 (1984), pp. 17–25; A. J. Davis and P. Slater, 'The good death: cross cultural attitudes about euthanasia', unpublished paper presented at the International Conference on Medicine and Ethics, Sydney, 1986; Pat Slater, 'The good death: registered nurses' concerns about ethical issues', *Australian Journal of Advanced Nursing*, 4 (June–Aug. 1987), pp. 16–28; *Report of the Study of Professional Issues in Nursing* (Melbourne: Health Department, 1988).

10 See, for example, the World Medical Association's *Declaration of Lisbon on the Rights of the Patient* (1981).

11 On interests, see ch. 5 of Helga Kuhse, *The Sanctity-of-Life Doctrine in Medicine: A critique* (1987). For a good working notion of 'interests' and 'well-being' see the report of the US President's Commission for the Study of Ethical Problems in Medicine and Biomedical and Behavioral Research, *Deciding to Forego Life-Sustaining Treatment* (March 1983). For a detailed philosophical discussion of well-being, see James Griffin, *Well-Being: its meaning, measurement and moral importance* (1986).

12 See, for example, Robert Young, *Personal Autonomy: Beyond negative and positive liberty* (1986); Dan Brock, 'Informed consent', in D. van de Veer and T. Regan (eds), *Introduction to Health Care Ethics* (1987), pp. 98–126. Gerald Dworkin, *The Theory and Practice of Autonomy* (1988); see also Thomas E. Hill, Jr, 'The importance of autonomy', in E. F. Kittay and D. T. Meyers (eds), *Women and Moral Theory* (1987), pp. 129–38.

13 See, for example, Thomas E. Hill, 'The importance of autonomy'; Brighid Kelly, 'Respect and caring: ethics and essence of nursing'; and Robin S. Dillon, 'Respect and care: toward moral integration', *Canadian Journal of Philosophy*, 22 (Mar. 1992), pp. 105–32.

14   See also, e.g., Marilyn Friedman, 'Beyond caring: the de-moralization of gender', in M. Hanon and K. Nelson (eds), *Science, Morality and Feminist Theory*, p. 106; Robin S. Dillon, 'Care and respect', in E. Browning Cole and S. Coultrap-McQuin (eds), *Explorations in Feminist Ethics: Theory and practice* (1992), pp. 69–81.

15   Nel Noddings, *Women and Evil* (1989), p. 133.

16   Sarah Hoagland, 'Some thoughts about "Caring"', in Claudia Card (ed.), *Feminist Ethics* (1990), p. 259.

17   At the time of writing, voluntary euthanasia can be practised lawfully in two jurisdictions only, under the *Rights of the Terminally Ill Act* in the Northern Territory of Australia and in the Netherlands. Euthanasia remains a criminal offence in the Netherlands, but Dutch doctors have been able to practise it for many years, under guidelines developed by the courts. In 1993 the practise was regularized by the Dutch parliament when it established in law a procedure on the implementation and reporting of cases of euthanasia.

18   See, for example, Sacred Congregation for the Doctrine of the Faith, *Declaration on Euthanasia* (1980). See also ch. 4 of Helga Kuhse, *The Sanctity-of-Life Doctrine in Medicine* (1986).

19   See also President's Commission for the Study of Ethical Problems in Medicine and Biomedical and Behavioral Research, *Deciding to Forego Treatment*, p. 89.

20   *Compassion in Dying versus State of Washington*, No. 94–3534, United States Court of Appeals, Ninth Circuit, 6 March 1996, 1966 WL 94848 (9th Cir.[Wash]).

21   Sacred Congregation of the Faith: *Declaration on Euthanasia*, p. 6.

22   For a statement of the Principle of Double Effect, see Catholic University of America, *New Catholic Encyclopaedia*, vol. 4 (1976), pp. 1020–2. For a critique of the principle, see Helga Kuhse, *The Sanctity-of-Life Doctrine in Medicine*, ch. 3.

23   Roger Hunt, 'Palliative care – the rhetoric–reality gap', in Helga Kuhse, *Willing to Listen – Wanting to Die* (1994), p. 125.

24   Helga Kuhse and Peter Singer, 'Voluntary euthanasia and the nurse: an Australian survey', *International Journal of Nursing Studies*, 30 (1993), p. 316.

25   Sarah Shannon, debating the distinction between terminating life support and assisted suicide on the Internet, 30 April and 2 May 1996. (Quoted with permission.)

26   T. Daniels, 'The nurse's tale', *New York Magazine*, 30 April 1979, as quoted by J. L. Muyskens, *Moral Problems in Nursing* (1982), p. 96.

27   Roger Hunt, 'Palliative care', in Helga Kuhse, *Willing to Listen* (1994), p. 125.

28 Timothy Quill, 'The ambiguity of clinical intentions', *New England Journal of Medicine*, 329 (1993), pp. 1039–40; see also Roger Hunt, ibid., pp. 125–6.

29 See also Holly Goldman, 'Killing, letting die and euthanasia', *Analysis*, 40 (1980), p. 224.

30 Nel Noddings, *Women and Evil* (1989), pp. 130–2.

31 Ibid., p. 132.

32 Ibid., pp. 132–3. Noddings is here quoting Daniel Maguire, *Death by Choice* (1984), p. 154.

33 Ibid., p. 133.

34 Pieter Admiraal, 'Listening and helping to die', in Helga Kuhse (ed.), *Willing to Listen*, p. 237. See also Roger Hunt, 'Palliative care', pp. 115–37. In some cases pain can be controlled only through the continuous infusion of opioids and sedatives or anaesthetics which will render the patient unconscious.

35 *British Medical Journal*, 305 (Sept. 1992), p. 731; *Lancet*, 340 (26 Sept. 1992), pp. 757–8, 782–3; *Bulletin of Medical Ethics* (1992), pp. 3–4; Peter Singer, *Rethinking Life and Death* (1994), pp. 139–40. (While there has been some – largely inconclusive – debate about whether it would have been possible to relieve Lillian Boyes' pain more adequately by some other means, it remains the case that in least some instances pain cannot satisfactorily be controlled.)

36 See, for example. Rodney Syme, 'From innocent to advocate', in Helga Kuhse (ed.), *Willing to Listen*, pp. 155–71.

37 See, for example, Helga Kuhse and Peter Singer, 'Doctors' practices and attitudes regarding voluntary euthanasia', *Medical Journal of Australia*, 148 (1988), pp. 623–7; Peter Baume and E. O'Malley, 'Euthanasia: attitudes and practices of medical practitioners', *Medical Journal of Australia*, 161 (1994), p. 137; Helga Kuhse and Peter Singer, 'Voluntary euthanasia and the nurse: an Australian survey', *International Journal of Nursing Studies*, 39 (1993), pp. 311–22; S. Aranda and M. O'Connor, 'Euthanasia, nursing and care of the dying: rethinking Kuhse and Singer', *Australian Nursing Journal*, 3 (1995), pp. 18–19; B. J. Ward and P. A. Tate, 'Attitudes among NHS doctors to requests for euthanasia', *British Medical Journal*, 308 (1994), pp. 1332–4; T. D. Kinsella and M. J. Verhoef, 'Alberta euthanasia survey I: physicians' opinions about the morality and legalization of active euthanasia', *Canadian Medical Association*, 148 (1993), pp. 1921–3; A. L. Black, J. I. Wallace, H. E. Starks and R. A. Pearlman, 'Physician-assisted suicide and euthanasia in Washington State: patient requests and physician responses', *Journal of the American Medical Association*, 275 (1996), pp. 919–25; J. G. Bachman

et al., 'Attitudes of Michigan physicians and the public toward legal-izing physician-assisted suicide and voluntary euthanasia', *New England Journal of Medicine*, 334 (1 Feb. 1996), pp. 303–9; Melinda Lee et al., 'Legalizing assisted suicide – views of physicians in Oregon', *New England Journal of Medicine*, 334 (1 Feb. 1996), pp. 310–15.

38   Roger Hunt, 'Palliative care', p. 127.
39   Ibid., pp. 120ff.; Pieter Admiraal, 'Listening and helping to die', pp. 238ff.
40   A close reading of Noddings' *Women and Evil* (pp. 122–55) suggests that – contrary to the impression created in her earlier book *Caring* – she may be advocating a somewhat similar approach to the one put forward here.
41   Helga Kuhse and Peter Singer, 'Voluntary euthanasia and the nurse', p. 318.
42   Ibid.
43   H. T. Engelhardt, Jr, *The Foundations of Bioethics* (1986), ch. 1.
44   John Stuart Mill, *On Liberty* (1960; first published 1859), p. 73. For a feminist defence of Mill's liberalism, see Gail Tulloch, *Mill and Sexual Equality* (1989).
45   Max Charlesworth, 'A good death', in Helga Kuhse (ed.), *Willing to Listen*, p. 214.
46   Ronald Dworkin, *Life's Dominion: An argument about abortion, euthanasia and individual freedom* (1993), p. 46.
47   *Timothy E. Quill, MD; Samuel C. Klagsbrun, MD; and Howard A. Grossman, MD, v. Dennis C. Vacco, Attorney General of the State of New York; George E. Pataki, Governor of the State of New York; Robert M. Morgenthau, District Attorney of New York County*, Docket No. 95–7028, 2 April 1996.
48   See also the Canadian case *Sue Rodriguez v. The Attorney General of Canada and the Attorney General of British Columbia*, Supreme Court of Canada, File No. 23467; 30 September 1993.
49   Helga Kuhse and Peter Singer, 'Voluntary euthanasia and the nurse', p. 314. A. S. Aranda and M. O'Connor, 'Euthanasia, nursing and care of the dying', found it to be 91 per cent. The views of doctors are similar. On this point, see Helga Kuhse and Peter Singer, 'Doctors' practices and attitudes' and Peter Baume and E. O'Malley, 'Euthanasia'.
50   *American Medical News* (8 Apr. 1996).
51   Sarah E. Shannon on the Internet.
52   D. Brock, 'Voluntary active euthanasia', *Hastings Center Report*, 22 (1992), p. 10.
53   For two recent discussions of this issue see, for example, S. Wear, S. Pagaipa and G. Logue, 'Toleration of moral diversity and the

conscientious refusal by physicians to withdraw life-sustaining treatment', *Journal of Medicine and Philosophy*, 19 (1994), pp. 147–59; Kevin Wildes, 'Conscience, referral, and physician assisted suicide', *Journal of Medicine and Philosophy*, 18 (1993), pp. 323–8.

54 Slippery slope arguments are philosophically very complex. In the standard writings on the alleged bad consequences of the legalization of voluntary euthanasia, they often do not amount to more than unfounded assertion. For two good recent discussions of slippery slope arguments, see W. van der Burg, 'The slippery slope argument', *Ethics*, 102 (1991), pp. 42–65; J. Burgess, 'The great slippery slope argument', *Journal of Medical Ethics*, 19 (1993), pp. 169–74. See also Helga Kuhse, 'Sanctity-of-life, voluntary euthanasia and the Dutch experience: some implications for public policy', in Paul Bayertz (ed.), *Sanctity of Life and Human Dignity* (1996), pp. 19–37.

55 P. J. van der Maas, J. J. M. van Delden, L. Pijnenborg and C. W. N. Looman, 'Euthanasia and other medical decisions concerning the end of life', *Lancet*, 338 (14 Sept. 1991), pp. 669–74.

56 Two Australian surveys have shown that every third respondent who has been asked to do so has practised voluntary euthanasia at least once. See Helga Kuhse and Peter Singer, 'Doctors' practices and attitudes regarding voluntary euthanasia' and Peter Baume and Emma O'Malley, 'Euthanasia: attitudes and practices'.

57 J. Griffiths, 'The regulation of euthanasia and related medical procedures that shorten life in the Netherlands', *Medical Law International*, 1 (1994), pp. 137–58.

58 On this point, see also Ian Kennedy, 'The quality of mercy: patients, doctors and dying', Upjohn Lecture delivered at the Royal Society, London, on 25 April 1994.

59 *New York Times*, 9 March 1996; *British Medical Journal*, 312 (1996), p. 464.

60 See also Ian Kennedy, 'The quality of mercy'.

61 See also Rita Manning, *Speaking from the Heart*, p. 74.

62 Mary Ann Warren, 'The moral significance of birth', in H. B. Holmes and L. M. Purdy (eds), *Feminist Perspectives in Medical Ethics*, p. 198.

Chapter 9 Nursing: The Slumbering Giant

1 Roland R. Yarling and Beverly J. McElmurry, 'Rethinking the nurse's role in "do not resuscitate" orders: a clinical policy proposal in nursing ethics', *Advances in Nursing Science*, 5 (July 1983), p. 8. (Italics in original.)

2 See, for example, Adele W. Pike, 'Moral outrage and moral discourse

in nurse–physician collaboration', *Journal of Professional Nursing*, 7 (Nov./Dec. 1991), pp. 351–63; and Catherine P. Murphy, 'The changing role of the nurse in making ethical decisions', *Law, Medicine and Health Care* (Sept. 1984), p. 174.

3 *Report of the Study of Professional Issues in Nursing* (Melbourne: Health Department of Victoria, 1988), p. 26.

4 Robert Zussmann, *Intensive Care: Medical ethics and the medical profession* (1992), p. 67.

5 The Editors, 'The right to die', *Nursing Life*, 4 (1984), pp. 18 and 20.

6 The literature on advocacy is vast. For some interesting models and discussions, see, for example, Sally Gadow, 'Existential advocacy: philosophical foundation of nursing', in S. F. Spicker and S. Gadow (eds), *Nursing: Images and Ideals – Open Dialogue with the Humanities* (1980), pp. 69–101; Lea Curtin, 'The nurse as advocate: a philosophical foundation for nursing', in *Advances in Nursing Science*, 1 (Apr. 1979), pp. 1–10; Natalie Abrams, 'A contrary view of the nurse as patient advocate', *Nursing Forum*, 17 (1978), pp. 259–67; Jean Jenny, 'Patient advocacy: another role for nursing', *International Nursing Review*, 26 (1979), pp. 176–81; Mary F. Kohnke, *Advocacy: Risk and reality* (1982); Ellen W. Bernal, 'The nurse as patient advocate', *Hastings Center Report*, 22 (July–Aug. 1992), pp. 18–23; Ann W. Bird, 'Enhancing patient well-being: advocacy or negotiation?', *Journal of Medical Ethics*, 20 (1994), pp. 152–6.

7 American Nurses' Association, *Code for Nurses with Interpretative Statements*, 1985.

8 Australian Nursing Council, *Code of Ethics for Nurses in Australia*, July 1993.

9 United Kingdom Central Council for Nursing, Midwifery and Health Visiting, *Code of Professional Conduct for the Nurse Midwife and Health Visitor*, 2nd edn (Nov. 1984).

10 See also Gerald Winslow, 'From loyalty to advocacy: a new metaphor for nursing', *Hastings Center Report*, 14 (1984), p. 39.

11 Roland R. Yarling and Beverly J. McElmurry, 'Rethinking the nurse's role', *Advances in Nursing Science*, 15 (1983), p. 8.

12 See, for example, the submission by the Australian Medical Association (AMA) to the Study of Professional Issues in Nursing, *Report of the Study of Professional Issues in Nursing*, p. 181. The submission states quite unequivocally that '[t]he views of the AMA are fundamentally predicated on the fact that the ultimate legal and ethical responsibility for the medical treatment of patients is the sole domain of medical practitioners.'

13 *Report of the Study of Professional Issues in Nursing*, p. 200.

14 Ibid.
15 See S. Coney, *The Unfortunate Experiment* (1988); also S. Coney and P. Bunkle, 'An "unfortunate experiment" at National Women's', *Metro* (June 1987), pp. 47–65.
16 Megan-Jane Johnstone, *Bioethics: A nursing perspective*, 2nd edn (1994), pp. 15–16.
17 Joy Bickley, 'What the cervical cancer inquiry means for nurses', *New Zealand Nursing Journal*, 81 (1988), p. 15, as cited by Megan-Jane Johnstone, *Bioethics*, p. 18.
18 See, for example, the case of Ms Bardenilla, as discussed by Sara Fry, 'Whistle-blowing by nurses: a matter of ethics', 37 (Jan./Feb. 1989), p. 56.
19 *Report of the Study of Professional Issues in Nursing*, p. 164.
20 See Megan-Jane Johnstone, *Nursing and the Injustices of the Law* (1994).
21 Bill Puka makes this point in 'The liberation of caring: a different voice for Gilligan's "Different Voice"', in M. J. Larrabee (ed.), *An Ethics of Care: Feminist interdisciplinary perspectives* (1993), pp. 215–39.
22 See also Gerald Winslow, 'From loyalty to advocacy', p. 38.
23 Gerald Winslow uses the term 'slumbering giant'.
24 Legislative Assembly of the Northern Territory, *Report of the Inquiry by the Select Committee on Euthanasia*, vol. 1 (May 1995)
25 Australian Nursing Council, *Code of Ethics for Nursing in Australia*.
26 American Nurses Association, *Code for Nurses*.
27 American Nurses Association, *Position Statement on Active Euthanasia* (1994); and American Nurses Association, *Position Statement on Assisted Suicide* (1994).
28 Helga Kuhse and Peter Singer, 'Voluntary euthanasia and the nurse: an Australian survey', *International Journal of Nursing Studies*, 30 (1993), pp. 311–22.
29 Ibid.
30 David A. Asch, 'The role of critical care nurses in euthanasia and assisted suicide', *New England Journal of Medicine*, 334 (23 May 1996), pp. 1374–9.
31 Ibid., p. 1378.
32 Terence Monmaney, '20 per cent of ICU nurses have aided death, survey finds', *Los Angeles Times* (23 May 1996), Part A, p. 1.
33 The SUPPORT Principal Investigators, 'A controlled trial to improve care for seriously ill hospitalized patients: the Study to Understand Prognoses and Preferences for Outcomes and Risks of Treatments (SUPPORT)', *Journal of the American Medical Association*, 274 (1995), pp. 1591–8.

34   I do not wish to enter the debate about whether professional organizations or bodies, such as hospitals, can have moral responsibilities. I take it that even if we are not able to ascribe moral responsibility to organizations, we can ascribe them to those charged with their leadership. For a somewhat different account of collective responsibility see James L. Muyskens, *Moral Problems in Nursing: A philosophical investigation* (1982), chs. 6 and 7.

35   Colleen Scanlon, 'Euthanasia and nursing practice – right question, wrong answer', *New England Journal of Medicine*, 334 (1996), pp. 1401–2.

36   David Asch, 'The role of critical care nurses', pp. 1374–5.

37   See, for example, the Sacred Congregation for the Doctrine of the Faith, *Declaration on Euthanasia* (1980).

38   David Asch, 'The role of critical care nurses', p. 1378.

39   Ibid.

40   See, for example, The SUPPORT Principal Investigators, 'A controlled trial' and David A. Asch, J. Hansen-Flaschen and P. N. Lanken, 'Decisions to limit or continue life sustaining treatment by critical care physicians in the United States – conflicts between physicians' practices and patients' wishes', *American Journal of Respiratory and Critical Care Medicine*, 151 (1995), pp. 288–92.

41   See note 37, ch. 8.

42   Andrew Jameton, *Nursing Practice: The ethical issues* (1984), p. 261.

43   Leah Curtin, 'Case Study X: cardiopulmonary resuscitation and the nurse', in Leah Curtin and M. Josephine Flaherty (eds), *Nursing Ethics: Theories and pragmatics* (1982), p. 294.

44   See, for example, Megan-Jane Johnstone, *Nursing and the Injustices of the law* (1994), p. 271.

45   For a proposal along similar lines, see James L. Muyskens, *Moral Problems in Nursing* (1982), pp. 34ff. See also Geoffrey Hunt, 'Nursing accountability – the broken circle', in Geoffrey Hunt (ed.), *Ethical Issues in Nursing* (1994), pp. 129–47.

46   *Report of the Study of Professional Issues in Nursing*, p. 168.

47   A. Young, D. Volker, P. T. Rieger and D. M. Thorpe, 'Oncology nurses' attitudes regarding voluntary, physician-assisted dying for competent, terminally ill patients', *Oncological Nursing Forum*, 20 (1993), pp. 445–51.

48   See *Report of the Study of Professional Issues in Nursing*, p. 182.

49   A view taken by, for example, J. A. Ashley, *Hospitals, Paternalism and the Role of the Nurse* (1976) and Mary Wollstonecraft, *A Vindication of the Rights of Women* (1967).

Bibliography

Abel-Smith, B. *A History of the Nursing Profession*, London: Heinemann, 1960.

Abrams, N. 'A contrary view of the nurse as patient advocate', *Nursing Forum*, XVII (1978), 258–67.

Adams, M. 'The compassion trap', in V. Gornick and B. K. Moran (eds), *Women in Sexist Society: Studies in power and powerlessness*, New York: New American Library, 1971.

Adams, R. M. 'Motive utilitarianism', *Journal of Philosophy*, 73 (1976), 467–81.

Adler, J. E. 'Particularity, Gilligan and the two-level view', *Ethics*, 100 (Oct. 1989), 149–56.

Admiraal, P. 'Listening and helping to die', in H. Kuhse (ed.), *Willing to Listen – Wanting to Die*, Melbourne: Penguin, 1994, 230–45.

Alcoff, L. 'Cultural feminism versus post-structuralism: the identity crisis in feminist theory', in Nancy Tuana and R. Tong (eds), *Feminism and Philosophy: Essential readings in theory, reinterpretation, and application*, Boulder, CO: Westview Press, 1995, 434–56.

Allmark, P. 'Can there be an ethics of care?', *Journal of Medical Ethics*, 21 (1995), 19–24.

—— 'Reply to Ann Bradshaw', *Journal of Medical Ethics*, 22 (1996), 13–15.

American Journal of Nursing (editorial) 'Where does loyalty to the physician end', *American Journal of Nursing*, 10 (January 1910), 230–1, and 'Where does loyalty to the physician end?', *American Journal of Nursing*, 10 (January 1910), 274–6.

American Nurses Association, *Code for Nurses with Interpretative Statements*, 1985.

—— *Position Statement on Active Euthanasia*, Washington, DC: American Nurses Association, 1994.

——— *Position Statement on Assisted Suicide*, Washington, DC: American Nurses Association, 1994.

American Psychiatric Association. *Diagnostic and Statistical Manual of Mental Disorders*, 3rd edn, Washington, DC: American Psychiatric Association, 1980.

Annas, G. J. 'The patient rights advocate; can nurses effectively fill the role?', *Supervisor Nurse*, 5 (July 1974), 21–5.

Annas, G. J. and Healey, J. M. 'The patient rights advocate: redefining the doctor–patient relationship in the hospital context', *Vanderbilt Law Review*, no. 243 (1974), 266–8.

Anscombe, G. E. M. 'Modern moral philosophy', *Philosophy*, 33 (1958), 1–19.

Aranda, S. and O'Connor, M. 'Euthanasia, nursing and care of the dying: rethinking Kuhse and Singer', *Australian Nursing Journal*, 3 (1995), 18–19.

Aristotle: 'Politics', in *The Basic Works of Aristotle*, ed. R. McKeon, New York: Random House, 1941, pp. 1113–1316.

Asch, D. A. 'The role of critical care nurses in euthanasia and assisted suicide', *New England Journal of Medicine*, 334 (23 May 1996), 1374–9.

Asch, D. A., Hansen-Flaschen, J. and Lanken, P. N. 'Decisions to limit or continue life-sustaining treatment by critical care physicians in the United States – conflicts between physicians' practices and patients' wishes', *American Journal of Respiratory and Critical Care Medicine*, 151 (1995), 288–92.

Ashley, J. *Hospitals, Paternalism and the Role of the Nurse*, New York: Teachers College Press, 1977.

Australian Nursing Council. *Code of Ethics for Nurses in Australia* (July 1993).

Bachman, J. G., Alcser, K. H., Doukas, D. J., Lichtenstein, R. L., Corning, A. D. and Brody, H. 'Attitudes of Michigan physicians and the public toward legalizing physician-assisted suicide and voluntary euthanasia', *New England Journal of Medicine*, 334 (1 February 1996), 303–9.

Baier, A. 'What do women want in a moral theory?', in M. J. Larrabee (ed.), *An Ethic of Care*, New York: Routledge, 1993, pp. 19–32. (The article was originally published in *Nous*, 19 (1985), pp. 53–63.)

Baker, R. 'Care of the sick and cure of the disease: comment on "The Fractured Image"', in S. F. Spicker and S. Gadow (eds), *Nursing: Images and ideals – opening dialogue with the humanities*, New York: Springer, 1980, pp. 41–8.

Balikci, A. *The Netsilik Eskimo*, Garden City, NY: The Natural History Press, 1970.

Baly, M. E. 'Florence Nightingale and "her" schools of nursing', *Humane Medicine*, 4 (1988), pp. 45–51.

Bandman, E. E. and Bandman, B. *Nursing Ethics in the Life Span*, Norwalk, CT: Appleton-Century Crofts, 1985.

Bates, E. and Lapsley, H. *The Health Machine: The impact of medical technology*, Ringwood: Penguin, 1985.

Baume, P. and O'Malley, E. 'Euthanasia: attitudes and practices of medical practitioners', *Medical Journal of Australia*, 161 (July 1994), 137–44.

Baumrind, D. 'Sex differences in moral reasoning: response to Walker's (1984) conclusion that there are none', in M. J. Larrabee (ed.), *An Ethic of Care*, New York: Routledge, 1993, pp. 177–92.

Bayles, M. 'Betwixt and between: juggling ethical responsibilities in today's nursing scene', *Canadian Nurse*, 78 (1982), 36–9.

Beauchamp, T. L. 'What's so special about the virtues?', in Earl E. Shelp (ed.), *Virtue and Medicine*, Dordrecht: Reidel, 1984, pp. 307–27.

Beauchamp, T. L. and Childress, J. F. *Principles of Biomedical Ethics*, 3rd edn, New York: Oxford University Press, 1989.

—— *Principles of Biomedical Ethics*, 4th edn, New York: Oxford University Press, 1995.

Benhabib, S. 'The generalized and the concrete other', in Marilyn Pearsall (ed.), *Women and Values*, Belmont, CA: Wadsworth, 1986.

Benjamin, M. and Curtis, J. 'Ethical autonomy in nursing', in Donald Van De Veer and Tom Regan (eds), *An Introduction to Health Care Ethics*, Philadelphia: Temple University Press, 1987, pp. 395–427.

—— *Ethics in Nursing*, 3rd edn, New York: Oxford University Press, 1992. (First published in 1981.)

Benner, P. 'The role of experience, narrative, and community in skilled ethical comportment', *Advances in Nursing Science*, 14 (1991), 1–21.

Benner, P. and Wrubel, J. *The Primacy of Caring: Stress and coping in health and illness*, Menlo Park, CA: Addison Wesley, 1989.

Bentham, Jeremy. *Principles of Morals and Legislation*, New York: Hafner, 1948.

Bernal, E. W. 'The nurse as patient advocate', *Hastings Centre Report*, 22 (July–August 1992), 18–23.

Bevis, E. O. 'Caring: a life force', in M. Leininger (ed.), *Caring: An essential human need*, Thorofare, NJ: Slack, 1981.

Bickley, J. 'What the cervical cancer inquiry means for nurses', *New Zealand Nursing Journal*, 81 (1988), 14–15.

Bird, A. W. 'Enhancing patient well-being: advocacy or negotiation?', *Journal of Medical Ethics*, 20 (1994), 152–6.

Bishop, A. and Scudder, J. R. Jr. *Caring, Curing, Coping*, Birmingham, AL: University of Alabama Press, 1985.

Bishop, S. and Weinzweig, Majorie (eds) *Philosophy and Women*, Belmont, CA: Wadsworth, 1989.

Black, A. L., Wallace, J. I., Starks, H. E. and Pearlman, R. A. 'Physician-assisted suicide and euthanasia in Washington State: patient requests and physician responses', *Journal of the American Medical Association*, 275 (1996), 919–25.

Black, M. 'Metaphor' in Max Black (ed.), *Models and Metaphors: Studies in language and philosophy*, Ithaca, NY: Cornell University Press, 1962, pp. 25–47.

Blattner, B. *Holistic Nursing*, Englewood Cliffs, NJ: Prentice Hall, 1981.

Blum, L. *Friendship, Altruism and Morality*, London: Routledge, 1980.

—— 'Iris Murdoch and the domain of the moral', *Philosophical Studies*, 50 (1986), 343–67.

—— 'Gilligan and Kohlberg: implications for moral theory', *Ethics*, 98 (April 1988), 472–91.

—— 'Moral perception and particularity', *Ethics*, 101 (July 1991), 701–25.

—— *Moral Perception and Particularity*, New York: Cambridge University Press, 1994.

Blustein, J. *Care and Commitment: Taking the personal point of view*, New York: Oxford University Press, 1991.

Bowman, G. *The Lamp and the Book*, London: Queen Anne Press, 1967.

Bradshaw, A. 'Yes! There is an ethics of care: an answer for Peter Allmark', *Journal of Medical Ethics*, 22 (February 1996), 8–12.

Brand, K. L. and Glass, L. K. 'Perils and parallels of women and nursing', *Nursing Forum*, 14 (1975), 169.

Brandt, R. B. *Ethical Theory*, Englewood Cliffs, NJ: Prentice Hall, 1959.

Brock, D. 'Informed consent' in D. van de Veer and T. Regan (eds), *An Introduction to Health Care Ethics*, Philadelphia: Temple University Press, 1987, pp. 98–126.

—— 'Voluntary active euthanasia', *Hastings Center Report*, 22 (March/April 1992), 10–22.

Brody, B. A. and Engelhardt, H. T. Jr (eds), *Bioethics: Readings and cases*, Englewood Cliffs, NJ: Prentice Hall, 1987.

Brody, Jane K. 'Virtue ethics, caring, and nursing', *Scholarly Inquiry for Nursing Practice, An International Journal*, 2 (1988), 87–96.

Broughton, John M. 'Women's rationality and men's virtues: a critique of gender dualism in Gilligan's theory of moral development', *Social Research*, 50 (August 1983), 597–642.

Buber, M. *I and Thou*, 3rd edn, trans. W. Kaufmann, Edinburgh: T. & T. Clark, 1970.

Buckle, S. 'Natural law' in P. Singer (ed.), *A Companion to Ethics*, Oxford: Blackwell, 1991, pp. 161–74.

Bullough, V. L. and Bullough, B. *The Care of the Sick: The emergence of modern nursing*, London: Croom Helm, 1979.

Burbridge, G. *Lectures for Nurses*, 4th edn, Glebe: Australian Medical Publishing Company, 1950.

Burg, W. van der 'The slippery slope argument', *Ethics*, 102 (1991), 42–65.

Burgess, J. 'The great slippery slope argument', *Journal of Medical Ethics*, 19 (1993), 169–74.

Callahan, J. C. 'Basics and background', in J. C. Callahan (ed.), *Ethical Issues in Professional Life*, New York: Oxford University Press, 1988, pp. 3–25.

Cannold, L., Singer, P., Kuhse, H. and Gruen, L. 'What is the justice/care debate *really* about?', *Midwestern Studies in Philosophy*, 20 (1996), pp. 357–77.

Card, C. 'Caring and evil', *Hypatia*, 5 (Spring 1990), 101–8.

Card, C. (ed.), *Feminist Ethics*, Lawrence: University of Kansas Press, 1990.

Carmichael, G. Jennings. *Hospital Children: Sketches of life and character at the Children's Hospital Melbourne*, Melbourne, 1891.

Carnell, E. J. *An Introduction to Christian Apologetics*, Grand Rapids, MI: Eerdmans, 1950.

Carper, B. 'The ethics of caring', *Advances in Nursing Science*, 1 (1979), 11–19.

Carse, A. L. 'The voice of care: implications for bioethical education', *Journal of Medicine and Philosophy*, 16 (1991), 5–28.

Catholic University of America. *New Catholic Encyclopaedia*, vol. 4, New York: McGraw-Hill, 1976.

Charlesworth, M. 'A good death', in H. Kuhse (ed.), *Willing to Listen – Wanting to Die*, Melbourne: Penguin, 1994, pp. 203–16.

Childress, J. F. 'Metaphor and analogy', in W. T. Reich (ed.), *Encyclopedia of Bioethics*, New York: Macmillan, 1995, pp. 1765–73.

Chodorow, N. 'Family structure and feminine personality', in M. Z. Rosaldo and L. Lamphere (eds), *Woman, Culture and Society*, Stanford: Stanford University Press, 1974.

—— *The Reproduction of Mothering*, Berkeley: University of California Press, 1978.

—— *Feminism and Psychoanalytic Theory*, New Haven: Yale University Press, Cambridge: Polity Press, 1989.

Cleland, V. S. 'Sex discrimination: nursing's most pervasive problem', *American Journal of Nursing*, 81 (1981), 1542–7.

Cocking, D. and Oakley, J. 'Indirect consequentialism, friendship and the problem of alienation', *Ethics*, 106 (1995), 86–111.

Colby, A. and Kohlberg, L. *The Measurement of Moral Judgment*, vol. 1, Cambridge: Cambridge University Press, 1987.

Cole, E. Browning, and Coultrap-McQuin, S. (eds), *Exploration in Feminist Ethics: Theory and practice*, Bloomington: Indiana University Press, 1992.

Committee of Inquiry into Allegations Concerning the Treatment of Cervical Cancer at National Women's Hospital and into Other Related Matters. *Report of the Cervical Cancer Inquiry*, Auckland: Government Printing Office, 1988.

Compassion in Dying versus State of Washington, No. 94–3534, United States Court of Appeals, Ninth Circuit, March 6, 1996, 1966 WL 94848 (9th Cir.[Wash]).

Coney, S. *The Unfortunate Experiment*, Auckland and Melbourne: Penguin, 1988.

Coney, S. and Bunkle, P. 'An "unfortunate experiment" at National Women's', *Metro* (June 1987), 47–65.

Cook, J. *Captain Cook's Journal 1768–71*, ed. W. S. L. Wharton, London: Elliott Stock, 1893.

Cooper, M. C. 'Gilligan's Different Voice: a perspective for nursing', *Journal of Professional Nursing*, 5 (1989), 10–16.

—— 'Reconceptualizing nursing ethics', *Scholarly Inquiry for Nursing Practice: An International Journal*, 4 (1990), 209–21.

Costello, S., Engelhardt, H. T., Jr and Gardell, M. A. 'Licensing, certification, and the restraint of trade: the creation of differences among the health care professions', in B. A. Brody and H. T. Engelhardt, Jr (eds), *Bioethics: Readings and cases*, Englewood Cliffs, NJ: Prentice Hall, 1987, pp. 89–95.

—— 'Case Study X: Cardiopulmonary Resuscitation and the Nurse', in L. Curtin and J. Flaherty, *Nursing Ethics: Theories and pragmatics*, Bowie, MD: Brade, 1982, pp. 293–4.

—— 'The nurse as advocate: a cantankerous critique', *Nursing Management* (May 1983), 9–10.

Curtin, L. 'The nurse as advocate: a philosophical foundation of nursing', *Advances in Nursing Science*, 1 (April 1979), 1–10.

—— 'Ethical issues in nursing practice and education', in *Ethical Issues in Nursing and Nursing Education*, New York: National League for Nursing, 1980.

Curtin, L. and Flaherty, J. *Nursing Ethics: Theories and pragmatics*, Bowie, MD: Brade, 1982.

Curzer, H. J. 'Is care a virtue for health care professionals?', *Journal of Medicine and Philosophy*, 18 (1993), 51–69.

—— 'Fry's concept of care in nursing ethics', *Hypatia*, 8 (Summer 1993), 174–83.

Dalley, G. *Ideologies of Caring*, Basingstoke: Macmillan, 1988.

Daly, M. *Gyn/Ecology: The metaethics of radical feminism*, Boston: Beacon Press, 1978.

Dancy, Jonathan. 'Caring about justice', *Philosophy*, 67 (October 1992), 447–66.

Daniels, T. 'The nurse's tale', *New York Magazine* (30 April 1979).

Davidson, Nicholas *Failure of Feminism*, Buffalo, NY: Prometheus, 1988.

Davies, Celia (ed.), *Rewriting Nursing History*, London: Croom Helm, 1980.

Davis, A. J. 'Are there limits to caring? Conflict between autonomy and beneficence', in M. Leininger (ed.), *Ethical and Moral Dimensions of Care*, Detroit: Wayne State University Press, 1990, pp. 25–32.

Davis, A. J. and Aroskar, M. A. *Professional Ethics and Institutional Constraints in Nursing Practice*, New York: Appleton-Century-Crofts, 1978.

—— *Ethical Dilemmas in Nursing Practice*, Norwalk, CT: Appleton-Century-Crofts, 1983.

Davis, A. J. and Slater, P. 'The good death: cross cultural attitudes about euthanasia', unpublished paper presented at the International Conference on Medicine and Ethics, Sydney, 1986.

Davis, Dena S. 'Nursing: an ethics of caring', *Humane Medicine*, 2 (1985), pp. 19–25.

Davis, Nancy (Ann). 'Contemporary deontology' in P. Singer (ed.), *A Companion to Ethics*, Oxford: Blackwell, 1991, pp. 205–18.

De Pledge, J. L. 'Nursing as a profession', *Nursing Record* (6 July 1893), 336.

Dickens, Charles. *Martin Chuzzlewit*, Harmondworth: Penguin, 1968.

Dickinson, D. (ed.), *Woman in the Nineteenth Century and Other Writings by Margaret Fuller*, Oxford: World's Classics, 1994.

Dillon, R. S. 'Respect and care: toward moral integration', *Canadian Journal of Philosophy*, 22 (March 1992), 105–32.

—— 'Care and respect', in E. Browning Cole and S. Coultrap-McQuin (eds), *Exploration in Feminist Ethics: Theory and practice*, Bloomington: Indiana University Press, 1992, pp. 69–81.

Dock, L. L. and Stewart, I. Maitland. *A History of Nursing*, 3rd edn, New York: G. P. Putnam's Sons, 1934.

Dock, S. 'The relation of the nurse to the doctor and the doctor to the nurse', *American Journal of Nursing*, 17 (1917), 394.

Donahue, M. P. 'The nurse – a patient advocate?', *Nursing Forum*, 17 (1978), pp. 143–51.

Dostoyevsky, F. *The Brothers Karamazov*, vol. 1, Harmondsworth: Penguin, 1964.

Dworkin, A. 'The politics of intelligence', in Elizabeth Frazer, Jennifer Hornsby and Sabina Lovibond (eds), *Ethics: A feminist reader*, Oxford: Blackwell, 1992, pp. 100–31.

Dworkin, G. *The Theory and Practice of Autonomy*, New York: Cambridge University Press, 1988.

Dworkin, R. M. *Taking Rights Seriously*, Cambridge, MA: Harvard University Press, 1977.

—— *Life's Dominion: An argument about abortion, euthanasia and individual freedom*, New York: Knopf, 1993.

Echols, A. 'The new feminism of yin and yang' in Ann Snitow, Christine Stansell and Sharon Thomson (eds), *Powers of Desire: The politics of sexuality*, New York: Monthly Review Press, 1983.

Ehrenreich, B. 'The purview of political action', in National League of Nursing, *The Emergence of Nursing as a Political Force*, New York, 1979.

Engelhardt, H. T. Jr. 'Physicians, patients, health care institutions – and the people in between: nurses', in Anne Bishop and John R. Scudder, Jr, *Caring, Curing, Coping*, Birmingham, AL: University of Alabama Press, 1985, pp. 62–79.

—— *The Foundations of Bioethics*, New York: Oxford University Press, 1986.

Faludi, S. *Backlash: The undeclared war against women*, London: Chatto & Windus, 1991.

Fay, Patricia. 'In support of patient advocacy as a nursing role', *Nursing Outlook*, 26 (April 1978), 252–3.

Finnis, J. *Natural Law and Natural Rights*, Oxford: Oxford University Press, 1980.

Flaherty, M. J. *Nursing Ethics: Theories and pragmatics*, Bowie, MD: Brady, 1982.

Fletcher, G., *An Essay on the Morality of Relationships*, New York: Oxford University Press, 1993.

Fletcher, N., Holt, J., Brazier, M. and Harris, J. *Ethics, Law and Nursing*, Manchester: Manchester University Press, 1995.

Flew, A. *God and Philosophy*, New York: Dell, 1966.

Fox, C. *Enough is Enough: The 1986 Victorian nurses' strike*, Kensington: University of New South Wales, 1991.

Freud, S. 'Some psychical consequences of the anatomical distinction between the sexes', in *The Standard Edition of the Complete Psychological Works of Sigmund Freud*, trans. and ed. James Strachey, vol. XIX, London: Hogarth Press, 1961.

Friedman, Marilyn 'Beyond caring' in M. Pearsall (ed.), *Women and Values*, Belmont, CA: Wadsworth, 1986.

—— 'Beyond caring: the de-moralization of gender', in M. Hanon and K. Nelson (eds), *Science, Morality and Feminist Theory*, Calgary: University of Calgary Press, 1987, pp. 87–110.

—— 'Care and context in moral reasoning', in Eva Feder Kittay and Diana T. Meyers (eds), *Women and Moral Theory*, Totowa, NJ: Rowman and Littlefield, 1987, pp. 190–204.

—— 'The practice of partiality', *Ethics*, 101 (July 1990), pp. 818–35.

—— 'The social self and the partiality debate', in Claudia Card (ed.), *Feminist Ethics*, Lawrence: University of Kansas Press, 1991, pp. 161–79.

—— *What Are Friends For? Feminist perspectives on personal relationships and moral theory*, Ithaca, NY: Cornell University Press, 1993.

Fry, S. T. 'The role of caring in a theory of nursing ethics', *Hypatia*, 4, no. 2 (Summer 1989), pp. 88–103.

—— 'Toward a theory of nursing ethics', *Advances in Nursing Science*, 11, no. 4 (1989), 9–21.

—— 'Whistle-blowing by nurses: a matter of ethics', *Nursing Outlook*, 37 (January/February 1989), 56.

—— 'The philosophical foundation of caring', in M. M. Leininger (ed.), *Ethical and Moral Dimensions of Care*, Detroit: Wayne State University Press, 1990, pp. 13–24.

Fuss, D. *Essentially Speaking: Feminism, nature and difference*, New York: Routledge, 1989.

Gadow, S. 'Existential advocacy: philosophical foundation of nursing', in S. F. Spicker and S. Gadow (eds), *Nursing: Images and ideals – open dialogue with the humanities*, New York: Springer, 1980, pp. 69–101.

—— 'Nurse and patient: the caring relationship', in A. Bishop and J. Scudder, *Caring, Curing, Coping: Nurse, physician, patient relationships*, Birmingham: University of Alabama Press, 1982, pp. 31–43.

Gawenda, M. 'The hospitals are sick. The symptoms start here', *Age* (Melbourne), *Saturday Extra* (19 October 1985), 2.

Gendreon, D. *The Expressive Form of Caring*, Toronto: University of Toronto Press, 1988.

Gilligan, C. *In A Different Voice: Psychological theory and women's development*, Cambridge, MA: Harvard University Press, 1982.

—— 'Reply by Gilligan', *Signs*, 11 (1986), 324–33.

—— 'Moral orientation and moral development', in Eva Feder Kittay and Diana T. Meyers (eds), *Women and Moral Theory*, Totowa, NJ: Rowman and Littlefield, 1987, pp. 19–33.

Gilligan, C. and Attanucci, J. 'Two moral orientations', in C. Gilligan, J. V. Ward and J. B. Bardige (eds), *Mapping the Moral Domain: A contribution to women's thinking on psychological theory and education*, Cambridge, MA: Harvard University Press, 1988.

Gilligan, C. and Wiggins, G. 'The origin of morality in early childhood relationships', in J. Kagan and S. Lamb (eds), *The Emergence of Morality in Young Children*, Chicago: University of Chicago Press, 1978.

Gilman, Charlotte Perkins. 'The unnatural mother' in *The Charlotte Perkins Gilman Reader*, ed. Ann J. Lane, New York: Pantheon, 1980, pp. 57–67.

Godden, J. O. 'No longer silent', *Humane Medicine*, 4 (1988), 1.

Goldman, H. 'Killing, letting die and euthanasia', *Analysis*, 40 (1980), 224.

Godwin, W. *An Enquiry Concerning Political Justice and its Influence on General Virtue and Happiness* [1793], ed. and abr. Raymond Preston, New York: Alfred Knopf, 1926.

—— *Thoughts Occasioned by the Perusal of Dr Parr's Spital Sermon*, London: Taylor and Wilks, 1801, reprinted in J. Marken and B. Pollin (eds), *Uncollected Writings by Willian Godwin*, Gainesville, FL: Scholars' Facsimiles and Reprints, 1968.

Green, K. *The Woman of Reason: Feminism, humanism and political thought*, Cambridge: Polity Press, 1995.

Greeno, C. C. and Maccoby, Eleanor E. 'How different is the "Different Voice"?', in M. J. Larrabee (ed.), *An Ethic of Care*, New York: Routledge, 1993, pp. 193–8.

Griffin, A. P. 'A philosophical analysis of caring in nursing', *Journal of Advanced Nursing*, 8 (1983), 289–95.

Griffin, J. *Well-Being: Its meaning, measurement and moral importance*, Oxford: Clarendon Press, 1986.

Griffith, J. 'The regulation of euthanasia and related medical procedures that shorten life in the Netherlands', *Medical Law International*, 1 (1994), 137–58.

Grimshaw, J. 'The idea of a female ethic', in Jean Grimshaw, *Feminist Philosophers: Women's perspectives on philosophical traditions*, Brighton: Wheatsheaf, 1986, pp. 187–226.

—— *Philosophy and Feminist Thinking*, Minneapolis: University of Minnesota Press, 1986.

—— 'The idea of a female ethic', in P. Singer (ed.), *A Companion to Ethics*, Oxford: Blackwell, 1991, pp. 491–9.

Grosz, E. 'A note on essentialism and difference', in S. Gunew (ed.), *Feminist Knowledge*, London: Routledge, 1990.

Haber, J. G. (ed.), *Absolutism and Its Consequentialist Critics*, Totowa, NJ: Rowman and Littlefield, 1994.

Haddon, C. 'Nursing as a profession for ladies', *St Paul's Monthly Magazine* (August 1871).

Hanford, L. 'Nursing and the concept of care: an appraisal of Noddings' theory', in G. Hunt (ed.), *Ethical Issues in Nursing*, London: Routledge (1994), pp. 181–97.

Harbison, J. 'Gilligan: a voice for nursing?', *Journal of Medical Ethics*, 18 (1992), 202–5.

Harding, S. *The Science Question in Feminism*, Ithaca, NY: Cornell University Press, 1986.

—— 'The curious coincidence of feminine and African moralities –

challenges for feminist theory', in Eva Feder Kittay and Diana T. Meyers (eds), *Women and Moral Theory*, Totowa, NJ: Rowman and Littlefield, 1987, pp. 296–315.

Hare, R. M. *The Language of Morals*, Oxford: Oxford University Press, 1952.

—— *Freedom and Reason*, Oxford: Oxford University Press, 1963.

—— *Moral Thinking*, Oxford: Clarendon Press, 1981.

—— 'Public policy in a pluralist society', in P. Singer, H. Kuhse, S. Buckle, K. Dawson and P. Kasimba (eds), *Embryo Experimentation*, Cambridge: Cambridge University Press, 1990, pp. 183–94.

—— 'Universal prescriptivism', in P. Singer (ed.), *A Companion to Ethics*, Oxford: Blackwell, 1991, pp. 451–63.

Harris, T. *Woman: The angel of the home and the saviour of the world*, Melbourne, 1890.

Harrison, B. Wildung. *Our Right to Choose: Toward a new ethics of abortion*, Boston: Beacon Press, 1983.

Health Call. *Health Complaints Advisory Link Annual Report – 1 May 1986–30 April 1987*, Melbourne: Health Call, 1987.

Hekman, S. J. *Moral Voices, Moral Selves*, Cambridge: Polity Press, 1995.

Hektor, L. M. 'Florence Nightingale and the women's movement: friend or foe?', *Nursing Inquiry*, 1 (1994), 38–45.

Held, V. *Rights and Goods: Justifying social action*, New York: Free Press, 1984.

—— *Feminist Morality: Transforming culture, society and politics*, Chicago: University of Chicago Press, 1993.

—— 'The meshing of care and justice', *Hypatia*, 10 (1995), 128–32.

Helm, P. (ed.), *Divine Commands and Morality*, Oxford: Oxford University Press, 1981.

Hill, T. E. Jr. 'The importance of autonomy', in Eva Feder Kittay and Diana T. Meyers (eds), *Women and Moral Theory*, Totowa, NJ: Rowman and Littlefield, 1987, pp. 129–38.

Hoagland, S. L. 'Some thoughts on "Caring"', in C. Card (ed.), *Feminist Ethics*, Lawrence: University of Kansas Press, 1991, pp. 246–63.

Hofling, C. K. et al.: 'An experimental study in nurse–physician relationships', *Journal of Nervous and Mental Disease*, 143 (1966), 171–80.

Holmes, Helen Bequaert. 'A call to heal medicine', *Hypatia* (special issue on feminist ethics and medicine.), 4, no. 2 (1989), 1–8.

Hooft, S. van. 'Caring and professional commitment', *Australian Journal of Advanced Nursing*, 4, no. 4 (1987), 29–38.

—— *Caring: An essay in the philosophy of ethics*, Niwot: University of Colorado Press, 1995.

Hooker, Brad. 'Rule consequentialism', *Mind*, 99 (1990), 67–77.

Hull, R. T. 'Defining nursing ethics apart from medical ethics', in J. E. Thompson and H. O. Thompson (eds), *Professional Ethics in Nursing*, Malabar, FL: Robert E. Krieger, 1990.

Hume, David. *A Treatise of Human Nature*, various editions (first published 1739–40).

——— *An Inquiry Concerning the Principles of Morals*, various editions (first published 1757).

——— 'Essay on suicide', in S. Gorovitz et al. (eds), *Moral Problems in Medicine*, Englewood Cliffs, NJ: Prentice Hall, 1976, pp. 381–7.

Hunt, G. 'Nursing accountability – the broken circle' in G. Hunt (ed.), *Ethical Issues in Nursing*, London: Routledge, 1994, pp. 129–47.

Hunt, R. 'Palliative care – the rhetoric–reality gap' in Helga Kuhse (ed.), *Willing to Listen – Wanting to Die*, Melbourne: Penguin, 1994, pp. 115–37.

Huttmann, B. 'One nurse's story: what I had to do for my patient Mac', *Nursing Life*, (January/February 1984), 21.

Jaggar, A. M. 'Human biology in feminist theory: sexual equality reconsidered', in Carl C. Gould (ed.), *Beyond Domination: New perspectives on women and philosophy*, Totowa, NJ: Rowman and Allanheld, 1984, pp. 21–42.

——— 'Feminist ethics: projects, problems, prospects', in Claudia Card (ed.), *Feminist Ethics*, Lawrence: University of Kansas Press, 1991, pp. 78–104.

James, J. Wilson. 'Isabel Hampton Robb and the professionalization of nursing in the 1890's', in M. J. Vogel and C. E. Rosenberg (eds.), *The Therapeutic Revolution: Essays in the Social History of Medicine*, Pennsylvania, 1979.

Jameton, A. *Nursing Practice: The ethical issues*, Englewood Cliffs, NJ: Prentice Hall, 1984.

——— 'Physicians and nurses: a historical perspective', in B. A. Brody and H. T. Engelhardt, Jr (eds), *Bioethics: Readings and cases*, Englewood Cliffs, NJ: Prentice Hall, 1987, pp. 66–74.

Jenny, J. 'Patient advocacy – another role for nursing?', *International Nursing Review*, 26 (1979), 176–81.

Johnstone, M. J. *Nursing and the Injustices of the Law*, Sydney: Harcourt Brace, 1994.

——— *Bioethics: A nursing perspective*, 2nd edn, Sydney: Harcourt Brace, 1995.

Jones, J. H. *Bad Blood: The Tuskegee syphilis experiment*, New York: Free Press, 1981.

Kant, I. 'On a supposed right to lie from altruistic motives' in *Critique of Practical Reason and Other Writings in Moral Philosophy*, trans. Lewis White Beck, Chicago: University of Chicago Press, 1949.

—— *Groundwork of the Metaphysics of Morals*, trans. H. J. Paton, London: Hutchinson, 1976.

—— 'On the distinction of the beautiful and sublime in the interrelations of the two sexes', in Mary Briody Mahowald (ed.), *Philosophy of Woman*, Indianapolis: Hackett, 1978, pp. 193–203.

Kaplan, G. T. and Rogers, L. J. 'The definition of male and female – biological reductionism and the sanctions of normality', in S. Gunew (ed.), *Feminist Knowledge, Critique and Construct*, London: Routledge, 1990, pp. 205–28.

Kegan, S. *The Limits of Morality*, Oxford: Oxford University Press, 1989.

Kelly, B. 'Respect and caring: ethics and essence of nursing', in M. M. Leininger (ed.), *Ethical and Moral Dimensions of Care*, Detroit: Wayne State University Press, 1990, pp. 67–79.

Kempen, S. van 'The nurse as client advocate', in Carolyn Chambers Clark and Carole A. Shea (eds), *Management in Nursing: A vital link in the health care system*, New York: McGraw Hill Book Company, 1979.

Kennedy, I. 'The quality of mercy: patients, doctors and dying', *Upjohn Lecture*, delivered at the Royal Society, London, on 25 April 1994.

Kinsella, T. D. and Verhoef, M. J. 'Alberta euthanasia survey I: physicians' opinions about the morality and legalization of active euthanasia', *Canadian Medical Association*, 148 (1993), 1921–3.

Kittay, E. Feder, and Meyers, D. T. (eds), *Women and Moral Theory*, Totowa, NJ: Rowman and Littlefield, 1987

Kohlberg, L. 'Stage and sequence: the cognitive development approach to socialization', in D. A. Goslin (ed.), *Handbook of Socialization Theory and Research*, Chicago: Rand McNally, 1969.

—— *The Philosophy of Moral Development*, San Francisco: Harper and Row, 1981.

—— *Essays in Moral Development*, vol. 1, San Francisco: Harper and Row, 1981.

Kohlberg, L., Levine, C. and Hewer, A. *Moral Stages: A current reformulation and response to critics*, Basel: S. Karger, 1983.

Kohnke, M. F. *Advocacy – Risk and Reality*, St Louis: C. V. Mosby, 1982.

Komorita, N. I., Doehring, K. M. and Hirchert, P. W. 'Perception of caring by nurse educators', *Journal of Nursing Education*, 30 (January 1991), 23–9.

Kosik, S. H. 'Patient advocacy or fighting the system', *American Journal of Nursing*, 72 (April 1972), 694–8.

Kroeger-Mappes, J. 'The ethic of care *vis-à-vis* the ethic of right: a problem for contemporary moral theory', *Hypatia*, 9 (Summer 1994), 108–31.

Kuhse, H. 'An ethical approach to IVF and ET: what ethics is all about', in W. Walters and P. Singer (eds), *Test-tube Babies,* Melbourne: Oxford University Press, 1982, pp. 22–35.

—— *The Sanctity-of-Life Doctrine in Medicine: A critique*, Oxford: Clarendon Press, 1987.

—— 'Caring is not enough: reflections on a nursing ethics of care', *Australian Journal of Advanced Nursing*, 11 (September–November 1993), 32–42.

—— 'Clinical ethics and nursing': "Yes" to caring, but "No" to a female ethics of care', *Bioethics*, 9 (1995), 207–19.

—— 'Sanctity-of-life, voluntary euthanasia and the Dutch experience: some implications for public policy', in Paul Bayertz: *Sanctity of Life and Human Dignity*, Dordrecht: Kluwer, 1996, pp. 19–37.

Kuhse, H. (ed.), *Willing to Listen – Wanting to Die*, Melbourne: Penguin, 1994.

Kuhse, H. and Singer, P. *Should the Baby Live? The Problem of Handicapped Infants*, Oxford: Oxford University Press, 1985.

—— 'Doctors' practices and attitudes regarding voluntary euthanasia', *Medical Journal of Australia*, 148 (1988), pp. 623–7.

—— 'The nature of ethical argument', in P. Singer, H. Kuhse et al. (eds), *Embryo Experimentation*, Cambridge: Cambridge University Press, 1990, pp. 37–42.

—— 'Individuals, humans and persons: the issue of moral status', in Peter Singer, Helga Kuhse et al.: *Embryo Experimentation*, Cambridge: Cambridge University Press, 1990, pp. 65–75.

—— 'Voluntary euthanasia and the nurse: an Australian survey', *International Journal of Nursing Studies*, 30 (1993), pp. 311–22.

Ladd, John. 'Some reflections on authority and the nurse', in S. F. Spicker and S. Gadow (eds), *Nursing: Images and ideals*, New York: Springer, 1980, pp. 160–75.

Lakoff, G. and Johnson, M. 'Conceptual metaphor in everyday language', *Journal of Philosophy*, 78 (August 1980), 435–86.

—— *Metaphors we Live by*, Chicago: University of Chicago Press, 1980.

Larrabee, M. J. (ed.), *An Ethic of Care*, New York: Routledge, 1993.

—— 'Gender and moral development: a challenge for feminist theory', in M. J. Larrabee (ed.), *An Ethic of Care*, New York: Routledge, 1993, pp. 3–16.

Lear, M. *Heartsounds*, New York: Simon & Schuster, 1980.

Lee, M. A., Nelson, H. D., Tilden, V. P., Ganzini, L., Schmidt, T. A. and Tolle, S. W. 'Legalizing assisted suicide – views of physicians in Oregon', *New England Journal of Medicine*, 334 (1 February 1996), pp. 310–15.

Leininger, M. 'Caring: the essence and central focus of nursing', in

The Phenomenon of Caring, Part V, Washington, DC: American Nurses' Foundation, Nursing Research Report 12, no. 1 (1977), 2–14.

—— 'Caring: a central focus of nursing and health care services', *Nursing and Health Care* (October 1980), pp. 45–59.

—— 'Caring is nursing: understanding the meaning, importance, and issues', in M. M. Leininger (ed.), *Care: The essence of nursing and health*, Detroit: Wayne State University Press, 1988, pp. 83–93.

—— 'The phenomenon of caring: importance, research questions and theoretical considerations', in M. Leininger (ed.), *Caring: An essential human need: Proceedings of Three National Caring Conferences*, Thorofare, NJ: Charles B. Slack, 1981.

Leininger, M. (ed.), *Caring: an essential human need: Proceedings of Three National Caring Conferences*, Thorofare, NJ: Charles B. Slack, 1981.

—— *Ethical and Moral Dimensions of Care*, Detroit: Wayne State University Press, 1990.

Levin, M. *Feminism and Freedom*, New Brunswick: Transaction Books, 1987.

Little, O. 'Seeing and caring: the role of affect in feminist moral epistemology', *Hypatia*, 10 (1995), 117–37.

Lloyd, G. *The Man of Reason: 'Male' and 'Female' in Western philosophy*, London: Methuen, 1984.

van der Maas, P. J. van, Delden, J. J. M., Pijnenborg, L. and Looman, C. W. N. 'Euthanasia and other medical decisions concerning the end of life', *Lancet*, 338 (14 September 1991), 669–74.

MacIntyre, Alasdair 'To whom is the nurse responsible?', in C. P. Murphy and H. Hunter (eds), *Ethical Problems in the Nurse–Patient Relationship*, Boston: Allyn and Bacon, 1983, pp. 78–83.

—— *After Virtue*, 2nd edn, Notre Dame, IN: University of Notre Dame Press, 1984.

Mackay, M. *Handmaidens of Medicine: Hospital nursing in Victoria 1880–1905*, unpublished Master of Economics thesis, Monash University, 1983.

MacKinnon, C. *Feminism Unmodified: Discourses on life and law*, Cambridge, MA: Harvard University Press, 1987.

McNeill, R. H. 'The ideal nurse', *Australasian Nurses Journal*, 8 (June 1910), 194.

Maguire, D. *Death by Choice*, Garden City, NY: Image Books, 1984.

Mahowald, Mary Briody (ed.), *Philosophy of Woman: An anthology of classic and current concepts*, Indianapolis: Hackett, 1978.

Manning, R. *Speaking from the Heart: A feminist perspective on ethics*, Lanham, MD: Rowman and Littlefield, 1992.

Marken, J. and Pollin, B. (eds), *Uncollected Writings by Willian Godwin*, Gainesville, FL: Scholars' Facsimiles and Reprints, 1968.

Martin, Jane Roland. *Reclaiming a Conversation: The ideal of the educated woman*, New Haven: Yale University Press, 1985.

Marx, K. 'The German ideology', in L. D. Easton and K. H. Gudat: *Writings of the Young Marx on Philosophy and Society*, New York: Doubleday Anchor, 1967.

—— 'Eighteenth Brumaire', in K. Marx and F. Engels, *Selected Works*, Moscow: Progress Publishers, 1975.

Mayeroff, M. *On Caring*, New York: Harper and Row, 1971.

Melosh, B. *'The Physician's Hand' – Work Culture and Conflict in American Nursing*, Philadelphia: Temple University Press, 1982.

Miles, S. H. and August, A. 'Courts, gender and "the right to die"', *Law, Medicine and Health Care*, 18 (Spring/Summer 1995), 85–95.

Mill, J. S. 'On Liberty', in E. A. Burtt (ed.), *The English Philosophers from Bacon to Mill*, New York: Modern Library, 1939, pp. 949–1041.

—— *On Liberty*, London: Dent, 1960. (First published 1859.)

—— *Utilitarianism*, London: Dent, 1960. (First published in 1861.)

—— 'On the subjection of women', in A. S. Rossi (ed.), *Essays on Sex and Equality*, Chicago: University of Chicago Press, 1970, pp. 125–242.

Mills, M., Davies, H. T. O. and Macrae, W. A. 'Care of dying patients in hospital', *British Medical Journal*, 309 (3 September 1994), 583–6.

Okin, S. Moller. *Women in Western Political Thought*, London: Virago, 1980.

—— *Justice, Gender, and the Family*, New York: Basic Books, 1989.

—— 'Reason and feeling in thinking about justice', *Ethics*, 99 (January 1989), 229–49.

Monmaney, T. '20 per cent of ICU nurses have aided death, survey finds', *Los Angeles Times* (23 May 1996), Part A, 1.

Moody-Adams, M. M. 'Gender and the complexity of moral voices', in Claudia Card (ed.), *Feminist Ethics*, Lawrence University Press of Kansas, 1990, pp. 195–212.

Moore, G. E. *Principia Ethica*, Cambridge: Cambridge University Press, 1978.

Morrow, H. 'Nurses, nursing and women', in *Facts About Nursing, 1986–1987*, New York: American Nursing Association, 1987.

Murphy, C. P. 'The changing role of nurses in making ethical decisions', *Law, Medicine and Health Care* (September 1984), 173–6.

Murphy, C. P. and Hunter, H. *Ethical Problems in the Nurse–Patient Relationship*, Boston: Allyn and Bacon, 1983.

Murphy, P. 'Helping Joanne die with dignity – a nursing profile in courage', *Nursing* (September 1990), 45–9.

Muyskens, J. L. *Moral Problems in Nursing: A philosophical investigation*, Totowa, NJ: Rowman and Littlefield, 1982.

Nelson, H. L. 'Against caring', *Journal of Clinical Ethics*, 3 (Spring 1992), 8–15.

Newton, L. H. 'A vindication of the gentle sister: comment on "The Fractured Image"', in S. F. Spicker and S. Gadow (eds), *Nursing Images and Ideals – Opening Dialogue with the Humanities*, New York: Springer, 1980, pp. 34–40.

—— 'In defence of the traditional nurse', *Nursing Outlook*, 29 (June 1981), 348–54.

Nightingale, F. *The Art of Nursing*, London: Claud Morris, 1946.

—— *Notes on Nursing*, London: Duckworth, 1952.

—— *Cassandra*, Old Westbury, NY: Feminist Press, 1979.

Noddings, N. *Caring: A feminine approach to ethics and moral education*, Berkeley: University of California Press, 1984.

—— *Women and Evil*, Berkeley: University of California Press, 1989.

—— 'A response', *Hypatia*, 5 (Spring 1990), 120–6.

—— 'In defense of caring', *Journal of Clinical Ethics*, 3 (Spring 1992), 15–18.

Northern Territory. Legislative Assembly. *Report of the Inquiry by the Select Committee on Euthanasia*, vol. 1, Darwin: Legislative Assembly of the Northern Territory, May 1995.

Nursing Life. 'The right to die – what 3504 nurses had to say about one of the most important – yet one of the "grayest" – issues in health care today', *Nursing Life*, 4 (1984), 17–25.

Nussbaum, M. C. 'Human functioning and social justice: in defence of Aristotelian essentialism', *Political Theory*, 20 (May 1992), 202–46.

—— 'Virtue revived', *Times Literary Supplement* (3 July 1992), 9–11.

Oakley, J. *Morality and the Emotions*, London: Routledge, 1992.

—— 'Virtue ethics', *Ratio*, 9, no. 2 (September 1996), pp. 128–52.

Ortony, A. (ed.), *Metaphor and Thought*, Cambridge: Cambridge University Press, 1979.

Paretsky, S. *Guardian Angel*, London: Penguin 1987.

Parker, R. Spreen. 'Nurses' stories: the search for a relational ethics of care', *Advances in Nursing Science*, 13 (1990), 31–40.

Perkins, J. *Women and Marriage in Nineteenth Century England*, Chicago: Lyceum, 1987.

Perry, C. M. 'Nursing ethics and etiquette', *American Journal of Nursing* (April 1906), 450–1.

Plato. 'Euthyphro' in *The Dialogues of Plato*, ed. R. M. Hare and D. A. Russell, trans. B. Jowett, vol. 1, London: Sphere Books, 1970, pp. 35–56.

President's Commission for the Study of Ethical Problems in Medicine and Biomedical and Behavioral Research. *Deciding to Forego Life-Sustaining Treatment*, Washington, DC: Government Printing Office, March 1983.

Puka, B. 'The liberation of caring: a different voice for Gilligan's "Different Voice"', in M. J. Larrabee (ed.), *An Ethic of Care*, New York: Routledge, 1993, pp. 215–39.

Purdy, L. 'Feminist healing ethics', *Hypatia*, 4 (1988), 9–14.

Putnam, D. 'Relational ethics and virtue theory', *Metaphilosophy*, 22 (1991), 231–8.

Quill, T. 'The ambiguity of clinical intentions', *New England Journal of Medicine*, 329 (1993), 1039–40.

T. E. Quill, S. C. Klagsbrun, and H. A. Grossman v. D. C. Vacco, G. E. Pataki, R. M. Morgenthau, Docket No. 95–7028, decided April 2, 1996, United States Courts of Appeals for the Second Circuit.

Quill, T. and Townsend, P. 'Bad news: delivery, dialogue and dilemmas', *Archives of Internal Medicine*, 151 (March 1991), 463–4.

Quinn, C. A. and Smith, M. D. *The Professional Commitment: Issues and ethics in nursing*, Philadelphia: W. B. Saunders, 1987.

Quint, J. C. 'Institutionalized practices of information control', *Psychiatry*, 28 (1965), 119–32.

Rachels, James. 'Can ethics provide answers?', *Hastings Center Report*, 10 (1980), 32–40.

—— *The Elements of Moral Philosophy*, 2nd edn, New York: McGraw Hill, 1993.

Railton, P. 'Alienation, consequentialism, and the demands of morality', in S. Scheffler, *Consequentialism and its Critics*, Oxford: Oxford University Press, 1988, pp. 93–133 (originally published in *Philosophy and Public Affairs*, 13 (1984), 134–71).

Rawls, John. *A Theory of Justice*, Oxford: Oxford University Press, 1973.

Raymond, J. G. 'Reproductive gifts and gift giving: the altruistic woman', *Hastings Center Report*, 20 (Nov./Dec. 1990), 7–11.

Reich, W. T. 'History of the notion of care', *Encyclopedia of Bioethics*, New York: Macmillan, 1995, pp. 319–31.

Report of the Commmittee of Inquiry into Human Fertilization and Embryology (Mary Warnock, chair), London: HMSO, cmnd 9314, 1984.

Rice, S. *Some Doctors Make you Sick*, Sydney: Angus and Robertson, 1988.

Rickard, M., Kuhse, H. and Singer, P. 'Caring and justice: a study of two approaches to health-care ethics', *Nursing Ethics*, 3 (1996), pp. 212–23.

Robb, I. Hampton. *Nursing Ethics: For hospital and private use*, 2nd edn, Cleveland: Kieckert, 1928.

Sue Rodriguez v. The Attorney General of Canada and the Attorney General of British Columbia, Supreme Court of Canada, File No. 23467, 30 September 1993.

Romain, D. 'Care and confusion', in Eve Browning Cole and Susan

Coultrap-McQuin (eds), *Explorations in Feminist Ethics: Theory and practice*, Bloomington: Indiana University Press, 1992.

Rousseau, Jean-Jacques. *Emile*, trans. Barbara Foxley, London: Dent, 1966.

Ruddick, S. 'Maternal thinking', *Feminist Studies*, 6 (Summer 1980), 342–67.

—— *Maternal Thinking: Toward a politics of peace*, Boston: Beacon Press, 1989.

Sacred Congregation for the Doctrine of the Faith. *Declaration on Euthanasia*, Vatican City, 1980.

Sadler, A. M. Jr, Sadler, B. L. and Bliss, A. A. *The Physician's Assistant: Today and tomorrow*, New Haven: Yale University Press, 1972.

Salvage, J. *The Politics of Nursing*, London: Heinemann, 1985.

Scanlon, C. 'Euthanasia and nursing practice – right question, wrong answer', *New England Journal of Medicine*, 334 (23 May 1996), 1401–2.

Scheffler, S. (ed.), *Consequentialism and Its Critics*, Oxford: Oxford University Press, 1988.

Schopenhauer, A. 'On women' in Mary Briody Mahowald (ed.), *Philosophy of Women: An anthology of classic and current concepts*, Indianapolis: Hacket, 1978, pp. 228–38.

Schultz, P. R. 'Noddings's *Caring* and public policy: a linkage and its nursing implications', in M. M. Leininger (ed.), *Ethical and Moral Dimensions of Care*, Detroit: Wayne State University Press, 1990, pp. 81–7.

Sher, G. 'Other voices, other rooms? Women's psychology and moral theory', in Eva Feder Kittay and Diana T. Meyers (eds), *Women and Moral Theory*, Totowa, NJ: Rowman and Littlefield, 1987, pp. 178–89.

Sherwin, S. 'Feminist and medical ethics: two different approaches to contextual ethics', *Hypatia*, 4 (1989), 57–72.

—— *No Longer Patient: Feminist ethics and health care*, Philadelphia: Temple University Press, 1992.

Shyrock, R. H. *The History of Nursing*, Philadelphia: Saunders, 1959.

Sidgwick, H. *The Methods of Ethics*, 7th edn, London: Macmillan, 1907.

Singer, P. (ed.), *A Companion to Ethics*, Oxford: Blackwell, 1991.

—— *Practical Ethics*, 2nd edn, Cambridge: Cambridge University Press, 1993.

—— *Rethinking Life and Death*, Melbourne: Text Publishing Company, 1994.

Singer, P., Cannold, L. and Kuhse, H. 'William Godwin and the defence of impartialism', *Utilitas*, 7 (May 1995), 67–86.

Slater, P. 'The good death: registered nurses' concerns about ethical issues', *Australian Journal of Advanced Nursing*, 4 (June/August 1987), 16–28.

Smart, J. J. C. 'An outline of a system of utilitarian ethics', in J. J. C. Smart and B. Williams, *Utilitarianism: For and against*, Cambridge: Cambridge University Press, 1973.

Snell, J. 'Dr Cox: The nurse's story', *Nursing Times*, 88 (7 October 1992), 19.

Sommers, C. Hoff. 'Filial morality', in Eva Feder Kittay and Diana T. Meyers (eds), *Women and Moral Theory*, Totowa, NJ: Rowman and Littlefield, 1987, pp. 69–84.

Sontag, S. *Illness as Metaphor*, New York: Farrar, Straus and Giroux, 1959.

Soskice, J. M. *Metaphor and Religious Language*, Oxford: Clarendon Press, 1985.

Spahn-Smith, C. 'Outrageous or outraged: a nurse's story', *Nursing Outlook* (October 1980), 624–5.

Spelman, E. *Inessential Woman*, Boston: Beacon Press, 1988.

Spicker, S. F. and Gadow, S. (eds), *Nursing: Images and Ideals–Opening Dialogue with the Humanities*, New York: Springer, 1980.

Stark, M. 'Introduction' in Florence Nightingale: *Cassandra*, Old Westbury, NY: Feminist Press, 1979.

Starr, P. *The Social Transformation of American Medicine*, New York: Basic Books, 1982.

Steinbock, B. (ed.), *Killing and Letting Die*, Englewood Cliffs, NJ: Prentice Hall, 1980.

Steinfels, M. 'Ethics, education and nursing practice', *Hastings Center Report*, 7 (August 1977), 20–1.

Stocker, M. 'The schizophrenia of modern ethical theories', *Journal of Philosophy*, 73 (1976), 453–66.

—— 'Values and purposes: the limits of teleology and the ends of friendship', *Journal of Philosophy*, 78 (1981), 747–65.

Strachey, R. *The Cause: A short history of the women's movement in Great Britain*, London: Bell, 1928.

Study for Professional Issues in Nursing. *Report of the Study of Professional Issues in Nursing*, Melbourne: Health Department, 1988.

Sumner, W. G. *Folkways*, Boston: Ginn, 1934.

SUPPORT Principal Investigators. 'A controlled trial to improve care for seriously ill hospitalized patients: the Study to Understand Prognoses and Preferences for Outcomes and Risks of Treatments (SUPPORT)', *Journal of the American Medical Association*, 274 (1995), 1591–8.

Syme, R. 'From innocent to advocate', in H. Kuhse (ed.), *Willing to Listen–Wanting to Die*, Melbourne: Penguin, 1994, pp. 155–71.

Tännsjö, T. 'In defence of theory in ethics', *Canadian Journal of Philosophy*, 25 (December 1995), 571–94.

Thomas Aquinas, St *Summa Theologica* in *The Basic Writings of Saint Thomas Aquinas*, ed. Anton C. Pegis, New York: Random House, 1946.

Thompson, I. E., Melia, K. M. and Boyd, K. M. *Nursing Ethics*, 2nd edn, Edinburgh: Churchill Livingstone, 1988.

Thornton, M. 'A fair day's pay for work of equal value', *Lamp*, 41, no. 8 (1984), pp. 11–16.

Tong, R. *Feminist Thought: A comprehensive introduction*, Boulder, CO: Westview, 1989.

—— *Feminine and Feminist Ethics*, Belmont, CA: Wadsworth, 1993.

Tracey, B. 'The ministering angel', *Lone Hand* (1 July 1908), p. 236.

Trembath, R. and Hellier, D. *All Care and Responsibility: A history of nursing in Victoria 1850–1934*, Melbourne: Florence Nightingale Committee, Victoria Branch, 1987.

Tronto, J. C. 'Beyond gender difference to a theory of care', *Signs*, 12 (1987), 644–63.

—— *Moral Boundaries: A political argument for an ethic of care*, New York: Routledge, 1993.

Tschudin, V. *Ethics in Nursing: The caring relationship*, London: Heinemann, 1986.

Tulloch, G. *Mill and Sexual Equality*, Hemel Hempstead: Harvester Wheatsheaf, 1989.

United Kingdom Central Council for Nursing, Midwifery and Health Visiting. *Code of Professional Conduct for the Nurse Midwife and Health Visitor*, 2nd edn, November 1984.

Walker, M. Urban. 'Moral understandings: alternative "epistemology" for a feminist ethics', *Hypatia*, 4, no. 2 (1989).

—— 'Partial Consideration', *Ethics*, 101 (1991), pp. 758–74.

Veatch, R. M. 'Medical ethics: an introduction', in R. M. Veatch (ed.), *Medical Ethics*, Boston: James Bartlett, 1989, pp. 3–26.

Veatch, R. M. and Fry, S. T. *Case Studies in Nursing Ethics*, Philadelphia: J. B. Lippincott, 1987.

Versluysen, M. Connor. 'Old wives' tales? Women healers in English history', in Celia Davies (ed.), *Rewriting Nursing History*, London: Croom Helm, 1980, pp. 175–99.

Victoria Health Department. *Report of the Study of Professional Issues in Nursing*, Melbourne: Health Department of Victoria, 1988.

Walker, L. J. 'Sex differences in the development of moral reasoning: a critical review', in M. J. Larrabee (ed.), *An Ethic of Care: Feminist and interdisciplinary perspectives*, New York: Routledge, 1993, pp. 157–76.

Walker, W. *A History of the Christian Church*, Edinburgh: T. & T. Clark, 1957.

Ward, P. J. and Tate, P. A. 'Attitudes among NHS doctors to requests for euthanasia', *British Medical Journal*, 308 (1994), 1332–4.

Warnock, M. *A Question of Life: The Warnock Report on human fertilisation and embryology*, Oxford: Blackwell, 1985.

Warnock, Mary (ed.), *Utilitarianism, On Liberty, and Essays on Bentham, by John Stuart Mill*, New York, New American Library, 1974.

Warren, M. A. 'The moral significance of birth', in H. Bequaert Holmes and L. M. Purdy (eds), *Feminist Perspectives in Medical Ethics*, Bloomington: Indiana University Press, 1992, pp. 198–215.

Warthen v. Toms River Community Memorial Hospital, 488 A.2d 229, NJ Super AD 1985.

Watson, J. *Nursing: Human science and human care*, Norwalk, CT: Appleton-Century-Crofts, 1985.

—— 'Introduction: An ethic of caring/curing/nursing *qua* nursing', in Jean Watson and M. A. Ray (eds), *The Ethics of Care and the Ethics of Cure: Synthesis and Chronicity*, New York: National League for Nursing, 1988, pp. 1–3.

Watson, J. and Ray, M. A. (eds), *The Ethics of Care and the Ethics of Cure: Synthesis and Chronicity*, New York: National League for Nursing, 1988.

Wear, S., Pagaipa, S. and Logue, G. 'Toleration of moral diversity and the conscientious refusal by physicians to withdraw life-sustaining treatment', *Journal of Medicine and Philosophy*, 19 (1994), 147–59.

Whitbeck, C. 'A different reality: feminist ontology', in Ann Garry and Marilyn Pearsall (eds), *Women, Knowledge, and Reality: Explorations in Feminist Philosophy*, Boston: Unwin Hyman, 1989.

Wildes, K. 'Conscience, referral, and physician assisted suicide', *Journal of Medicine and Philosophy*, 18 (1993), 323–8.

Wilkinson, J. M. 'Moral distress in nursing practice: experience and effect', *Nursing Forum*, 99, no. 1 (1987), pp. 16–29.

Williams, B. 'A critique of utilitarianism' in B. Williams and J. J. C. Smart (eds), *Utilitarianism: For and against*, Cambridge: Cambridge University Press, 1973, pp. 73–150.

—— 'Persons, character and morality', in *Moral Luck*, Cambridge: Cambridge University Press, 1981.

Williams, B. *Ethics and the Limits of Philosophy*, Cambridge, MA: Harvard University Press, 1985.

Williams, K. 'Ideologies of nursing: their meanings and implications', in R. Dingwall and J. McIntosh (eds), *Readings in the Sociology of Nursing*, Edinburgh: Churchill Livingstone, 1978, pp. 36–44.

—— 'From Sarah Gamp to Florence Nightingale: a critical study of hospital nursing systems 1840–1897', in Celia Davies (ed.), *Rewriting Nursing History*, London: Croom Helm, 1980.

Winslow, G. R. 'From loyalty to advocacy: a new metaphor for nursing', *Hastings Center Report*, 14 (June 1984), 32–40.

Wolf, S. 'Moral saints', *Journal of Philosophy*, 79 (1982), 419–39.

Wollstonecraft, M. *A Vindication of the Rights of Woman (1792)*, New York: Norton, 1967.

Wong, D. B. *Moral Relativity*, Berkeley: University of California Press, 1984.

—— 'Relativism', in P. Singer (ed.), *A Companion to Ethics*, Oxford: Blackwell, 1991, pp. 442–50.

Woodham-Smith, C. *Florence Nightingale*, London: Penguin, 1951.

Woodruff, A. 'Divided loyalties – the nurse's dilemma', in Royal Nursing Federation, *Ethics – Nursing Perspectives*, vol. 1, South Melbourne: Royal Australian Nursing Federation, 1987, pp. 37–44.

World Medical Association. *Declaration of Lisbon on the Rights of the Patient*, 1981.

Yarling, R. R. and McElmurry, B. J. 'Rethinking the nurse's role in "do not resuscitate" orders: a clinical policy proposal', *Advances in Nursing Science*, 15 (July 1983), 1–12.

Young, A., Volker, D., Rieger, P. T. and Thorpe, D. M. 'Oncology nurses' attitudes regarding voluntary, physician-assisted dying for competent, terminally ill patients', *Oncology Nursing Forum*, 20 (1993), 445–51.

Young, R. *Personal Autonomy: Beyond negative and positive liberty*, London: Croom Helm, 1986.

Zussman, R. *Intensive Care: Medical ethics and the medical profession*, Chicago: University of Chicago Press, 1992.

Index